The BIG
Astrology Guide
Volume One

The BIG Astrology Guide

Volume One

A wide-ranging, thoroughly fascinating and educational book, all about the key branches of Astrology.

Volume One covers:

Sun Signs

Rising Signs & the Midheaven

The Planets

Aspects

~ ~ ~

Volume Two covers:

Moon Signs

Predictive Astrology

A Miscellany of Interesting Facts.

The BIG
Astrology Guide
Volume One

Sasha Fenton

Zambezi Publishing Ltd

Published in 2021 by
Zambezi Publishing Ltd
22 Second Avenue, Camels Head,
Plymouth, Devon PL2 2EQ (UK)
www.zampub.com   email: zambezipub@gmail.com

British Library Cataloguing-in-Publication Data:
A catalogue record for this book is available from
the British Library

Typeset by Zambezi Publishing Ltd, Plymouth UK
Printed and bound in the UK by Lightning Source (UK) Ltd
(Volume 1) ISBN: 978-1-903065-93-8
(Volume 2) ISBN: 978-1-903065-94-5

The Big Astrology Guide is a revised and updated, **two-volume** compilation of the
following books, with additional content:
Sasha Fenton's Moon Signs (ISBN: 978-1-903065-74-7)
Sasha Fenton's Rising Signs (ISBN: 978-1-903065-75-4)
Sasha Fenton's Planets in Astrology (ISBN: 978-1-903065-76-1)
Sasha Fenton's Reading the Future (ISBN: 978-1-903065-77-8)

About the Author

Sasha turned a childhood interest in palmistry and astrology into a career when she was in her twenties, later adding Tarot and developing her psychic abilities. She worked as a professional consultant from 1974 onwards, learning her trade in the best way possible - by doing readings for clients. She reduced her workload when her writing career took off, and over the past twenty-five years, has mainly concentrated on writing and publishing, but she still does the occasional professional reading to keep her skills relevant.

Books

At present, Sasha's tally is 140 books, published by a number of mainstream publishers around the world. This now includes her three Tudorland novels.

Magazines and Papers

Sasha wrote the stars page for Woman's Own magazine for six years and for the Sunday People's Weekend Magazine for a couple of years before that. She wrote a syndicated column for many local papers and about 3,000 articles and columns for papers and magazines of all kinds, mainly for the UK market but some for Australia.

TV and Radio

Sasha has broadcast on many BBC and independent radio stations in the UK, with several regular spots that carried on for many years. She had her own spot on United Artists television for five years. Sasha now broadcasts from time to time on internet radio stations and podcasts around the world.

Festivals

Sasha has given talks and workshops at hundreds of festivals in the UK and overseas, including the large Mind, Body and Spirit festivals in London and Australia.

Organisations

Former President of the British Astrological and Psychic Society (BAPS)
Former Chair of the Advisory Panel on Astrological Education (APAE)
Former member of the Executive Council of the Writers' Guild of Great Britain

Zambezi Publishing Ltd

Sasha and her husband, Jan Budkowski, opened Zambezi Publishing in November 1996 and have since published over 300 books as an independent publisher. Most of our work is now co-editions and packaging projects. We have worked with Sterling Publishing Inc, Red Wheel Weiser, Charlesbridge, Parragon, Welbeck and Quarto.

Other Books by the Author

Astrology

Astrology East and West

Astrology for Living

Astrology for Wimps

Astrology in Focus: Decans and Dwaads

Astrology in Focus: How to Find Your Rising Signs

How to Read Your Star Signs

In Focus: Astrology – *(Writing as Roberta Vernon)*

Sasha Fenton's Moon Signs

Sasha Fenton's Planets

Sasha Fenton's Reading the Future

Sasha Fenton's Rising Signs

Sun Signs

Ten years of contributions to Llewellyn's Sun Sign Book

The Hidden Zodiac

The Magic of Astrology

The Moon in Focus

Understanding Astrology

Understanding the Astrological Vertex

Astrology / Numerology

Astro-Numerology: A Small Handbook

In Focus: Numerology

With the Late Jonathan Dee

Astro-guides – from 1995 to 2000 *(72 full sized books)*

Forecasts 2001

Forecasts 2002

Star*Date*Oracle

Sun Signs Made Simple

The Moon Sign Kit

Your Millennium Forecasts

Palmistry

Hand Reading

In Focus: Palmistry

Learning Palmistry

Living Palmistry

Modern Palmistry

Simply Palmistry

The Book of Palmistry

The Living Hand

Tarot

Elementary Tarot

Fortune-Telling by Tarot Cards

How to Find Love in the Tarot - *(ebook only)*

Super Tarot

Tarot in Action!

Tarot Masters *(chapter contribution)*

The Tarot

Chinese

Chinese Divinations

Elementary I Ching

Feng Shui for the Home

The Flying Stars

Health

In Focus: Chakra Healing – *(writing as Roberta Vernon)*

Diabetes: An Everyday Guide

Simply Chakras

Divination

Body Reading

Dream Meanings

Dreams *(with Jan Budkowski)*

Fortune-Teller's Handbook

Fortune-Teller's Workbook

Fortune-Telling by Tea Leaves

How to Be Psychic

Spells

Spells in Focus

Tea Cup Reading

The Aquarian Book of Fortune Telling

Publishing, Business and Finance

Prophecy for Profit *(with Jan Budkowski)*

Self-Publishing with Stellium

The Money Book *(with Jan Budkowski)*

Fiction – The Tudorland Series

Sophie's Inheritance *(book one)*

Lucy's Dilemma *(book two)*

Emily's Mistake *(book three)*

In Progress

Astrological Planetary Cycles

Astrology: The Complete Guide *(two volumes)*

Cross my Palm With Silver - *(Autobiography)*

Maisie – *(the fourth Tudorland novel)*

Revised Tarot in Action

Contents

The BIG Astrology Guide

Volume One

SUN SIGNS

Sun Sign Aries

March 21 to April 19
Planet: Mars
Symbol: The Ram
Gender: Masculine
Element: Fire
Quality: Cardinal
Number: One

Arians are quick, intelligent and somewhat impulsive, courageous and usually decent and honest. They are often described in astrology books as pioneering, but I have never met a pioneering Aries. One possible exception was my Aries father, because he was a designer and engineer who invented early versions of many everyday objects that we see around us today. Most Arians love their families, and they are good to their parents, in-laws, partners, children and other relatives. They are very sociable, so their homes are often filled with friends and relations having a great time together. They are not frightened of taking on home improvements, but not all are particularly good at it, so their efforts can be a bit hit and miss.

Aries people are hard workers who turn up on time and do what their job requires of them, and they soon move up the ladder to take on a supervisor position. Their great sense of humour and helpful nature ensures that they get on with colleagues and have many friends.

Many Arians are competitive, so they are often sporty or into dancing, acting or anything else that involves competing with others. If they have a downside, it is a tendency to overdo things, so they may spend too much time on their hobbies and interests, while some may overindulge when it comes to food and alcohol.

They love children and are good with them, but they may not be keen on pets and animals. They love spending any spare money that they have on clothes, and they are always nicely dressed. A downside is how they come out fighting if someone says something they don't like, because they can be aggressive.

The Aries Childhood

The father is usually hard working and probably a builder, mechanic or engineer, but the mother may be weak or feckless. The father may push the mother around, so she loses whatever bit of confidence she might have had, and she might try to numb her inner pain by becoming a drinker.or by sinking into some form of mental illness. Whatever happens, she may not be much support to the child,.

Aries Careers

Arians are bright, quick and clever, and they have a natural gift for engineering, design, especially computer software and games and so forth. Many find work in the motor industry and may work as garage mechanics. They love to work alongside others and meet people during their working day, and while they may fancy taking the top spot, they actually excel in middle management.

They like to feel that what they do is of service to humanity, which may be why so many are interested in politics, either as a primary career or as an interest outside their regular work. They prefer to work in large organisations, so you will find many of them in the police, armed forces, fire service and education. They can be excellent teachers, probably due to their affinity with young people while some work in the sports arena. Others love music and may play an instrument for a living or as a hobby.

Aries and Money

Arians are not drawn to the world of high finance, and they may not be great at organising their personal finances either, so they choose lovers and partners who are good at budgeting and who may take over this aspect of their lives for them. They can be spontaneously generous, but some are selfish where money is concerned.

Aries and Love

There are three types of Arian, one who moves around from one lover to the next, and another who is a natural family person. The third type may have a relationship or two but ends up settling for life alone, probably with many friends in place of partners. The family man or woman is very devoted to the partner and the children, but even they can stray if there is too much temptation around. They have a reputation for being good lovers.

Health

Aries rules the head, the eyes, and the upper jaw. They can be prone to leukaemia.

Sun Sign Aries Celebrities	
Elton John	Steven Segal
Maria Carey	Lady Gaga
Sarah Jessica Parker	Russell Crowe

Sun Sign Taurus

April 20 to May 20
Planet: Venus
Symbol: The Bull
Gender: Feminine
Element: Earth
Quality: Fixed
Number: Two

Taurus people are devoted to their families, and they work hard both in the home and outside it. Taureans are capable and often clever, so they can create things of beauty. They are friendly and sociable, and they are great hosts and good company. Many are religious, especially if they come from a religious family background, and they tend to follow the rules and be conventional.

They are capable, honest, intelligent, decent and hardworking, but they don't like it when others rush them, so they are best in a job where they can take their time and do things thoroughly. The average Taurus is better at marriage than any other sign of the zodiac because they want to be part of a happy family. Most Taureans are emotionally supportive and genuinely appreciative of anything that the partner does for them. They love their children and encourage them as much as possible, without having unrealistic expectations of what their children can achieve.

Taureans are good with animals, either in farming or as pet owners, and most have cats, dogs and small animals around, especially if they have children who also love pets.

They are the most reliable people of the zodiac, and they do what they say they will. The downsides to this sign are obstinacy and their tendency to have silly ideas and bees in their bonnets. An unpleasant form of behaviour that some Taureans like to indulge in is to embarrass and hurt others just because they can.

The Taurus Childhood

There is a hint of poverty or shortage in the family background, making the child grow up feeling that they need to earn good money and save as much as possible. Taurus children can face the problem of having a sibling that the parents prefer, and feeling second class thereafter.

Taurus Careers

Taureans are good with their hands, so they are great cooks, wonderful gardeners and artists with a talent for home décor. Another field that attracts Taurus is banking, home loans, insurance and anything to do with money. They are good in business but not necessarily keen on taking the top job.

Many choose to work in construction, furniture manufacture, and farming or food production; for instance, Sir James Dyson, who invented the bag-free vacuum cleaner, is an example. He's said to be stubborn and a hard businessman who is now a billionaire. Others enjoy farming or raising cattle. People of this sign love to work with their hands and create beauty, which is why many of them work as hairdressers, makeup artists and dress designers. Many Taureans are musical and will become singers or musicians as a job or as a side-line. A few excel at sports, especially boxing and tennis.

Taurus and Money

Taureans are sensible, capable and good with money, so they don't indulge in get-rich-quick schemes or waste their money on anything. If they buy something for the house or buy themselves a car, it will be serviceable and likely to last a long time. Many are in banking, accountancy or insurance. They have common sense, and they are good at handling money on behalf of others. Some can be tight-fisted, which comes from a fear of poverty or of being without enough funds to get by.

Taurus and Love

This is the steadiest sign of the zodiac, so these people are likely to choose the right partner in the first place and stay with them for as long as possible. If the marriage breaks down, they will eventually meet someone else and be as reliable and loving towards them as they tried to be before. They can put up with a lot, and they will even care for partners who have poor health. They are good at committing themselves to a relationship. People tell me they are good lovers. Single Taurean men may choose a good=looking "trophy" girlfriend, but the relationship doesn't last.

Taurus and Health

This sign rules the lower jaw, throat and neck, so Taurus people get sore throats and tonsillitis or perhaps spondylitis of the neck. Even though there is nothing in astrology to account for it, many Taurus people get arthritis in the knees.

Sun Sign Taurus Celebrities	
David Beckham	George Clooney
Cher	Andy Murray
Shirley MacLaine	Barbra Streisand

Sun Sign Gemini

May 21 – June 21
Planet: Mercury
Symbol: The Twins
Gender: Masculine
Element: Air
Quality: Mutable
Number: Three

Geminis are intelligent and quick-minded, but they may speak rather slowly, so they don't always come across as bright. Many of them find it hard to make their minds up or come to an important decision, so they can linger in situations longer than they should.

These capable and intelligent people do reasonably well at school and use their brains and their skills to make a good life for themselves. They have a knack for driving and are good with mechanical things, so they may become cab drivers or run driving schools. Many are comfortable with figure work and with computers which gives them a certain amount of status in their community, something they need. Geminis have a strong sense of responsibility, so they worry when things seem to be out of their control.

Geminis make good parents, and they ensure that their children have plenty of intellectual stimulation. Gemini homes are filled with books, music and evidence of their interests, and the children are encouraged to fulfil their potential. Interestingly, the Gemini make their surroundings pleasant and comfortable, so it is a pleasure to visit them in their homes. Some are very fond of small animals and get the love from them that they so need.

They have a wonderful sense of humour, but their downside is that they can be cutting and hurtful towards others.

The Gemini Childhood

Gemini is supposed to be the sign of the twins, as the constellation is that of the mythical twins, Castor and Pollux, but I have long considered this to be the sign of the orphan in real life. Something goes wrong in childhood, and there are many reasons why this may be. I have known Geminis, whose mothers dumped them on others to bring up, while others had cruel and abusive mothers. Yet when the mother is old and alone, Gemini takes care of her while others let her get on with it. Fathers may want to be good to the child, but the mother may not allow it.

Even those who have a reasonably good childhood find it hard to fit in with others at school and elsewhere, so even if their home life is good, they have trouble at school. There's always something that makes the Gemini jittery, unsettled, unsafe and worried when young, and it often spills over into adulthood, making them nervy and even somewhat neurotic.

Gemini Careers

Geminis are drawn to office jobs, perhaps processing invoices or working on rotas and so on. Their aptitude for figures leads many of them to work in banking or as accountants. Some are drawn to medicine, complementary medicine, psychology, dentistry and weight-loss clinics. Others work in obvious Gemini jobs, such as telephone operators, taxi drivers or temporary office workers. Many major tennis stars are Gemini, making sense, as this sign rules the shoulders, arms and hands. Others find work as journalists and broadcasters. Some become self-employed, but most prefer to work for someone else.

Gemini and Money

These people are reasonably good with money, mainly because they fear poverty and do their best to keep money coming in. They like to stay busy, so they prefer to work than to sit around doing nothing. Some spend quite freely, while others are careful.

Gemini and Love

Geminis marry young due to a need to create a happy family of their own, and this is fine if it works out but not so well if it goes wrong. They can fall in love with married people and spend years hanging around and waiting for the person to leave their partner for them. Unfortunately, this rarely, if ever, works out. If they are lucky in love, they make excellent partners, as they are kind, supportive and generous. Some find love later in life and become happy at long last.

Health

Gemini rules the upper chest, the bronchial tubes, the shoulders, arms and hands. Geminis get chest infections, but they also suffer from broken elbows, wrists and arms. Many have bad teeth or receding lower jaws and spend years having orthodontic treatment.

Sun Sign Gemini Celebrities	
Joan Collins	Boris Johnson
Xi Jinping	Nicole Kidman
Sir Paul McCartney	Donald Trump

Sun Sign Cancer

June 22 to July 22
Planet: The Moon
Symbol: The Crab
Gender: Feminine
Element: Water
Quality: Cardinal
Number: Four

Emotions drive Cancerians so they can be moody. Some go about things in convoluted ways, but for the most part, they are intelligent, capable and good in business. Cancer people are efficient and effective when they want to be, but they can be lazy when they don't feel inspired. Although shy, their charm, diplomacy, and salesmanship make them look like an easy touch or someone who can be pushed around; this isn't so, because this is a strong sign, and it's hard to pull the wool over the eyes of these subjects. Cancerians are cautious, they don't make decisions quickly, and they fear losing their security, so they can't bring themselves to gamble or take chances.

Although they love their homes and do their best to make them comfortable and happy havens, Cancerians love to travel and see the world, and they are particularly fond of the sea, so they enjoy taking cruises. The social side of this adds to their enjoyment. Some are good cooks, and they find cooking a pleasant and relaxing hobby. Cancer people have vivid imaginations, which they turn to good effect by writing romantic books or creating scripts for television plays. This is an intuitive sign that can be very psychic.

Cancerians are real family people who won't let down their parents, partners or children. They can be a bit clingy, expecting their children to stay close to them even when they are grown up and have families of their own. Cancerians are courageous, and they can put up with a lot without complaining. This is a kind-hearted sign for the most part, although there is another side to this sign that can make it moody, possessive, cruel and destructive.

I have noticed that sun sign Cancer people usually have good hearing, and they can be pretty sensitive to loud noises. While on the subject of hearing, Cancerians are wonderful listeners, so they make great counsellors, due to their ability to really hear people and understand them.

The Cancer Childhood
The chances are that the Cancer child is the oldest in the family, or the one with the greatest sense of responsibility, and the one who is most happy to help its parents around the home. This child is a blessing to its parents because it does well at school and causes no trouble, and it is relatively slow to grow up. There is often a lot of love between the child and its father.

Cancer Careers
Cancerians are great at fulfilling public needs, so you will find them catering and running pubs or even burger bars. These are wise business people, and they are good at figure work and bookkeeping. They love to run their own show, such as small shops, online businesses, care homes for the elderly or animal sanctuaries, or they can find work in the travel trade. Oddly enough, they can tolerate any noise and disturbance at work, but they need peace and quiet at home.

Cancer and Money
Cancer people are not big spenders, so they take care of their money, but they enjoy travel and will happily spend money for that purpose. They are generous to their loved ones, but they don't give much away to those outside the family.

Cancer and Love
When these subjects fall in love, they really mean business, and they stay loyal and loving to the object of their affections for ever and a day. They aren't the most sexual of people, but they show their love by cooking for their partners and looking after them. If the love affair breaks down, they find it impossible to let go, and they do all they can to keep the love affair going, often making themselves miserable in the effort.

Cancer and Health
These people are pretty strong, but the weak spots are the lungs,

breasts, and arthritis tendencies. They can be prone to cancer, especially breast cancer.

Sun Sign Cancer Celebrities	
50 Cent	Camilla Parker Bowles
Tom Cruise	Meryl Streep
Prince William	Richard Branson

Sun Sign Leo

July 23 – August 22
Planet: The Sun
Symbol: The Lion
Gender: Masculine
Element: Fire
Quality: Fixed
Number: Five

Leos are somewhat shy, although they cover it up well, and while they don't need to be the centre of attention, they do need to be respected. Leos have high standards, making them excellent employees who can be relied on to do a good job. These subjects are determined, and they have the sticking power, but their staying power means they may put up with difficult situations at home or work too long. They can't stand physical discomfort, so they need a pleasant and comfortable home.

There is a side to Leo that never really grows up, so they are extremely good with children, and their patience makes them good teachers. They can cope when relationships fall apart, and they tend to move on and not try to cling to the past but losing their children in a divorce is more than they can bear. Leos are good to their parents, as long as the parents are nice to them, but they are too independent to be tied to their parents' apron strings.

Leos do well in all forms of business, and if they are the ambitious type, they can reach the very top. They are extremely hard working and can sometimes work so hard that they make themselves ill. They love a comfortable lifestyle, and if they can become wealthy, they will really go for it. These people are kind-hearted, generous and sociable, and they love to entertain others, but they don't enjoy being taken for a ride or being surrounded by lame ducks or scroungers. Leos can become extremely downhearted when things go wrong, and it takes time for them to recover their equilibrium. Some Leos are reasonably sporty, but they seem to excel at swimming, while some love to dance.

A slight downside to this sign is that some are know-alls, and another is a tendency to become hypochondriacs; while the ailments are real, some Leos can wallow in them.

The Leo Childhood

Most have good childhoods, although their parents (especially the father) might be somewhat old fashioned or authoritarian or set down rules that they find restrictive. They may be considered special in some way, either because they have many siblings of the opposite sex or because they are clever or talented. Leos are slow to develop, and they don't do well at school, but they often take extra lessons and classes later and have successful careers when they know what they want to be.

Leo Careers

Leos are well organised and hardworking, and they have a knack for business. Although they aren't usually hands-on engineers, they understand engineering principles, and they are comfortable with computers. Most Leos are creative, although this may play out in creating a business of their own. Many become teachers or sports coaches. Some are drawn to the world of jewellery and expensive clothes or high-end furniture and goods.

Leo and Money

Leos love to spend money and they love to have the best of everything, but they work hard, and they earn the money they need for their extravagance, so nobody can really blame them. They are extremely generous and wonderful hosts, so their friends and family are always well looked after.

Leo and Love

Leos fall in love very quickly, they can meet someone and just know that is the one for them, so they keep on loving the other person even if this is not reciprocated. This sign is loyal, devoted and very affectionate – even playful – and also very sexy. If love goes well for Leos, they are the happiest people in the world, but if it doesn't, they can plunge into depression. They are wildly generous to their partners, but if they eventually discover that they are being taken for fools, they become furious.

Health

Leos are either very fit indeed or suffer constantly with their health, yet despite this, they rarely take time off work or give in to health problems. The sign traditionally rules the heart and the spine, and many Leos suffer from spinal problems. Leos have more heart problems than other signs, but fewer instances of cancer, and they can suffer from inflammation of the bowels.

Sun Sign Leo Celebrities	
Arnold Schwarzenegger	Barack Obama
Roger Federer	Charlize Theron
Madonna	Jennifer Lopez

Sun Sign Virgo

August 23 – September 22
Planet: Mercury & Chiron
Symbol: The Maiden
Gender: Feminine
Element: Earth
Quality: Mutable
Number: Six

Virgos are clever and their minds hold whole encyclopaedias of information, which they can access at the speed of light, so they can be guaranteed to win quizzes. Some are devoted to the service of others, and many are in the health services or in other careers that benefit humanity. Some Virgos are dedicated workers who become wealthy due to their brainpower and capacity for long hours and hard work. While some are family people, my experience is that most Virgos do better in a kind of loose arrangement, where they have a partner but don't spend much time with them. They are good to their parents, even though the parents are often selfish and not good to them.

The famed Virgo tidiness is a myth, but Virgos have a photographic memory, and they know exactly where to put their hands on everything, so they hate it when someone clears up their stuff or interferes with their territory. They can be fusspots and perfectionists, and their high standards can make them difficult partners. They can be critical and fault-finding, but they are also their own worst enemies, so they criticise themselves and get upset indeed if they think they have done something wrong.

Many Virgos work from home and their homes are often filled with friends and family. A Virgo friend never lets others down, and they have a terrific sense of humour.

The Virgo Childhood

Virgos don't have happy childhoods, and this may be because their parents separate or because their parents don't love them or because school is a nightmare. Some Virgo children are palmed off onto others. In contrast, other children are given harsh discipline and shouted at, none of which is needed, because they have a cooperative nature and are desperate for approval. Virgos are good at friendship, and their friends are often a better source of love and comfort than their parents. Despite this, the Virgo child rushes around and helps its parents when they get old while others in the family can't be bothered.

Some Virgo youngsters do well at school, while others continue their studies in something that interests them or that helps them get a decent job later on. They are knowledgeable, and they escape the real world by reading or playing on their computers.

Virgo and Money

These people are thrifty and careful with money, probably because they rarely have much of it. They work hard, but choose jobs that don't pay well or work in creative fields where the work is fun, but the money is lacking. They are generous to their friends, but only up to a point, as they don't like people who take advantage of them.

Virgo and Love

Many Virgos are not tactile, so they don't go in for cuddles and affection, but this doesn't mean they are unloving; it just means they show their love in other ways. They will cook for their lovers, make sure they are comfortable and happy, and they will keep their lovers' spirits up if they need cheering up. After a childhood that didn't give the Virgo the security they needed, they might get into a relationship when young and have children quickly in an effort to create a happy family of their own. If the partnership falls apart, they will marry again after a while.

Virgo Careers

Virgo careers fall into two categories. The first would be office work, such as secretary, bookkeeper, filing clerk or go-fer. But banking, big business and services that benefit the public can fit the bill. However, the other Virgo type loves to entertain, so many become actors, singers, entertainers, presenters, and broadcasters. Many write for a living, either as journalists or novelists. Some are drawn to the world of health and might become doctors and nurses, or work in the alternative health world.

Health

Virgos can suffer from bowel problems while others have diabetes. Some soothe their jangling nerves by being heavy smokers. Oddly enough, their feet can give them trouble.

Sun Sign Virgo Celebrities	
Beyoncé Knowles	Cameron Diaz
Charlie Sheen	Keanu Reeves
Shania Twain	Prince Harry

Sun Sign Libra

Planet:	Venus
Symbol:	The Scales
Gender:	Masculine
Element:	Air
Quality:	Cardinal
Number:	Seven

Librans are sophisticated, intelligent, good companions and good listeners. They are knowledgeable, diplomatic, sympathetic and able to fit in with any company. They are attractive, well dressed and great fun for a night out or a short holiday. They love meals out, having a laugh and going to events. They are good dancers who know how to enjoy themselves, especially with a drink or two inside them. They love going to classy places and being part of the in-crowd.

Having said all of the above, living with them day after day can be difficult, because they are lovely when they want to be and moody and aggressive when they don't. There are even Librans who can start a row in an empty room. Some Librans are not at all confrontational, and these subjects hate to dwell on ugly, unpleasant or hurtful things, so they tend not to look back on bad times but to look at life with rose-coloured glasses.

Librans can find conventional marriage restricting, and while they love their children, they can't take too much of their company. They prefer to work and provide the money for the children and let someone else do the donkey work of bringing the children up. Despite their laid-back demeanour, Librans work hard and create a wonderful lifestyle for themselves and their families. Librans are quite good at do-it-yourself, and some do quite extensive work on their homes, which end up being tasteful and welcoming. They rarely do this kind of work for a living, though.

They have a powerful sense of justice and will work hard for the underdog; some even join organisations that help people in need. They can be kind and soft-hearted. Oddly enough, there is a slight attachment to religion, probably just an interest in a particular kind of religion that they read about.

Librans find it hard to make their minds up, and they tend to dither when making decisions.

The Libran Childhood

It's pretty challenging to get Librans to talk about their childhood or their school days because they tend to put it in a box marked "the past" and forget about it. Nothing about their childhood is bad, but there is often a lack of contact with the father, either because he left the household when they are young or because he works in a job that keeps him away from home. They may lose touch with their parents and siblings when they grow up.

Librans and Money

This sign is hard to read where money is concerned because they can be careful in some ways and spendthrift in others. They love to buy things that look good, and they'll spend money on travel, especially travel in comfort. They are clever and lucky when it comes to earning money, so it rarely matters if they overspend at times.

Libra in Love

Librans fall in love with those who are not available to them, leading them to have an idealised love for their partner. alternatively, they may be deeply in love for a while, get bored and wander off. Not all Librans are faithful to their partners, as their natural curiosity takes them into other directions, and their charm and looks make it easy for them to attract new lovers. They are said to be extremely good lovers.

Libra Careers

Many Librans act as agents while others are in business or perhaps in the legal world or trade union organisers. Another Libran career is in the world of beauty, which may be hairdressing, nail art, stage and film makeup, dress designing. Set designing and art of all kinds and much else that is creative. Many have musical talent and work in the music business or are involved in music in some way. One Libran who I knew was an army drummer. Some run restaurants, hotels, garden design or book illustration. Many are great cooks.

Health

Librans can suffer from diabetes or heart disease, and their throats are vulnerable, so they get tonsillitis, colds, flu and bronchitis, and I have known one or two who have had throat cancer. Librans have sensitive skin and can get eczema or psoriasis.

Sun Sign Libra Celebrities	
Catherine Zeta-Jones	Deepak Chopra
Matt Damon	Simon Cowell
Snoop Dog	Kim Kardashian

Sun Sign Scorpio

October 23 – November 21
Planet: Mars & Pluto
Symbol: The Scorpion
Gender: Feminine
Element: Water
Quality: Fixed
Number: Eight

Scorpios are efficient, effective and thorough, and they study the subjects that interest them in great depth. They aren't naturally attuned to modern technology, and they dislike bookkeeping, but they can do these things if they must. Their talent is getting on with people, and they are broadminded with a great sense of humour, so they are good to be around. They are slow to trust others, but if they like someone, they become the best of friends, though someone only has to misbehave with them once, and that will be the end of the friendship. They can't forgive or forget. Their primary interest is their family, and they are especially good with children, which is why many Scorpios end up taking care of grandchildren.

If you want to understand where Scorpios are coming from, the answer is that they are coming from their last emotion, so they can take decisions based on the way they feel. Scorpio's main fears are loneliness and boredom, and they need calm and laid-back partners who take little notice of their changeability or moods.

Scorpios are extremely loyal, and their loyalty not only encompasses their loved ones, but it extends to everyone they deal with in business and personally. They don't like change for the sake of it, so they keep to the same faces around them, and they don't move to a new house or change their jobs easily, either. These people can be sacrificial, perhaps giving up too much for the sake of others

They are intelligent, sensible, they love to read, and they think deeply.

They do have some unpleasant sides to them, but most of the time, they are fine. One downside is an inability to control some of their appetites, so some overeat, while others overdo the drinking or can't stop themselves from spending money. They have a sexy reputation, but I doubt that it is born out in reality. They love a good holiday, time spent in the sun, visiting interesting places and being with people whose company they enjoy.

The Scorpio Childhood
There doesn't seem to be much wrong with the childhood, as they are wanted children who are well treated. They do well at school and get decent jobs when they finish their education. They get on reasonably well with their relatives and siblings, although there might be a bit of jealousy or sibling rivalry. They can excel at sports, and many are musical. I have noticed a certain amount of poverty and hardship in the Scorpio child's family background, which makes them work hard to create security for themselves and their own families in due course.

Scorpio and Money
This is an all or nothing sign, and that applies to financial matters as much as it does to other things, so Scorpios are either sensible or senseless where money is concerned. Some are generous, while others are incredibly tight-fisted. Some spend freely on alcohol and having a good time while others are aesthetic and only spend money on an occasional book. It's hard to tell.

Scorpio in Love
Despite their powerful emotions, I think there is an element of calculation in this sign, so to some extent, they choose the right kind of partner. They are intensely loyal and will put up with a lot, but they can pick fights over things that don't matter.

Careers
Many Scorpios are drawn to the world of health and healing, as doctors, opticians, dentists, nurses, care workers and so on. Some go in for complementary therapies, while others take up psychology and life coaching. Many are attracted to the armed forces, the police, forensic work, the fire service, paramedic work and ambulance driving. Scorpios are intuitive, and many are psychic. Linked with their interest in healing and psychology, it isn't surprising to find many of them working as mediums, healers and tarot readers. Whatever field they are in, Scorpios

prefer to work as backroom people rather than in the limelight.

Health

Scorpio rules the reproductive organs and the lower spine. Many have sensitive stomachs and suffer from indigestion, and most can't cope with

Sun Sign Scorpio Celebrities	
Bill Gates	Tamsin Outhwaite
Joe Biden	Julia Roberts
Katy Perry	Leonardo Di Caprio

spicy food. They also suffer from heart ailments.

Sun Sign Sagittarius

November 22 – December 21
Planet: Jupiter
Symbol: The Centaur
Gender: Masculine
Element: Fire
Quality: Mutable
Number: Nine

Sagittarians don't sit still for long or stay indoors for long, because they soon feel restricted. They don't want to be confined to an office job, so their work takes them from place to place and allows them to meet various people. Sagittarians have quick minds, but they are also good with their hands, and many of them do amazing do-it-yourself jobs in their homes.

Sagittarians can listen to those they respect, and they can sop up information very quickly, but they can also believe they are right when they aren't. They can be pulled in two directions at once, wanting stability on the one hand and adventure on the other, so they suffer from a certain amount of confusion.

They can have a foot in more than one country, with parents who have emigrated from some other place. This means they live with one culture, religion and set of beliefs inside the home and a completely different setup outside, and they seem to cope with this. Some are emigrants who can speak two or three languages. They are broadminded and happy to mix with people of different cultures, and they are comfortable and happy in the company of older people.

Sagittarians are intuitive and often psychic, which leads many of them to explore the world of spiritualism. They are rarely conventional. They are kind-hearted, fun to be with, and generous to those who they love, but oddly stingy to those outside their immediate group of friends and loved ones. They can be unpleasant and hurtful if they think someone is getting at them.

These subjects don't do stress very well, so they simply disappear over the horizon if things get them down. In some cases, this leads them to go from job to job without sticking to anything for long.

The Sagittarian Childhood

The Sagittarian childhood can be anything from all right to downright awful. There can be too much religion or repression in their school or their household, and too much disapproval and discouragement. There will be a lack of cuddles and comfort, and it could be impossible to please their parents or win their approval. It is a shame because these children are intelligent, talented and kind.

Sagittarius and Money

Sagittarians work hard because they like to have money to spend and something behind them if things go wrong. They are generous to their loved ones but not otherwise. They are lucky even when they gamble, and they don't worry overmuch about money.

Sagittarius in Love

Some are happy to be in a conventional relationship with a partner and children, but others won't stay with the same person for more than two weeks at a time. Some mean well, but their boredom and stress thresholds are so low that they can't help moving on. If they find the right person and get the support they need, they are extremely loyal and cooperative. Sagittarians aren't very tactile, so they do better with a partner who doesn't want much in the way of cuddles.

Careers

The best career for Sagittarians is teaching, either in conventional education or running training courses or as sports coaches. Another career path is that of ministers of religion. Others are mediums, astrologers, palmists and so on. Many Sagittarians are tradespeople, such as plumbers, electricians etc. In contrast, others work in the travel trade, as agents or holiday reps, or those who accompany tourists and tell them about the places they are visiting.

Some Sagittarians go into broadcasting or some aspect of show business where they can entertain people and make them laugh. It is hard to categorise them as they can be unconventional.

Health

The Sagittarian weak spots are the hips and thighs, so they must be careful not to fall and break these areas. The other vulnerable area is the liver, so they shouldn't drink too much alcohol or overeat fatty food.

Sun Sign Sagittarius Celebrities	
Brad Pitt	Britney Spears
Christina Aguilera	Jay Z
Taylor Swift	Keith Richards

Sun Sign Capricorn

December 22 to January 20
Planet: Saturn
Symbol: The Goat
Gender: Feminine
Element: Earth
Quality: Cardinal
Number: Ten

The people of this sign are classy and intelligent, and they don't like smutty or down-market things of any kind. Capricorns are ambitious, and if there is a hill to climb, just like the mountain goat that's their symbol, they will clamber upwards. Most are hardworking, and they may overdo it at times because they hate to see themselves as lazy or wasters of time. They dislike being rushed, so they need time to get jobs done correctly. These subjects like to know where they are from one day to the next.

Capricorns love family life, and they are extremely good to their parents. They can be pleasant friends, but their real love is reserved for their relatives, especially the older generation. They are happy to get involved in do-it-yourself work or gardening, and they can be pretty good cooks, although they have to be careful not to eat too many of the nice things they make. They are reliable, both at work and within the family.

These people love to travel on business, to meet clients and see the world. They enjoy travel for pleasure and taking holidays in pleasant places, but they aren't into camping or roughing it. Some Capricorns are afraid of poverty – perhaps due to a family history of not having enough to manage on, and some lack confidence even when they do well in life.

Some Capricorns are very talkative, and others can become involved with peculiar ways of life. It seems as if these Capricorns are heaven bent on going against the normal rules of behaviour for this sign. Most are sane, sensible and capable, though.

The Capricorn Childhood
These children are loved and wanted, but life may be challenging for their families because the parents may have to work hard to keep things going. These children are shy and unwilling to stand out of the crowd, so they get on with their schoolwork quietly and read a book if they have nothing else to do. They may not be very sporty, but they usually enjoy dancing, especially country dancing or ballroom dancing. They need encouragement to make friends and to have fun.

Capricorn and Money
This sign has a reputation for thrift, which comes from the realisation that money doesn't grow on trees and that things can go wrong in life. The family background may have been poor, so this subject grows up knowing that they need to have something put away for a rainy day. Some are stupidly tight-fisted, which can irritate others. The more normal ones enjoy spending money on their homes, holidays, and status symbols, such as a nice car.

Capricorn in Love
These people are shy, and they don't go from one partner to the next. They prefer to be alone than to be with someone who makes them unhappy. Capricorns don't fall in love easily, but they are sincere when they do so. They are real family people who will do all they can to support their partners and care for their children. They are loyal and dependable. However, some rogue Capricorns can't be trusted to behave well, while others are more interested in getting on in their jobs than putting effort into their relationships.

Careers
Publishing is a good choice for this sign, as is any job that requires a head for details. They like business and are happy working for a large corporation, especially if their job involves spreadsheets or accountancy. They make excellent secretaries and bookkeepers, as well as intelligent salespeople. They can work in the legal sphere, especially where details are concerned, or they can be an assistant to a rising politician, keeping her diary and ensuring she is well briefed. Some are experts in the field of antiques.

Health

Capricorn is a long-lived sign, and these people are usually strong and healthy, but they can have chronic problems, such as asthma, eczema and arthritis. Deafness is common too.

Sun Sign Capricorn Celebrities	
Nicholas Cage	Catherine, Duchess of Cambridge
Denzel Washington	Kate Moss
Michelle Obama	Tiger Woods

Sun Sign Aquarius

January 21 – February 18
Planet: Saturn & Uranus
Symbol: The Water Carrier
Gender: Masculine
Element: Air
Quality: Fixed
Number: Eleven

This is a hard sign to categorise, because there are so many different kinds of Aquarian. Many are unconventional, and a large number of them make a point of looking "different". In the words of an astrologer friend of mine, lots of Aquarian women choose to dress in old curtains! Indeed, I once knew an Aquarian who wore Native American Indian garb every day, despite working in an ordinary office job. Having said that, many Aquarian women dress smartly and have lovely homes, while others live in a mess.

Aquarians have strong views that are very black and white, so despite their reputation for being broadminded, they can be very blinkered and only believe what they want to believe. Some are politically extreme, some are religious, and some are even racist.

These subjects are humanitarian, and they dislike injustice. Some are passionate about the needs of children, while others fight hard for the rights of animals. However, they can be uninterested in family life, and a lot of them avoid having children themselves.

Most people of this sign share a thirst for knowledge and a love of books, while modern technology and the internet are made for Aquarius because they need information at their fingertips. They can be amazingly knowledgeable, especially about their specialist subjects, and they are highly intelligent. Their minds work quickly, but they speak slowly, so they don't always look as bright as they are.

The Aquarian Childhood

These people can have a perfectly normal and happy childhood, but this is not always the case. It seems as if the weak link is the father, because in many cases, the mother brings up the children alone because the father isn't around much. Some Aquarians drift away from the family once they grow up, but once again, there is no hard and fast rule with this. With a bit of luck, these children get a good education equipping them for life as an adult.

Aquarius and Money

Aquarians are not great spenders, probably because they don't have much money to spare. They live in small houses with extraordinarily little in the way of material goods. They aren't particularly generous, but they are humanitarian and will give time to local causes and help the needy. There really are no rules to this sign.

Aquarius in Love

Aquarians find the person they want to be with when they are young, after which they try hard to make it work. If the relationship doesn't work out, they move on and find someone else. Despite their reputation for independence, they like to be in a partnership, although they need space to come and go, and they also give their partners room to get on with their own interests. Aquarians feel more deeply about their partners than appears to be the case to outsiders, and if the partner leaves or dies, they become very distressed indeed.

Careers

Aquarians can cope with an ordinary office job, but they prefer to do something more interesting. Some work in education, while others are in the social services, where they can help people in trouble. They work in local government and charitable institutions. They embrace new technology, and were among the first to get into computers. The upper echelon of astrology is full of Aquarians. Something as unusual as creating or breaking codes and cyphers could suit this unusual sign, while others deliver yachts to rich people by sailing them from one side of the world to the other. Some can be found in publishing, but more would be into broadcasting, film, or in any original, inventive and unusual sphere of work.

Health

This is a strong sign on the whole, but the weak points are the lungs - which are subject to bronchitis and asthma - or the spine, the Achilles tendon, the ankles and the skin.

Sun Sign Aquarius Celebrities	
Ellen DeGeneres	Geena Davis
Jennifer Aniston	John Travolta
Justin Timberlake	Sheryl Crowe

Sun Sign Pisces

February 19 – March 20
Planet: Jupiter & Neptune
Symbol: The Fishes
Gender: Feminine
Element: Water
Quality: Mutable
Number: Twelve

There is always an element of chaos in the life of a Pisces, so if they are successful at their work, their family life is in a mess, but if their family life is fine and they are coping at work, their finances are in meltdown. They live on the brink of disaster, and nothing that well-meaning friends or relatives try to do helps them, because as soon as one intractable problem is solved, the Piscean will find another. Yet, they never fall into the abyss. These subjects live according to their own rules, and they do precisely what suits them most of the time.

Pisceans are creative, artistic, musical and lucky. They don't lead conventional lives, but they are happy in their own way. They love their families, and most of them are wonderful with children, even if they are a bit lax and forgetful with their own children at times. Some are real earth mothers whose homes and gardens are beautiful places for children to grow up in, and they often choose to look after their grandchildren, because they love to have their little ones around. They are great cooks and hosts, and they often have people staying in their homes. They enjoy life more than most people do, and their friends are lucky to be able to join in the fun with them. These people are sensitive, kind and highly intuitive, and they have wonderful senses of humour.

Where business is concerned, they can sense opportunities and take advantage of them, so they are often surprisingly successful in their chosen field. They are remarkably shrewd, and while they may choose an unusual way of life, they often turn out to be the real winners of the zodiac.

The Pisces Childhood

Some Pisces children have poor health, probably due to asthma, bronchitis and lung infections. They may spend time in a hospital or a convalescent home, which helps them develop their creativity or spirituality. They aren't great scholars, and they may have dyslexia, but they have a talent for music, singing, dancing, drama, art or sports, especially water sports. They are gentle and attractive children who make friends easily. They love animals and will find a way of spending time with them, perhaps by helping out at a place where animals are kept. Their parents may be too busy to take much notice of them, but they don't take much notice of their parents either, so that usually works out well for them.

Pisces and Money

The Piscean ability to live on little or no money is one of the great mysteries of life. They work in creative fields where they don't earn much, but they have what they need; they entertain friends, keep their families together and eat and drink well. They may not have the outer trappings of smart cars, the latest gadgets and beautiful clothes, but they have what they want.

Pisces in Love

These people fall in and out of love on a reasonably frequent basis. If they find the right partner early, and if the partner is interesting enough for them to stay put, they can have a relatively conventional marriage-type relationship. However, if they find the partner boring, they move on quickly, and some keep moving, never really settling down. Some are extremely hurtful, spiteful and jealous of a partner who becomes successful.

Pisces Careers

Pisces attracts people to an odd range of careers, and many of them work in New Age jobs, such as palmistry, mediumship, and healing. They are attracted to anything that helps others, such as hospitals, charities, psychology, social work and childcare. They make wonderful salespeople, or they can work in catering, hotels or the travel trade. A surprising number go into politics, the most famous being Mikhail Gorbachev, while others are artists, musicians and film-makers.

Health

Once these people reach adulthood, they are relatively healthy, although they suffer from chest infections in the winter. Some drink too much. Tradition tells us that their feet are troublesome.

Sun Sign Pisces Celebrities	
Bruce Willis	Daniel Craig
Lupita Nyang'o	Justin Bieber
Rachel Weisz	Rihanna

The BIG
Astrology Guide
Volume One

RISING SIGNS AND THE
MIDHEAVEN

The Rising Sign and the Ascendant

THE OUTER MANNER

The rising sign frequently rules a person's outer manner, mindset and career choices, but this isn't an absolute rule. One can argue that the rising sign represents the kind of person our parents, teachers and childhood friends wanted us to be, while the Sun, Moon and other planets show our true selves.

Many of us project the ascendant when we are in new situations. We often choose to use it as a shield that hides and protects the real personality, thereby allowing us to assess a new situation before revealing our true feelings. It would be terrific if astrologers could categorically say that the rising sign invariably rules the outer manner and appearance, but, as in other areas of life, few things are cast in stone. Nevertheless, the rising sign is fascinating.

The ascendant is so important, that without knowing exactly what is rising, the astrologer is partially working in the dark. If nothing else, an exact ascendant marks the starting point of the astrological houses and it sets the position of such astrological features as the descendant, midheaven, Imum Coeli, part of fortune, east point, vertex and much else.

Are the Ascendant and Rising Sign the Same Thing?

The terms are often used interchangeably, but the ascendant refers to the exact position within the rising sign. For instance, you might have had Taurus rising when you were born, but your ascendant may be 18 degrees of Taurus.

What is the Rising Sign?

The following list shows you exactly what the rising sign and the ascendant actually are:

- Starting at the place where you were born and noting the time of day or night, take an imaginary, horizontal line around the earth until you find the spot where the sun was rising. If you were born at night, this will be on the other side of the earth.

- If you were born in the northern hemisphere, drop another imaginary line down from that point to the place along the ecliptic (also known as the zodiac) and see what sign lies there, and what exact degree of that sign you drop down to.
- If you were born in the southern hemisphere, you take a line up from that point to the place along the ecliptic (also known as the zodiac) and see what sign lies there, and what exact degree of that sign you reach up to.

N.B: While you *can* work out the ascendant by hand, it involves two ephemerides and a lot of mathematical calculations. The easiest way is to use software, which could be anything from an app for your phone that may cost less than £10, to an astrological program, such as Solar Fire or Winstar.

Appearance
Many people look far more like their rising sign than their Sun sign, while others are a combination of both. However, there are people whose appearance is strongly influenced by other factors on their birthchart, along with inherited factors, such as race, colour and family likeness.

Several years ago, I read of a survey that had been carried out with 100 subjects. About 45 per cent looked like their Sun sign and about another 40 per cent resembled their rising sign, while the remainder looked like either their Moon sign or the sign in which their chart ruler was placed. The chart ruler is the planet associated with the rising sign. For example, in the case of Libra rising, the ruling planet is Venus. I'm not sure that one survey of 100 people proves much, but it's interesting. It's possible that the outward projection of the rising sign is more apparent in our mannerisms and behaviour than our looks. I've noticed that, whenever I or any other astrologer has been daft enough to try and guess a person's Sun sign, we often come up with their rising sign.

It's always interesting to take a look at a family group to see how the signs are distributed within it. Frequently, one person's Sun is the rising sign of another and the Moon sign or the MC of yet a third. It's also interesting to note the factors on the birthcharts of close associates to see whether they connect with our Sun, Moon, Asc, Dsc, MC or IC.

Do We Outgrow Our Rising Sign?
There is a theory that many people are far more like their Moon sign or their rising sign during the first thirty years, becoming more like their Sun

sign later on. Another theory is that the progression of the ascendant from one sign to the next weakens the rising sign's influence and allows the subject to grow and change. These are both worthwhile theories, as long as you are flexible about them and don't consider them to be written in tablets of stone.

Signs of Long and Short Ascension

During the course of a 24-hour day in the tropics, the signs rise at more or less two hourly intervals, but the further away one moves from the equator the more distorted this movement becomes. This means that at certain times of the year in Britain, we can see the sign of Cancer taking as much as two-and-three-quarter hours to rise over the horizon, while at certain times of the year, Pisces will take little more than twenty minutes to do so.

Therefore, in our part of the world, it's far easier to find people who have the longer ascension signs of Cancer and Leo rising than the shorter ascension signs of Pisces or Aries. In the southern hemisphere, the signs of longest ascension are Capricorn and Aquarius, while the shorter signs are Virgo and Libra.

Abbreviations	
Some astrological abbreviations in this book are:	
Ascendant:	Asc
Descendant:	Dsc
Medium Coeli/MC:	MC
Imum Coeli/Nadir:	IC

Finding Your Rising Sign

The rising sign finder table that you will see in a moment is suitable for births in any part of the world. This will give you a fairly accurate rising sign, unless you are on the cusp of two signs, in which case, read both of them in this book and you will soon see which one applies to you.

N.B: If you were born in the UK during British Summer Time (BST), or elsewhere during Daylight Saving Time, please deduct one hour from your time of birth.

Sooner or later, you will want to know the exact location of your ascendant (the exact degree of the sign that was rising). You can find this initially by finding an astrological service online, or by buying an app/program as mentioned above.

Things change, however, but a Google search for terms such as "free astro chart" will find what's on tap. You could visit an astrologer, send off to Equinox for a computerised chart and report, or you could buy your own astrology software. Amazon.co.uk sometimes carries amazingly inexpensive, effective and easy-to-use software packages, but again, things change, so you need to look for yourself, or do an internet search.

THE QUICK AND EASY RISING SIGN FINDER

Birthdate	Aries	Taurus	Gemini
ARI 21 to 31 Mar	5.30am to 6.29am	6.30am to 7.44am	7.45am to 9.29am
01 to 10 Apr	5.00am to 5.59am	6.00am to 7.14am	7.15am to 8.59am
11 to 20 Apr	4.15am to 5.14am	5.15am to 6.29am	6.30am to 8.14am
TAU 21 to 30 Apr	3.30am to 4.29am	4.30am to 5.44am	5.45am to 7.29am
01 to 10 May	3.00am to 3.59am	4.00am to 5.14am	5.15am to 6.59am
11 to 21 May	2.30am to 3.29am	3.30am to 4.44am	4.45am to 6.29am
GEM 22 to 31 May	2.00am to 2.59am	3.00am to 4.14am	4.15am to 5.59am
01 to 10 Jun	1.30am to 2.29am	2.30am to 3.44am	3.45am to 5.29am
11 to 21 Jun	12.45am to 1.44am	1.45am to 2.59am	3.00am to 4.44am
CAN 22 to 30 Jun	12.00am to 12.59am	1.00am to 2.14am	2.15am to 3.59am
01 to 11 Jul	11.30pm to 12.29am	12.30am to 1.44am	1.45am to 3.29am
12 to 22 Jul	11.00pm to 11.59pm	12.00am to 1.14am	1.15am to 2.59am
LEO 23 to 31 Jul	9.45pm to 10.44pm	10.45pm to 1.59pm	12.00am to 1.44am
01 to 11 Aug	9.15pm to 10.14pm	10.15pm to 11.29pm	1.30pm to 1.14pm
12 to 23 Aug	8.30pm to 9.29pm	9.30pm to 10.44pm	10.45pm to 12.29am
VIR 24 to 31 Aug	7.30pm to 8.29pm	8.30pm to 9.44pm	9.45pm to 11.29pm
01 to 11 Sep	7.00pm to 7.59pm	8.00pm to 9.14pm	9.15pm to 10.59pm
12 to 22 Sep	6.15pm to 7.14pm	7.15pm to 8.29pm	8.30pm to 10.14pm
LIB 23 to 30 Sep	5.30pm to 6.29pm	6.30pm to 9.44pm	9.45pm to 11.29pm
01 to 11 Oct	5.00pm to 5.59pm	6.00pm to 7.14pm	7.15pm to 8.59pm
12 to 23 Oct	4.15pm to 5.14pm	5.15pm to 6.29pm	6.30pm to 8.14pm
SCO 24 to 31 Oct	3.30pm to 4.29pm	4.30pm to 5.44pm	5.45pm to 7.29pm
01 to 11 Nov	2.45pm to 3.44pm	3.45pm to 4.59pm	5.00pm to 6.44pm
12 to 22 Nov	2.15pm to 3.14pm	3.15pm to 4.29pm	4.30pm to 6.14pm
SAG 23 to 30 Nov	1.30pm to 2.29pm	2.30pm to 3.44pm	3.45pm to 5.29pm
01 to 11 Dec	12.45pm to 1.44pm	1.45pm to 2.59pm	3.00pm to 4.44pm
12 to 21 Dec	12.15pm to 1.14pm	1.15pm to 2.29pm	2.30pm to 4.14pm
CAP 22 to 31 Dec	11.15am to 12.14pm	12.15pm to 1.29pm	1.30pm to 3.14pm
01 to 11 Jan	10.45am to 11.44am	11.45am to 12.59pm	1.00pm to 2.44pm
12 to 20 Jan	10.15am to 11.14am	11.15am to 12.29pm	12.30pm to 2.14pm
AQU 21 to 31 Jan	9.30am to 10.29am	10.30am to 11.44am	11.45am to 1.29pm
01 to 10 Feb	9.00am to 9.59am	10.00am to 11.14am	11.15am to 12.59pm
11 to 18 Feb	8.15am to 9.14am	9.15am to 10.29am	10.30am to 12.14pm
PIS 19 to end Feb	7.30am to 8.29am	8.30am to 9.44am	9.45am to 11.29am
01 to 10 Mar	7.15am to 8.14am	8.15am to 9.29am	9.30am to 11.14am
11 to 20 Mar	6.30am to 7.29am	7.30am to 8.44am	8.45am to 10.29am

Birthdate	Cancer	Leo	Virgo
ARI 21 to 31 Mar	9.30am to 11.59am	12.00pm to 2.44pm	2.45pm to 5.29pm
01 to 10 Apr	9.00am to 11.29am	11.30am to 2.14pm	2.15pm to 4.59pm
11 to 20 Apr	8.15am to 10.44am	10.45am to 1.29pm	1.30pm to 4.14pm
TAU 21 to 30 Apr	7.30am to 9.59am	10.00am to 12.44pm	12.45pm to 3.29pm
01 to 10 May	7.00am to 9.29am	9.30am to 12.14pm	12.15pm to 2.59pm
11 to 21 May	6.30am to 8.59am	9.00am to 11.44am	11.45am to 2.29pm
GEM 22 to 31 May	6.00am to 8.29am	8.30am to 11.14am	11.15am to 1.59pm
01 to 10 Jun	5.30am to 7.59am	8.00am to 10.44am	10.45am to 1.29pm
11 to 21 Jun	4.45am to 7.14am	7.15am to 9.59am	10.00am to 12.44pm
CAN 22 to 30 Jun	4.00am to 6.29am	6.30am to 9.14am	9.15am to 11.59am
01 to 11 Jul	3.30am to 5.59am	6.00am to 8.44am	8.45am to 11.59am
12 to 22 Jul	3.00am to 5.29am	5.30am to 8.14am	8.15am to 10.59am
LEO 23 to 31 Jul	1.45am to 4.00am	4.15am to 6.59am	7.00am to 9.44am
01 to 11 Aug	1.15am to 3.44am	3.45am to 6.29am	6.30am to 9.14am
12 to 23 Aug	12.30am to 2.59am	3.00am to 5.44am	5.45am to 8.29am
VIR 24 to 31 Aug	11.30pm to 1.59am	2.00am to 4.44am	4.45am to 7.29am
01 to 11 Sep	11.00pm to 1.29am	1.30am to 4.14am	4.15am to 6.59am
12 to 22 Sep	10.15pm to 12.44am	12.45am to 3.29am	3.30am to 6.14am
LIB 23 to 30 Sep	9.30pm to 11.59pm	12.00am to 2.44am	2.45am to 5.29am
01 to 11 Oct	9.00pm to 11.29pm	11.30pm to 2.14am	2.15am to 4.59am
12 to 23 Oct	8.15pm to 10.44pm	10.45pm to 1.29am	1.30am to 4.14am
SCO 24 to 31 Oct	7.30pm to 9.59pm	10.00pm to 12.44am	12.45pm to 3.29am
01 to 11 Nov	6.45pm to 9.14pm	9.15pm to 11.59pm	12.00am to 2.44am
12 to 22 Nov	6.15pm to 8.44pm	8.45pm to 11.29pm	11.30pm to 2.14am
SAG 23 to 30 Nov	5.30pm to 7.59pm	8.00pm to 10.44pm	10.45pm to 1.29am
01 to 11 Dec	4.45pm to 7.14pm	7.15pm to 9.59pm	10.00pm to 12.44am
12 to 21 Dec	4.15pm to 6.44pm	6.45pm to 9.29pm	9.30pm to 12.14am
CAP 22 to 31 Dec	3.15pm to 5.44pm	5.45pm to 8.29pm	8.30pm to 11.14pm
01 to 11 Jan	2.45pm to 5.14pm	5.15pm to 7.59pm	8.00pm to 10.44pm
12 to 20 Jan	2.15pm to 4.44pm	4.45pm to 7.29pm	7.30pm to 10.14pm
AQU 21 to 31 Jan	1.30pm to 3.59pm	4.00pm to 6.44pm	6.45pm to 9.29pm
01 to 10 Feb	1.00pm to 3.29pm	3.30pm to 6.14pm	6.15pm to 8.59pm
11 to 18 Feb	12.15pm to 2.44pm	2.45pm to 5.29pm	5.30pm to 8.14pm
PIS 19 to end Feb	11.30am to 1.59pm	2.00pm to 4.44pm	4.45pm to 7.29pm
01 to 10 Mar	11.15am to 1.44pm	1.45pm to 4.29pm	4.30pm to 7.14pm
11 to 20 Mar	10.30am to 12.59pm	1.00pm to 3.44pm	3.45pm to 6.29pm

Birthdate	Libra	Scorpio	Sagittarius
ARI 21 to 31 Mar	5.30pm to 8.14pm	8.15pm to 10.59pm	11.00pm to 1.29am
01 to 10 Apr	5.00pm to 7.44pm	7.45pm to 10.29pm	10.30pm to 12.59am
11 to 20 Apr	4.15pm to 6.59pm	7.00pm to 9.44pm	9.45pm to 12.14am
TAU 21 to 30 Apr	3.30pm to 6.14pm	6.15pm to 8.59pm	9.00pm to 11.29pm
01 to 10 May	3.00pm to 5.44pm	5.45pm to 8.290pm	8.30pm to 10.59pm
11 to 21 May	2.30pm to 5.14pm	5.15pm to 7.59pm	8.00pm to 10.29pm
GEM 22 to 31 May	2.00pm to 4.44pm	4.45pm to 7.29pm	7.30pm to 9.59pm
01 to 10 Jun	1.30pm to 4.14pm	4.15pm to 6.59pm	7.00pm to 9.29pm
11 to 21 Jun	12.45pm to 3.29pm	3.30pm to 6.14pm	6.15pm to 8.44pm
CAN 22 to 30 Jun	12.00pm to 2.44pm	2.45pm to 5.29pm	5.30pm to 7.59pm
01 to 11 Jul	11.30am to 2.14pm	2.15pm to 4.59pm	5.00pm to 7.29pm
12 to 22 Jul	11.00am to 1.44pm	1.45pm to 4.29pm	4.30pm to 6.59pm
LEO 23 to 31 Jul	9.45am to 12.29pm	12.30pm to 3.14pm	3.15pm to 5.44pm
01 to 11 Aug	9.15am to 11.59am	12.00pm to 2.44pm	2.45pm to 5.14pm
12 to 23 Aug	8.30am to 11.14am	11.15am to 1.59pm	2.00pm to 4.29pm
VIR 24 to 31 Aug	7.30am to 10.14am	10.15am to 12.59pm	1.00pm to 3.29pm
01 to 11 Sep	7.00am to 9.44am	9.45am to 12.29pm	12.30pm to 2.59pm
12 to 22 Sep	6.15am to 8.59am	9.00am to 11.14am	11.45am to 2.14pm
LIB 23 to 30 Sep	5.10am to 8.14am	8.15am to 10.59am	11.00am to 1.29pm
01 to 11 Oct	5.00am to 7.44am	7.45am to 10.29am	10.30am to 12.59pm
12 to 23 Oct	4.15am to 6.59am	7.00am to 9.44am	9.45am to 12.14pm
SCO 24 to 31 Oct	3.30am to 6.14am	6.15am to 8.59am	9.00am to 11.29am
01 to 11 Nov	2.45am to 5.29am	5.30am to 8.14am	8.15am to 10.44am
12 to 22 Nov	2.15am to 4.59am	5.00am to 7.44am	7.45am to 10.14am
SAG 23 to 30 Nov	1.30am to 4.14am	4.15am to 6.59am	7.00am to 9.29am
01 to11 Dec	12.45am to 3.29am	3.30am to 6.14am	6.15am to 8.44am
12 to 21 Dec	12.15am to 2.59am	3.00am to 5.44am	5.45am to 8.14am
CAP 22 to 31 Dec	11.15pm to 1.59am	2.00am to 4.44am	4.45am to 7.14am
01 to 11 Jan	10.45pm to 1.29am	1.30am to 4.14am	4.15am to 6.44am
12 to 20 Jan	10.15pm to 12.59am	1.00am to 3.44am	5.45am to 6.14am
AQU 21 to 31 Jan	9.30pm to 12.14am	12.15am to 2.59am	3.00am to 5.29am
01 to 10 Feb	9.00pm to 11.44pm	11.45pm to 2.29am	2.30am to 4.59am
11 to 18 Feb	8.15pm to 10.59pm	11.00pm to 1.44am	1.45am to 4.14am
PIS 19 to end Feb	7.30pm to 10.14pm	10.15pm to 12.59am	1.00am to 3.29am
01 to 10 Mar	7.15pm to 9.59pm	10.00pm to 12.44am	12.45am to 3.14am
11 to 20 Mar	6.30pm to 9.14pm	9.15pm to 11.59pm	12.00am to 2.29am

Birthdate	Capricorn	Aquarius	Pisces
ARI 21 to 31 Mar	1.30am to 3.14am	3.15am to 4.29am	4.30am to 5.29am
01 to 10 Apr	1.00am to 2.44am	2.45am to 3.59am	4.00am to 4.59am
11 to 20 Apr	12.15am to 1.59am	2.00am to 3.14am	3.15am to 4.14am
TAU 21 to 30 Apr	11.30pm to 1.14am	1.15am to 2.29am	2.30am to 3.29am
01 to 10 May	11.00pm to 12.44am	12.45am to 1.59am	2.00am to 2.59am
11 to 21 May	10.30pm to 12.14am	12.15am to 1.29am	1.30am to 2.29am
GEM 22 to 31 May	10.00pm to 11.44pm	11.45pm to 12.59am	1.00am to 1.59am
01 to 10 Jun	9.30pm to 11.14pm	11.15pm to 12.29am	12.30am to 1.29am
11 to 21 Jun	8.45pm to 10.29pm	10.30pm to 11.44pm	11.45pm to 12.44am
CAN 22 to 30 Jun	8.00pm to 9.44pm	9.45pm to 10.59pm	11.00pm to 11.59pm
01 to 11 Jul	7.30pm to 9.14pm	9.15pm to 10.29pm	10.30pm to 11.29pm
12 to 22 Jul	7.00pm to 8.44pm	8.45pm to 9.59pm	10.00pm to 10.59pm
LEO 23 to 31 Jul	5.45pm to 7.29pm	7.30pm to 8.44pm	8.45pm to 9.44pm
01 to 11 Aug	5.15pm to 6.59pm	7.00pm to 8.14pm	8.15pm to 9.14pm
12 to 23 Aug	4.30pm to 6.14pm	6.15pm to 7.29pm	7.30pm to 8.29pm
VIR 24 to 31 Aug	3.30pm to 5.14pm	5.15pm to 6.29pm	6.30pm to 7.29pm
01 to 11 Sep	3.00pm to 4.44pm	4.45pm to 5.59pm	6.00pm to 6.59pm
12 to 22 Sep	2.15pm to 3.59pm	4.00pm to 5.14pm	5.15pm to 6.14pm
LIB 23 to 30 Sep	1.30pm to 3.14pm	3.15pm to 4.29pm	4.30pm to 5.29pm
01 to 11 Oct	1.00pm to 2.44pm	2.45pm to 3.59pm	4.00pm to 4.59pm
12 to 23 Oct	12.15pm to 1.59pm	2.00pm to 3.14pm	3.15pm to 4.14pm
SCO 24 to 31 Oct	11.30am to 1.14pm	1.15pm to 2.29pm	2.30pm to 3.29pm
01 to 11 Nov	00.45am to 12.29pm	12.30pm to 1.44pm	1.45pm to 2.44pm
12 to 22 Nov	10.15am to 11.59am	12.00pm to 1.14pm	1.15pm to 2.14pm
SAG 23 to 30 Nov	9.30am to 11.14am	11.15am to 12.29pm	12.30pm to 1.29pm
01 to 11 Dec	8.45am to 10.29am	10.30am to 11.44am	11.45am to 12.44pm
12 to 21 Dec	8.15am to 9.59am	10.00am to 11.14am	11.15am to 12.14pm
CAP 22 to 31 Dec	7.15am to 8.59am	9.00am to 10.14am	10.15am to 11.14am
01 to 11 Jan	6.45am to 8.29am	8.30am to 9.44am	9.45am to 10.44am
12 to 20 Jan	6.15am to 7.59am	8.00am to 9.14am	9.15am to 10.14am
AQU 21 to 31 Jan	5.30am to 7.14am	7.15am to 8.29am	8.30am to 9.29am
01 to 10 Feb	5.00am to 6.44am	6.45am to 7.59am	8.00am to 8.59am
11 to 18 Feb	4.15am to 5.59am	6.00am to 7.14am	7.15am to 8.00am
PIS 19 to end Feb	3.30am to 5.14am	5.15am to 6.29am	6.30am to 7.29am
01 to 10 Mar	3.15am to 4.59am	5.00am to 6.00am	6.15am to 7.14am
11 to 20 Mar	2.30am to 4.14am	4.15am to 5.29am	5.30am to 6.29am

An Example of the Method in Action
- Jack was born at 8.35 p.m. BST (British Standard Time) on 31 July 1968.
- Deduct one hour for BST and make the birth time 7.35 p.m.
- The 31st of July is in the first (uppermost) of the three Leo rows.
- The penultimate column shows a birth time of 7.30 p.m. to 8.44 p.m.
- The column is headed "Aquarius", so it shows that Jack has the sign of Aquarius on the ascendant.
- Furthermore, we can see that he only just comes inside the limits of this birth time, so this gives him an early degree of Aquarius rising.

This quick method is not fully accurate, so check it with your app/program. An accurate computer reading confirms that Jack's ascendant is 5° Aquarius.

The Zodiac

The signs of the zodiac are always listed in the following order, and they change on or about the following dates; you need to check the correct date change for any particular year, by asking an astrologer, checking in an ephemeris or by some other means, such as an Internet search.

	SIGN	DATES
1	Aries	21 Mar – 20 Apr
2	Taurus	21 Apr – 21 May
3	Gemini	22 May – 21 Jun
4	Cancer	22 Jun – 22 Jul
5	Leo	23 Jul – 23 Aug
6	Virgo	24 Aug – 22 Sep
7	Libra	23 Sep – 23 Oct
8	Scorpio	24 Oct – 22 Nov
9	Sagittarius	23 Nov – 21 Dec
10	Capricorn	22 Dec – 20 Jan
11	Aquarius	21 Jan – 18 Feb
12	Pisces	19 Feb – 20 Mar

The odd-numbered signs (Aries, Gemini, Leo, Libra, Sagittarius and Aquarius) are masculine/positive/yang in character. This suggests extroversion, confidence and assertiveness, and the ability to solve problems with courage and enterprise. The even-numbered signs (Taurus, Cancer, Virgo, Scorpio, Capricorn and Pisces) are feminine/negative/yin in character. These suggest introversion, shyness and passivity, the ability to nurture, conserve and to solve problems by intuitive means.

I've noticed that the feminine signs are more attuned to business than the masculine ones, and that they make the best sales people. Why is this? Well, it's only a theory, but to my mind, the masculine signs have traditionally been the soldiers, warriors and the political thinkers and planners, while the feminine signs have traditionally taken care of the tribe's business, the treasury and the financial and physical well being of the group. Feminine sign people have an ability to read the omens and see which way things are moving. Finally, these people are persuasive and they can sell a dream, so they really do make good sales people.

The signs are grouped into the ancient elements of fire, earth, air and water:

Elements	SIGNS
The fire signs:	Aries, Leo and Sagittarius
The earth signs:	Taurus, Virgo and Capricorn
The air signs:	Gemini, Libra and Aquarius
The water signs:	Cancer, Scorpio and Pisces

The signs are also grouped into the ancient qualities of cardinal, fixed and mutable:

Qualities	SIGNS
The cardinal signs:	Aries, Cancer, Libra and Capricorn
The fixed signs:	Taurus, Leo, Scorpio and Aquarius
The mutable signs:	Gemini, Virgo, Sagittarius and Pisces

The Fire Signs – Aries, Leo Sagittarius

The key ideas here are of energy, enthusiasm and optimism. These people need to be in the centre of whatever is going on, thoroughly involved and even directing. Fire people take the initiative and throw their enthusiasm, intuition and faith behind any enterprise. They never quite relinquish their childhood and are therefore very much in tune with young people and young ideas.

Fire people are egotistic, headstrong and sometimes arrogant, but they are also generous, warm-hearted and spontaneously kind, preferring to help others wherever possible than taking advantage of them. Fire people get things started; they create activity, but need a back-up team to fill in the details for them. These people are quick to grasp an idea and tackle it with gusto, treating life like a kind of game, complete with the sportsman's sense of fair play. They find it impossible to save for a rainy day, but will invariably find a way to earn money when in trouble. Oddly enough, fire people are often very materialistic, measuring their self-worth by their ability to accumulate money and possessions and by having an expensive lifestyle. These people are quick to anger, but rarely sulk.

When a fire sign is on the ascendant, the outer manner is friendly, uncritical and non-hostile, which makes these people good mixers and excellent public relations executives.

- Aries rising gives a well-organised, slightly military bearing, which makes them fit well into any kind of paramilitary or civil service organisation.
- Leo rising subjects have a dignified and rather formal manner that inspires confidence.
- Sagittarius risers have a cheerful, pleasant and rather witty outer manner that suits all kinds of teaching, training and public speaking situations.

The Earth Signs – Taurus, Virgo, Capricorn

The key ideas here are of practicality and security. Earth is concerned with structure and slow growth, as well as conventional behaviour and concrete results. This element is connected with physical things that can be touched and held and which perform a function. Earth people are sensible; they take their time over everything and tend to finish every task that they start. They are shrewd and careful, usually very good at figure work. They are surprisingly dexterous, so they don't often drop or break anything.

Earth people hate to waste anything and they are careful with their money. However, they are invariably generous to their own families. They need a secure home and a solid financial base; requirements that make them appear materialistic to others. Earthy types like to socialise among small groups of familiar people who appreciate their intelligence and dry sense of humour. They may lack spontaneity and can be too cautious and fussy at times, but they are reliable and capable. It takes time to get to know these folk, as they prefer to hang back in social situations, while in business situations they behave in a rather formal manner. Earth people are suspicious of the motives of others and are extra sensitive to hurt. They are slow to fall in love, but when they do, they will remain loyal and faithful to their partner in the majority of cases.

When an earth sign is on the ascendant, the outer manner is shy, serious and cautious, but they send out pleasant and tactful signals.

- Taurus risers are sociable and they are often musical, creative or artistic.
- Virgo risers are shy until they get to know people.
- Capricorn risers are friendly and they dress well.

The Air Signs – Gemini, Libra, Aquarius

The key idea here is of communication. Air people are concerned with ideas and theories of all kinds, including education, networks and news. They seek answers to questions and then go on to enlighten other people. The network of their nervous system is always on the alert and sometimes over-stretched. These people may be serious-minded intellectuals who are highly involved with the education system or the media, or they may be chirpy, happy-go-lucky types who pick up their street-wise knowledge from the tabloid newspapers and the local pub. They can be found arguing, exploring ideas and becoming excited by means and methods that can apply to anything from the way the universe was formed to a recent football game. They make good journalists, shopkeepers, teachers and travellers, because they are always up-to-date.

Although kind hearted and genuinely concerned with humanity, they can forget their many friends when they are out of sight. They cannot deal with emotional dependency on the part of others, as this drains them, leaving them exhausted and irritable. Air rising subjects love gadgets, especially those that help them communicate or travel, such as computers, fancy telephones and a good fast car. These people may be too talkative.

When an air sign is on the ascendant, the subject is friendly and sociable, but also independent and somewhat detached.

- The Gemini riser is constantly busy, but always ready to chat.
- The Libra riser is good-looking and pleasant company.
- The Aquarian riser can be very friendly or very hostile.

The Water Signs – Cancer, Scorpio, Pisces

The key ideas here are of emotion, intuition and feeling. These people may spend their lives helping others, or at least involving themselves in human problems. They are attached to the kind of matters that bring beginnings, endings and transformations to the lives of others. Watery people respond slowly when asked a question and may appear slow to grasp a new concept, but this is deceptive, because they are filtering the ideas through their layers of intuition before accepting them. Being slow to change, they prefer familiar surroundings and the closeness of family and friends.

Water people are often quite tense and they can worry themselves into illness. They need a lot of understanding, as their moods and emotions make them changeable and unfathomable at times. They are the kindest of friends, often giving practical and sensible help when it's needed, but they cannot take too much neurotic dependence from others. These people are hypersensitive, creative and often psychic. They can appear withdrawn and distant in some cases, but they desperately need stable relationships with plenty of love and affection.

When a water sign is on the ascendant the subject will hide his true feelings. He fears the world around him; he feels a strong need to protect himself, and also in some cases, to protect the helpless. What you see is definitely not what you get with these people.

- Cancerians appear chatty and helpful and they do well in any situation that requires tact.
- Scorpio risers use many different forms of camouflage, one of their favourites being offensiveness and an off-putting manner. It's always worth being patient with such people, because there is often a reason for their difficult attitude, and the reward is usually worth the effort.
- Pisces risers may appear soft and gentle or abrupt and offensive, depending upon their choice of camouflage. The signals they give out are consciously or subconsciously chosen for their effect, making them appear fierce, friendly, peaceful or docile depending upon their choice of mask.

Cardinal Signs – Aries, Cancer, Libra, Capricorn

Cardinal people cannot be held under anyone's thumb, they need to take charge of their own world. Their energies may be directed towards themselves, their homes and families or to the wider world of work and politics. The cardinal signs, being on the angles of a birthchart, provide the energy and initiative to get things moving.

Fixed Signs – Taurus, Leo, Scorpio, Aquarius

Fixed people have the strength and endurance to see things through and to uphold the status quo. They rarely change their homes, careers or partnerships, preferring to live with an existing situation rather than face uncertainty. Fixed people are loyal and dependable, but also very obstinate. They project an image of strength that is an effective shield for their considerable vulnerability.

Mutable Signs – Gemini, Virgo, Sagittarius, Pisces

These people can adapt to the prevailing circumstances at any given time while, at the same time, managing to alter a situation to suit themselves. Mutable people can steer projects through periods of transition as well as bringing things to a conclusion. They work in fields where things, jobs or people pass through their hands and then come to an end or leave to go on their way. Although gentle and likable, mutable people can be ruthless when the need arises.

Aries Rising

RULED BY MARS

*The whole art of war consists of getting at what is
on the other side of the hill.*
ARTHUR WELLESLEY, 1ST DUKE OF WELLINGTON

Aries is a cardinal sign, so it likes its own way and it's also a fire sign, which implies enthusiasm and impulsiveness. It's masculine/positive in its approach, which suggests an outwardly extrovert nature. Aries rising is a sign of short ascension, which means that it only applies in the northern hemisphere for a very short period of time in any day, making these people rather thin on the ground, north of the equator; It is a sign of medium ascension in the southern hemisphere.

Early Experiences

Many Aries rising children are born into military families who move about from one place to another. They may also spend a part of each year at boarding school, so the child experiences feelings of strangeness, dislocation and of distance from family and familiar surroundings. Self-reliance and some measure of self-centredness are natural for Aries risers, even if their childhood experiences don't force this upon them, and this can make it difficult for them to form successful family relationships later on. The Aries riser may opt for a life in the services, where he becomes part of a larger family-type group. Several years ago, I did a horoscope for a middle-aged lady who was coming to the end of a service career. She told me that it had been a good life full of travel and fellowship, and that she wasn't quite sure what she was going to do with her time now that she was becoming a civilian.

Aries risers who grow up in a normal, stay-at-home family, often experience discord and conflict. There may be a difficult relationship between the child and his parents, and this is especially true of the father/son relationship. There can't be two bosses in one family, and in this case, neither wants to concede any kind of authority to the other. It's quite usual for the two to be very different in character with little real understanding between them; so, it seems that neither can really approve of the other and there could be some noisy disagreements.

It's worth remembering that an Aries rising nature makes for a noisy, bouncy and rather bumptious child whose restless behaviour and argumentative ways can aggravate even the most saintly of parents. In some cases, the parents are sporty and adventurous, and they encourage a kind of gung-ho bravery in the child. This is all very well if the child is also an outdoor and athletic type, but it isn't so great otherwise.

Women who have this rising sign may not fall into the traditional feminine role. This does not imply that all Aries rising women are gay, or that they are militant feminists. On the contrary, these women get on very well with men, enjoying their company and sharing their interests. Some women prefer not to marry, either living an independent life with or without boyfriends or finding happiness within a career. Those who do marry and have a family need an interesting career outside the home in order to sop up their extra energy and give them something worthwhile to do. Fortunately, these days, there is plenty of scope for the sporty, extrovert, enthusiastic Aries rising woman to have the unrestricted, independent kind of lifestyle that she needs.

The IC is concerned with family matters, and your IC is in probably in the family-minded sign of Cancer. This makes you a surprisingly caring family member, even to the extent of sacrificing a great deal for your loved ones.

Many Aries rising people come from small families and there may be little contact with relatives. Aries rising children, therefore, don't have the opportunity of benefiting from a wider family group, and this leaves them with only their parents' views and values to fall back on. Frequently, these values are distorted and lacking in common sense. Furthermore, the Aries risers are often only-children, or so separated in age and type from the other siblings that they feel like an only child.

It's likely that one or both parents disliked you or saw no value in you. There was no discernible reason for this; you were simply viewed as an irritation or an inconvenience. This leads many of you to seek self-validation through marriage, often marrying young and choosing an older partner, or someone who is deemed wiser and more competent at the game of life. If the marriage doesn't work out, you may begin to philander. There is no guarantee that second or subsequent relationships work out either, unless you are able to go through a good deal of self-analysis and reach a stage where you can finally throw off the distorted lessons of your childhood.

Some Aries rising people succeed in one-to-one relationships, but then face difficulties in relating to their children, either leaning too far towards the position of authority and dominance, or overdoing the nurturing role by clinging to them and sacrificing on their behalf for far too long. All Aries rising subjects have the sign of Capricorn on their midheaven, and it seems as if top of the chart (Capricorn) leads to too much authority, while the bottom of the chart (Cancer) leads to too much clinging.

However, nothing stays the same forever; children grow up and relationships come and go. With a bit of luck, you can learn from life. Perhaps in compensation, Aries rising subjects often make lots of good friends, while others make a viable family out of a couple of pet animals.

Basically, this is neither the best nor the worst sign to have on the ascendant. There may have been loneliness in childhood, but this seems to breed self-reliance and doesn't usually cause you to have any difficulty in relating to others later on in life. Aries rising is a sociable sign and on the whole, a cheerful and optimistic one. The worst fault is a tendency to break out in sudden attacks and loud, abusive behaviour that is completely unwarranted.

Appearance

Remember to make allowances for racial differences, family tendencies and the influence of the rest of your birthchart when looking at astrological appearances.

The Aries influence would suggest a medium to small stature with a strong and muscular body that may run to fat later. Your arms and shoulders are strong and you can lift and carry surprisingly heavy weights for your size. Your face is broad across the eyes and may be rounded with a rather large head for your body. Aries rising eyes are neither protruding nor deep set, they stare out honestly from under thick, arched eyebrows.

Aries rising women can do a lot with eye make-up, as there is a rather large and flat area of eyelid to play with. The hair may be reddish in colour, quickly going grey. Men of this sign lean towards baldness - well, they do say that bald men are sexy! Women may moan about their hair or dislike their round faces.

Outer Manner

You present yourself in a cheerful, friendly, non-hostile manner, but may find it hard to conceal your contempt for those whose minds and actions are slower than your own. Not being easily influenced, you prefer to make up your own mind about everything, and you can appear rather opinionated. Others see you as quick, clever and courageous, but they may become annoyed by your tendency to push yourself to the front of every queue and to fight for the best of whatever is going. Your sense of humour and child-like appeal can help you get away with murder - especially with the opposite sex.

The Midheaven

The midheaven shows the subject's aims and ambitions, public standing and attitude to work outside the home. It can often throw light on strange or unexpected behaviour in a way that even the Sun, Moon and Ascendant don't always address. Some rising signs usually have only one possible MC, while others can have two or even three possible MCs, depending on the time of year in which a person was born, along with the hemisphere and latitude of birth.

In the northern hemisphere, Aries rising can only have a Capricorn MC, but in the southern hemisphere, it is just possible for those born with very late Aries rising to have an Aquarian MC.

The MC also shows the type of person whom you find attractive, so someone whose sun sign was the same as your MC could make you very happy.

Aries/Capricorn

Despite not showing much interest in studying while young, you may return to study later in order to gain some specific qualification, because you have more ambition than is immediately obvious to outsiders.

This MC suggests that you work best in a well-ordered structure, perhaps in a large public service organisation. Some of you prefer to run your own well-planned businesses. You are determined and capable. Your leadership qualities and common sense attitude to money can lead to great success, but this could well come rather late in life. You prefer to start something new, but if you do take over an existing position or an existing team, you soon reorganise it to reflect your own personal style.

You could be drawn to the Arian careers of engineering, building, public service or the armed services, or to the Capricorn ones of business and banking. You may be interested in national or local politics as a career. Your brain is excellent and, if the rest of the chart backs this up, you could find a future in the academic world but you also like to work in an area that helps the public or that improves the environment. You may spend several years coasting along in a job until a change of circumstances propels you towards success.

Aries/Aquarius

This rare combination adds idealism to the personality and it makes you far more interested in the future than in the past. This Asc/MC combo can give you truly inspired ideas and great intuition, so you may become a wonderful inventor or revolutionary. However, this combination is not good for practicality or even basic common sense in some cases. You really must try to keep your feet on the ground and avoid getting so hung up about something that you become a bore or you will lose that great gift of sociability and popularity that is such a large part of your success.

The Descendant

When Aries is rising, the descendant is Libra. The fiery, enthusiastic Aries is attracted to the calm detachment of Libra, including this sign's pleasantness, good taste and desire for harmony and balance. Librans are often good looking and stylish too, but Librans like to argue and once they start, they don't know when to stop.

Love and Relating

Your most attractive features are generosity, honesty, spontaneous kindness and a sense of humour. To be honest, as long as your partner is humourous, intelligent and tolerant of your daft behaviour, you will be happy and so will your partner. You need an independent partner who has work and interests of their own, or better still, someone who doesn't need to be waited on hand and foot. However, you need them within phone-shot so that you can have your needs attended to immediately! Aries risers don't require a terribly domesticated partner, but you do need help in the house and with the children, as you are not especially domesticated or tidy yourself.

Your partner must give you space, not only for your career, but also for your hobbies and interests. You need to be able to take off from time to time, either on business trips or sporting holidays with a group of mates. Your partner must understand that there is a side of you that needs this kind of freedom, and that this doesn't constitute either a lack of loyalty or a dereliction of duty.

You love your children very deeply, and want the best for them, often going to great lengths to educate them. Try not to dominate your children or to show impatience, especially if they seem slow, timid, introverted or clumsy. If you behave impatiently to this kind of child, he will freeze up, making him even more awkward and withdrawn, and will subsequently deprive you of the special kind of warmth that you could have from a loving parent/child relationship.

With your abundance of energy, sex is an obvious necessity, and even a slightly dodgy relationship will work for you if the sexual side is good. In some ways, you suit a moody, changeable partner who varies in his or her sexual needs and responses from one day to the next, so that you can avoid your pet hate - boredom.

Health

Traditionally, Aries rules the head down as far as the upper jaw. Therefore, headaches, eyes, ears, sinuses and the upper teeth are trouble spots. Some Aries rising subjects suffer from acne well into adult life. You have neither the time nor the nature to give in to illness, but sudden fevers and accidents are possibilities. You can become quite ill at times, but will bounce back quickly, because your resistance is generally high. You enjoy food and may be a drinker, therefore weight gain could present a problem later in life. However, if you maintain your preference for an active life, you quickly use up the extra calories. Arian skin is often very pale and delicate, so you have to put on plenty of sunscreen, and even cover up on very sunny days.

Additional Information

- You may have a quiet voice, and possibly a slightly high one.
- Some of you love animals, and you may particularly enjoy horse riding.
- You may like travel, hunting of various kinds and chasing after any kind of dream.
- You spend freely on clothes, although you don't always look after them properly.
- You will probably have a lifelong interest in sports, both as a spectator and as a participant. You particularly like team sports and anything to do with speed.

ARIES RISING CELEBRITIES	
John Lennon	Joe Cocker
Billy Graham	Bette Midler
Joan Baez	Martina Navratilova

Taurus Rising

Ruled by Venus

Shall I compare thee to a summer's day?
Thou art more lovely and more temperate:
Rough winds do shake the darling buds of May,
And summer's lease hath all too short a date.
WILLIAM SHAKESPEARE, SONNET

Taurus is a fixed sign, which means that Taureans like to stay with a situation and see it through. It's also an earth sign, which implies practicality and a stubborn nature. It's feminine/negative, which suggests introversion. This is a sign of short ascension in the northern hemisphere, so only a few people are born each day with this ascendant. However, it's not quite as short as Pisces or Aries, so there are a few more of you around than there are of the latter two. It is a sign of medium ascension in the southern hemisphere.

Early Experiences

Taurus rising suggests comfort, and this was certainly true of your childhood. All the earth signs place an emphasis on the need for material security and, in the case of any earth sign on the ascendant, the parents may accumulate money and goods in reaction to their own experiences of childhood poverty. They probably had to work very hard in order to make a home and bring up children. By the time you came along, your parents may have got over the early struggles, or may have still been trying to get it all together. Either way, the message given to the Taurus rising child is one of the need for security, comfort and, better still, wealth.

The old-fashioned virtues of a steady job, money in the bank and solid family life were programmed into you, but it's also possible that values of crass materialism and the devil-take-the-hindmost could also have been pushed upon you. This is fine if you have the same kind of requirements elsewhere in your birthchart, but not so good if you have a gamut of planets in a completely different type of sign. Another and far more serious problem is that, although you were taken care of materially, you may have suffered emotional deprivation. One person with Taurus rising that I know had a mother who suffered badly from depression, which made her unavailable to the child.

When a rising sign is both earthy and fixed, there is a strong possibility that one or both of the parents behaved in an authoritarian manner. Approval may have been given and withheld in subtle ways, making you withdrawn and rather mulish in return. Another possibility is that your father was a slightly awesome figure. However, there is much that's good about this rising sign, and one could do a lot worse than to be born with a Taurean ascendant.

Your parents' outlook was conservative and their behaviour expressed moderation, commonsense, practicality and kindness. You were encouraged to be kind, thoughtful and conscientious. In the unlikely event that you grew up in anything other than the nuclear family, this would have been because one of your parents died. You are unlikely to have witnessed open discord or divorce at first hand. Civilised, unexpressed discontent might have been the order of the day in your parent's household.

You may have grown up with parents who were wrapped up in one another, leaving you emotionally stranded, so that you learned to demand nothing and to avoid bringing the familiar look of irritation to their faces. If you were lucky enough to find another relative or perhaps a person outside the family to whom you could relate, the situation would not have been quite so bad. You may have been at odds with a brother or sister, either envying them for being more successful and more acceptable to your parents than you were, or on the other hand, you may have despised them for being dull, incompetent and irritating. This situation would also have caused you to hide your real feelings, to become devious or to boil inwardly. On occasions, your rage would be towering, frightening and quite destructive. As you grew older, you managed to avoid scenes and ignore unpleasantness, but when pushed, you might erupt in anger or retreat into a world of silent withdrawal that's incomprehensible to others.

Many of you love gardening, because you can enjoy both the scent and beauty of the flowers and growing good things to eat. It's possible that your parents were farmers or landscape gardeners, because there is a natural feeling for the land and all that it produces. The twin messages of conservatism and conservation would lead you to create and to build rather than destroy, and to continue rather than to bring things to a close.

Your family may have been instrumental in introducing you to the world of music, dance or art. You have a natural appreciation of beauty and harmony, so you would have enjoyed these things. If your home life was stable and your parents loving, united and caring, the situation at school may have been a problem. You were not the kind of child to cause trouble at school, and disruption and disobedience is hardly your way of doing things. Nevertheless, unless the rest of the chart is an intellectual one, you were probably slow to catch on, especially in the years before adolescence.

If your parents and teachers accepted you as you were without trying to get you to perform miracles, your school life would have been pleasant, if rather unproductive. However, your teachers may have made you feel worthless and a failure. Worse still, Taurus risers are not the sportiest of children. Many are plump and they all hate to feel cold, wet and uncomfortable. Neither you nor your parents could see any value in romping around on a muddy sports field, although a Sunday afternoon tramp across the field with a dog was quite another matter. Your natural talent and interests lay in the areas of art and music. Nowadays, these interests are fostered for both sexes, but in the days when boys had to be boys and self-expression was not on the curriculum, this could have caused some suffering.

You probably enjoyed working with natural substances such as wood or clay, and you like to cook nice food. Many Taurus rising subjects develop an interest in reading, maths and finance, and they go on to educate themselves later in life at their own pace.

Appearance
Remember to make allowances for racial differences, family tendencies and the influence of the rest of your birthchart when looking at astrological appearances.

Taurus rising women look luscious when young, but have to guard against weight gain later in life. Your complexion is clear, your eyes are marvellous and, in white races, your skin is rather pale and luminous. Your pleasant smile and gentle manner add to your attractive looks. It's fairly common for members of this rising sign to have a "Churchillian" appearance around the mouth.

Outer Manner
Your outer manner is pleasant and slightly reserved, but friendly and non-hostile. You enjoy a chat with neighbours or colleagues from the office, you probably enjoy listening to office gossip and jokes. You have a good clean sense of humour that doesn't depend upon cruelty or sarcasm for effect. You appear slow moving to others, preferring to make your way

through life at quite a gentle pace. Some Taurus risers give an appearance of hardness, especially in business situations.

The Midheaven

The midheaven shows the subject's aims and ambitions, his public standing and his attitude to work outside the home. It can often throw light on strange or unexpected behaviour in a way that even the Sun, Moon and Ascendant don't always address. Some rising signs usually have only one possible MC, while others can have two or even three possible MCs, depending on the time of year in which a person was born, along with the hemisphere and latitude of birth.

In the case of births in the UK and in similar (northern) latitudes, the Taurus rising midheaven is always in Capricorn. In much of the United States, people who have a late degree of Taurus on the ascendant may have Aquarius on the MC.

Taurus/Capricorn

Capricorn, like Taurus, is an earth sign, but it's cardinal in nature, whereas Taurus is fixed. This cardinality on the MC may be one of the reasons why so many Taurus risers go in for running their own show, by owning their own businesses. You produce or supply goods that are practical and useful. You may run a shop, a gardening service, something in the farming or farm-supply line or a small factory. Many of you work in the building trade. Your love of beauty and your subtle sense of touch could lead you into the fields of dressmaking, cooking and craftwork. Some of you take up beauty therapy or become involved with the cosmetic industry, possibly as make-up artists. Many others find their way into the entertainment world, often as singers. However, life being what it is, many Taurus rising people actually work in offices and banks. The Capricorn connection gives a fondness for big business and banking, while the Taurean thoroughness ensures that errors are few.

Taurus/Aquarius

Generally speaking, Taurus rising subjects resist pressure and dislike hectic or worrying jobs, but the Taurus/Aquarius combination is a little more able to cope with this. Remember that these are both fixed signs that need to do things at their own pace and do them in their own way. The ingenuity of Aquarius could produce a competent wheeler-dealer or someone who reaches the top in an unusual career. The combination of these two could produce a show-business impresario, the owner of a respected art gallery or auction house, or a top editor. This combination adds determination and stubbornness.

Despite the fact that the midheaven is supposed to represent one's direction in life, it can also show the type of person who might attract you, especially if you require a partner who is in sympathy with your goals. Therefore, a partner who has a strong Capricorn or Aquarius emphasis on the chart could appeal to you.

The Descendant

Your descendant is in Scorpio, so you are attracted to strong, determined people. You seem to be looking for the fireworks that accompany the Scorpio, either in the form of uncertain moods or sexual energy. I have no evidence of a particularly high incidence of Taurus/Scorpio relationships, but I think that this combination would work quite well. Both partners need stability in relationships, both are happier in familiar surroundings than with a life of constant change, and both are dutiful family members who are also orientated towards getting on in life. There is much in common but there are times when Scorpio's moods might be hard for Taurus to take. Both signs prefer commitment to playing the field.

Love and Relating

You can cope with a financially independent partner or even one who is heavily involved with a career, just as long as the emotional security is there. You need the love that might have been missing during your childhood. You like to know where your partner is, also what they are doing - not because you distrust them, but because you feel safer if there are no mysteries going on around you. You also like your partner to be around at mealtimes.

A couple of female acquaintances of mine who live with Taurus rising men, tell me that they are very well looked after in bed! On a more serious note, what Taurus rising subjects like best and need most are emotional security and a peaceful home. The adult Taurus rising subject may still suffer the residual effects of the childhood lack of closeness and touch.

Health

Taurus is a robust sign with good powers of recovery. The weak spots are the neck, throat, thyroid gland and the lower teeth. You may be prone to diabetes.

Additional Information

- If these people finds a partner, they never really let go; for instance, one Taurus rising person left his wife for another woman, and then had an affair with his wife, eventually returning to her.
- Some can be argumentative and hurtful, while others can be very stingy, even over small and inconsequential things. Some don't like to hold hands or be touched.
- These people rarely drop anything, so they are probably good at catching a ball. They are also very dexterous.
- Some are practical and sensible, others are the complete opposite, it seems that there are no half measures with this sign.
- Most seem to love cats.
- Many have a conventional day job and an absorbing hobby, such as singing or dancing.
- Some are religious.

TAURUS RISING CELEBRITIES	
Dionne Warwick	Amelia Earhart
Mia Farrow	Liza Minelli
George Lucas	Robert Kennedy

Gemini Rising

Ruled by Mercury
The flower that smiles today
Tomorrow dies:
All that we wish to stay
Tempts and then flies.
What is this world's delight?
Lightening that mocks the night.
Brief even as bright.
PERCY BYSSHE SHELLEY, MUTABILITY

This sign is mutable, which implies flexibility of mind, and an air sign, which implies an intellectual approach to everything. It's masculine/ positive, suggesting an outwardly extrovert nature.

Early Experiences
If you have this rising sign, your childhood may have been unsatisfactory, emotionally deprived or even something of a horror story; there may even have been a mystery surrounding your origins. If your childhood was genuinely all sweetness and light, I suggest that you actually re-check your birth time! I call this the "orphan's ascendant", because there is a feeling of being left out in the cold. A surprisingly high proportion of orphans, fostered and adopted children seem to be born with Gemini rising. Many people who started out with two parents in the normal manner seem to mislay one or both of them somewhere along the way!

Even if you were brought up in a normal nuclear family, there would have been feelings of isolation and of being a square peg in a round hole. All this would have been bad enough for the silent, withdrawn type who is given to hiding his feelings and putting on an act of dumb acceptance, but you need to communicate and to connect with other people on an intellectual level. You also like to analyse yourself and the world around you in order to put it into a sensible and meaningful kind of order.

There may have been difficulty in your dealings with brothers and sisters and you may have grown up in a patched-together extended family. If you came from a large family, you may have missed out in the rush to gain your parent's attention, or you may be so different from your natural parents and siblings that you appear to have originated from a different planet.

You were probably one of the younger children, or even actually the youngest child in the family, born to parents for whom the novelty of parenthood had rather worn off. Older siblings may have pushed you around, and your parents might have ignored you or left you with minders, while your mother went out to earn much-needed extra money. Something may have gone badly wrong early in your childhood, maybe the death of a parent or some kind of financial disaster.

You may have been acutely aware that the people with whom you had been left, looked after you under sufferance or for money. It could have been all but impossible to please them Even in a more normal family, there is a feeling of being the odd one out. You may have been an academic child in a practical family, or a school failure in a family where the only things that counted were brains and exam papers. You may have had a personal or religious outlook that was different from the rest of the family.

If your childhood was tolerable, you will have gained from the better side of this ascendant. The benefits are exposure to books, ideas and teaching aids of one kind or another from an early age. You were encouraged to read, write and to express yourself. If self-expression in the form of too much talking was discouraged, you will have been encouraged by your teachers to write, draw and make things. Being restless and lively, you enjoyed sports or dancing and you could have achieved a high standard. It's possible that you enjoyed being involved in some kind of youth organisation, but probably not for long, as you hate to be regimented. Even as an adult, you enjoy movement and often do most of your thinking while walking or exercising in the local swimming pool. Gemini risers have an inventive streak and are often dexterous, so you can always find something to do. You like animals and pets, as they love you without judging you.

You are surprisingly ambitious and there is a feeling that, if you can develop a level of strength, power and self-esteem, you can avoid being laughed at and shoved out of the way. There are some among you who go through a sticky marriage or two before you realise that you have a right to be loved and to be treated decently. Gemini rising people are workers, and this is your salvation. You probably have two or more careers going at once, together with a couple of committee positions to boot. You need to feel important and one day, you realise with a jolt that you *are* important and no one talks down to you any more. The Gemini rising clown disappears then, being replaced by the Gemini rising ringmaster.

Appearance

Remember to make allowances for racial differences, family tendencies and the influence of the rest of your birthchart when looking at astrological appearances.

You may have pretty awful problems with your teeth, requiring years of wire braces or even operations to alter the shape of your jaws. Your hair may be fine and in need of a lot of attention. Your hands and feet are neat, and you try to maintain a rather stylish and youthful appearance throughout life. Your chic, attractive clothes reflect your busy super-modern lifestyle. Your car is an important part of your turnout, and this is small, neat, sporty and fast.

Outer Manner

Your outer manner is cheerful, confident and friendly. Some of you can be offensive and upsetting at times, but your sharp-edged cleverness is a shield that protects your vulnerability and shaky sense of self-esteem. You can appear strong, efficient and businesslike, but if you feel threatened in any way, you can be cutting and hurtful. Females with this sign on the ascendant give an appearance of capability and efficiency that doesn't seem to detract from their femininity. The Gemini rising mind is masculine and the mental processes are logical and orderly, more suited to the engineer or computer programmer than anyone's idea of a dizzy woman.

You use your hands while talking and may be emphatic when excited about something. You remain young looking throughout life. You may actually fear old age, but your attitude and appearance guarantee that you remain youthful, even when old. Your quick mind and sense of humour are delightful. Your friendly, non-hostile manner wins you many friends.

The Midheaven

The midheaven shows the subject's aims and ambitions, his public standing and his attitude to work outside the home. It can often throw light on strange or unexpected behaviour in a way that even the Sun, Moon and Ascendant don't always address. Some rising signs usually have only one possible MC, while others can have two or even three possible MCs, depending on the time of year in which a person was born, along with the hemisphere and latitude of birth.

It's possible for those who were born in southern areas of Europe or the USA to have Capricorn on the MC, but for British births, the MC will be Aquarius.

Gemini/Capricorn

Those of you who have Capricorn on the MC are ambitious and determined, looking for security and advancement. You can put your mind to the job and get on with it in a way that other people can only envy. You can turn your communicating skills to good account by sticking at a job and climbing slowly up the career ladder. The earth sign quality of Capricorn suggests that you are probably attracted to work where the values are material, such as in business, banking and large corporations, because you feel a need to achieve something solid by your efforts. This combination could make you a highly skilled and ambitious operator. Alternatively, you could find a comfortable job and stick with it for years without going any higher, as long as there were plenty of new faces around for company and entertainment.

Gemini/Aquarius

The vast majority of Gemini rising subjects, however, have Aquarius on the mid-heaven and this brings both vision and humanitarianism into the picture. A measure of idealism in your choice of career, coupled with your need to communicate, leads you towards the whole area of teaching and training others. If you follow any of the other typically Gemini careers, such as sales representative, journalist, writer, broadcaster or telephonist, you will still try to help people, both on a personal day-to-day basis or by means of communicating useful or instructive ideas.

Gemini's ruling planet is Mercury. In mythology, the Roman god, Mercury, was a messenger who worked for all the gods, but especially for Apollo. Indeed, he was Apollo's errand-boy and he did a good deal of his boss's dirty work, often getting the blame for it, which is a familiar situation, even today!

Another, more satisfying side of this god's work was healing, and this still draws Mercurial people even now. Strictly speaking, the healing attributes are often laid at the feet of the other Mercury-ruled sign of Virgo, but Geminians do their bit in their own way. The idealistic Aquarian midheaven coupled with the Gemini need to help can lead to a medical or nursing career, although the need to communicate often manifests itself in some kind of counselling work. Therefore, psychiatry, marriage guidance or the counselling side of astrology could appeal to you, either as a full-time occupation or as a satisfying sideline.

The presence of such forward looking air signs on both the ascendant and mid-heaven gives an interest in information technology and communications, both from an engineering point of view and by working directly in the broadcasting field. Some Gemini rising subjects become Tarot readers or spiritual healers.

The MC can throw some light on the kind of partners you choose, both in business and in personal life. You may be attracted to people who reflect the values of the sign on your midheaven.

The Descendant
When Gemini is rising, the descendant is in Sagittarius. In theory, you should find yourself especially attracted to Sagittarians. In practice, you could be attracted to any one of the 12 signs – or none of them! Perhaps you look for Sagittarian values in your friends. The Sagittarian values are intelligence, broadmindedness and a taste for adventure.

If your ascendant is late in Gemini, much of your seventh house will be in Capricorn, which will encourage you to seek out a reliable and responsible kind of partner, perhaps one who is in a position of power and influence.

Love and Relating
This is above all a sign of the intellect, so a stimulating partner is a necessity. You can even put up with an absolute rat more easily than you can a boring partner. It hardly needs to be stressed that the old familiar triangle of "safe partner and thrilling but unreliable lover" could have been made for you. Even a thrilling but unreliable partner is all right, just as long as you can still enjoy your first real loves, which are your work and your hobbies!

Gemini risers are curious, so you probably experimented with sex quite early in life and there is an element of the "don't die wondering" syndrome here. To be honest, you can live without sex, as long as you are creatively occupied, but your need for comfort and company will soon draw you back to companionship. Your greatest need is to communicate, so you are bound to take the needs of a partner into account.

Health
Gemini rules the arms, shoulders, wrists and hands, also the bronchial tubes and lungs. Therefore, asthma, bronchitis and rheumatism are all possible complaints. Strained ligaments and broken wrists are common, too. Your nerves are delicate, so you could expect skin eruptions, allergies, migraine and nervous bowel problems. You may have an occasional spell of hysteria due to overstretched nerves, or as a result of

too much worry. If ever a sign benefited from meditation, massage and relaxation techniques, this is the one.

Additional Information

- All are good with words, either as politicians, writers or broadcasters.
- I've come across cases where the subject's parents were literally on their deathbeds before apologising to the subject for being so dreadful to them. Yet the Gemini rising child was always extremely good to the parent.
- As babies and children, Gemini rising subjects are so quick to develop that they are light years ahead of others around them. This causes jealousy and resentment.

GEMINI RISING CELEBRITIES	
Charlie Sheen	Gregory Peck
Michelle Pfeiffer	Hillary Clinton
Drew Barrimore	Neil Armstrong

Cancer Rising

Ruled by the Moon
*Keep the home fires burning, while
Your hearts are yearning,
Though your lads are far away they
Dream of home.*
LENA GUILBERT FORD, KEEP THE HOME FIRES BURNING

Cancer is a feminine/negative sign that belongs to the water group, but we must remember that it's a cardinal sign, which implies strength and determination. Even though Cancer is deemed to be a gentle sign, oriented towards the feminine principles of home and family, people with this sign rising know what they want and won't do without it for long. This is a sign of long ascension; therefore, there are many people with this sign on the ascendant, at least in the northern hemisphere.

Early Experiences
You were probably well cared for by at least one of your parents and never left for long periods with strangers, nor were you badly treated. Very few people have a perfect childhood, and one could argue that a completely trouble-free childhood is a poor training for adult life. It's better if a little rain does fall from time to time, so that one learns to use an umbrella! This sign is especially associated with the mother, mother figure or anybody who took on the nurturing role.

Your childhood home would have been fairly comfortable, with a slight emphasis on materialism. You were a wanted child; possibly the first one born into the family, and you were able to have your parent's exclusive attention for a few years at least. Even though it's likely that you were the eldest child in the family, you stayed young at heart.

You have a responsible attitude and a slightly dignified manner. You didn't get into any ridiculous escapades when you were young, and neither did you find it necessary to play the part of the clown. You were quiet and rather cautious, a bit inclined to cling to your parents and reluctant to move on, out into the world. This attitude tends to change later, when the progressed ascendant moves from cautious Cancer into adventurous Leo.

There is some evidence of religious or spiritual messages being handed out by your parents, and these are accepted or rejected later in life, according to your changing views and circumstances. Your parents may have encouraged you to follow in their footsteps, but you weren't pressured into doing so. In all probability, you had a good relationship with your father, but he might have been a slightly remote figure, being wrapped up in his work or personal interests.

Some Cancer rising subjects have a sneaking contempt for their fathers, considering them to be weak, but sometimes, the father becomes seriously ill either in a dramatic way which frightens the child, or in a lingering way which requires permanent care and attention. One Cancer rising friend of mine told me that his father had a weak and frequently ulcerated stomach, which meant the father needed to eat very carefully, whilst also being protected from worry. This ensured that the mother was the power in the family, so reinforcing the typical Cancerian respect for the power of the mother. Incidentally, unless there are hard aspects from the planet Saturn to your ascendant, you were probably born easily.

Many Cancer rising subjects experience some kind of problem in connection with their schooling, especially during the secondary or college phase of their education. This stems more from peer group pressure than actual education problems. You were probably rather slow and lazy when young, as you were more inclined to sit and dream rather than to get down to work.

However, the desire to conform and a growing awareness that the road to adult success begins with school achievement, ensures that you catch up later and then leave your classmates behind. This increase of academic speed may bring a jealous and spiteful response from your erstwhile school friends. You don't seem to go through the same kind of rebellious phase as other teenagers, although there is some evidence that the famed Cancer rising attitude of obedience to parental wishes doesn't last forever. A time will come when you quietly but firmly reject your parents' preferences in favour of a career or lifestyle of your own choice. Despite these changes of direction, you tend to remain affectionately close to your parents throughout their lives.

Appearance

Remember to make allowances for racial differences, family

tendencies and the influence of the rest of your birthchart when looking at astrological appearances.

Cancer rising subjects are attractive rather than beautiful, with chubby features, full cheeks, lips and a nicely shaped nose. Your chest and rib cage are large and your shoulders and arms well covered. This gives males a slightly top heavy look, while females frequently have an hourglass type of figure. Some are chunky and solid looking rather than chubby, and those types often have quite heavily lined foreheads. In white races, the skin is pale and the hair can range from fair to almost black, and it's usually strong and abundant, with a will of its own. Your height is probably small to average, and you have to watch your weight later in life. Your hands and feet are small and neat. Both sexes like to look neat, clean and well turned out.

Outer Manner

Most Cancer rising subjects get over their early shyness and become outgoing adults, often with a talent for salesmanship and the more pleasant kind of company politics. You prefer to pour oil on troubled waters than to stir up a storm. At work, you always appear to be cheerful and friendly. You may have troubles in your life, but you don't blab about them or ever appear downhearted, but when you get home, you can be moody, miserable, angry, irritable and very hard to live with. You can even totally ignore your partner – sometimes for months on end!

You are a bit shy, being rather modest and retiring in new company. You do not really seek friendship and you are not terribly interested in people outside your immediate family. You hate to look outrageous, or to draw attention to yourself or to make a public fool of yourself. You obey the rules, and are generally very civilised in your manner. You are good to talk to because you are such a good listener.

The Midheaven

The midheaven shows the subject's aims and ambitions, public standing and attitude to work outside the home. It can often throw light on strange or unexpected behaviour in a way that even the Sun, Moon and Ascendant don't always address. Some rising signs usually have only one possible MC, while others can have two or even three possible MCs, depending on the time of year in which a person was born, along with the hemisphere and latitude of birth. In the case of Cancer rising, the MC can be Aquarius, Pisces or Aries.

Cancer/Aquarius

There is some conflict here, because Cancer rising seeks security while Aquarius seeks freedom. In resolving this conflict, you may behave in one way dealing with friends and family and in another when pursuing your worldly ambitions. If the signs are allowed to blend rather than conflict, you could be drawn to one of the caring professions, due to the fact that these are both caring signs. Counselling work is a possibility, as is medicine, veterinary work and, of course, teaching. In business, Cancer rising wants to drive a hard bargain, while Aquarius wants to be friends with the world, but both can be tough in business and both hide their true feelings from others. The intuitive skills of astrology, palmistry, graphology, numerology and the Tarot etc. may appeal to you, possibly enough to make a part-time or full-time living from them. Political activity is a natural for you, so you could be drawn to work in the civil service, local government or you may choose to serve on committees.

Cancer/Pisces

This mixture produces a sentimental person for whom continuity is important. You probably prefer to stay in a job where you feel yourself to be appreciated as part of a successful team. The Pisces element can bring confusion regarding your aims, so you could drift along, hoping for the best rather than reaching for a specific goal. If Neptune (the ruler of Pisces) is well aspected in your chart, career muddles will be less of a problem. The combination does not usually bring any burning ambitions; you just want a happy working life and contentment at home. Some of you prefer to work from home or spend your energies looking after children or animals.

The travel trade may attract you, or you may have to travel in connection with your work. You may have an interest in the medical world, osteopathy, aromatherapy or other complementary therapies. All the Cancer/Pisces people whom I know seem to consult alternative medical practitioners either in addition to, or in place of conventional doctors. You find it quite easy to accept the idea of spiritual healing and psychic or mediumistic work, probably due to your own highly developed level of intuition. You have a natural affinity with money and budgeting, therefore finance work (which also requires intuition) and fund raising for a charity are possible interests.

Cancer/Aries

This combination brings together two cardinal signs, so you would be unlikely to blindly follow any course of action that was against your own interests. The charm of the Cancerian ascendant masks your willfulness to some extent. You could make a good politician or diplomat because you appear to be sociable and reasonable, but you are usually able to make your point. If you want to, you can push your way to the top by sheer hard work and by keeping your goals clearly in sight, however some of you can't be bothered to make the effort.

You probably prefer self-employment to being part of a team, and may be interested in a mixture of the rather muscular Aries type of job and the gentler, more domestic, Cancerian type. This could lead you to run a small building concern, or to employ a group of gardening contractors or a battalion of office cleaners. Both Cancer, which is associated with patriotism and history, plus Aries, which has military inclinations, lead to an interest in military matters. This could suggest a career in the services (especially the navy), the police or part-time involvement with a paramilitary organisation. You might be interested in the Scout movement or something similar. Whatever you choose to do, you won't allow the grass to grow under your feet. Other interests, whether as hobbies or as a career, include cooking, teaching, child-care, engineering, interior design and decorating.

The Descendant

Your descendant is Capricorn, which is a conventional sign, so you look for safe and secure relationships. You are sincere in your dealings with others and you seek the same sincerity from them. You need practical partner who can stand on their own two feet and who have a sense of personal dignity. You are very caring and dutiful in your attitude to others, even when the relationship is a detached one, such as a close colleague at work. You don't appreciate people whose eccentricities include a lack of personal principles, laziness or stupidity, and you appreciate efficiency. You may be attracted to a partner who is ambitious or outstanding, but you must resist the urge to curb or control them.

I haven't noticed any prevalence of Cancer/Capricorn marriages; however, these two signs have much in common, so this could work quite well. Both signs understand the other's attachment to his or her family. Both parties will look after parents, in-laws and grandparents, in addition to children and stepchildren. The cautious attitude suggested by this descendant makes you slow to get into relationships, and inclined to marry later in life than usual.

Love and Relating

Your caution and shyness mean that you are slow to get off the ground in this area of life, and many of you seem to wait until your thirties before marrying and having children; when you do, your intentions are that you stay married, preferably for life. It's possible that this very sense of commitment is one reason for your hesitancy. Another peculiarity of this rising sign is that you are probably most comfortable with a partner who is quite a bit younger or older than you are. You are protective towards your partner, but you may take this a bit too far, becoming a bit of a mother hen.

Cancer rising is not a notably sexy sign. Typical comments are that an affectionate cuddle is as important as sex, and that sex is part of a larger relationship rather than as an end in itself. You need to love and be loved and to have the love of a family around you, and this includes parents, siblings and children. You adore your own children and can give a great deal of love and affection to other people's children, too.

Health
Traditionally, the areas that give you trouble are the stomach, breasts and the lower end of the lungs. Many Cancer rising subjects seem to have weak throats, and bronchitis, and many suffer from rheumatism.

Additional Information
- You are shrewd, but wealth may elude you, possibly because you are too lazy to follow through on a good idea, or because you financially support other family members.
- Some Cancer rising subjects are very tight-fisted, others are just short of money.
- You must watch a tendency to be cruel. You may think you are defending yourself against potential attack, but in reality, all you may be doing is hurting others for no reason.
- Surprisingly, you are flirtatious and sometimes a little bit outrageous, but you don't mean anything by this behaviour.

CANCER RISING CELEBRITIES	
Steven Spielberg	Bill Gates
Ian McShane	Robert De Niro
Michelle Obama	Mae West

Leo Rising

Ruled by the Sun

I suppose that means that I shall have to die beyond my means.

OSCAR WILDE - ON BEING PRESENTED WITH A DOCTOR'S BILL FOR AN OPERATION TOWARDS THE END OF HIS LIFE.

Leo is a masculine, positive sign that's fixed in quality; therefore, the subject will present a confident, capable and reliable image to the world. This is a sign of long ascension, which implies that there are a lot of these people about, but oddly enough, we seem to run across far fewer Leo rising subjects in daily life than we do their immediate neighbours, Cancer and Virgo rising. There is no astrological reason for this discrepancy, but there may be some less obvious ones.

Leo rising infants are not strong and they don't all survive the first months of infancy. Secondly, these subjects don't seem to lead ordinary lives; they become captains of industry, sports champions or stars in the entertainment world, which suggests that they are not to be found in the local pub or at the office. Thirdly, this is a royal sign and is actually well represented within the royal family. Even the younger George Bush has Leo rising! Therefore, this sign carries a pedigree, or thinks it should have one.

Early Experiences

You were a wanted child, but there may have been a problem with your father. He may have been too authoritarian or he may have left the family, or even died. Perhaps someone else came along and pushed you around. I've come across some Leo rising subjects who had success-story fathers who had a very high opinion of themselves, and who made their children feel inadequate, probably because they saw their children as potential rivals. Some fathers considered their offspring too much like hard work. The relationship with the mother seems to be much easier, although the situation can reverse, with the father being the favourite parent.

In happier households, you would have been encouraged to develop your talents and abilities, but also to conform to set patterns of thought and behaviour. Your parents were traditional in outlook, possibly following some kind of religious belief. Later in life, you question your parents' beliefs and find your own philosophy or religious outlook. You may become interested in spiritual matters, meditation and alternative or complementary medicine.

Your parental home was probably comfortable and your parents fairly well off. They may not have been rich, but they would have been respected in their community. Your parents believed in staying together and working out their problems within the family. Although home life was comfortable and peaceful, you do not seem to have been spoiled or over-indulged. Having said this, I've met one subject whose father died, leaving her mother to find work as a servant at the house of a very wealthy family. Nobody set out to hurt the child, but she couldn't help feeling like a second-class citizen in comparison with the wealthy children around her. There is usually something weird about the childhood when Leo is rising. You would have been told you that you were special in some way, which led to some measure of isolation. Your parents may have favoured you because you were the first child to be born to the family, an only child, or a child of one sex among siblings of the opposite sex. You may have been a much-loved late addition, born when your parents had money to spare, so that your childhood was different to that experienced by your siblings.

Leo rising children are often talented. Many are musical, but some are academic, artistic, creative, dexterous, sporty or mediumistic. A talented child, especially if he comes from a non-talented family, always stands a little apart from others. Whatever has been the cause, the effect is a feeling of being different and of isolation, although this is less noticeable when the rest of the birthchart inclines the child towards good relationships.

Appearance

Remember to make allowances for racial differences, family tendencies and the influence of the rest of your birthchart when looking at astrological appearances.

Leo risers are quite distinctive, so you are probably tall with a slow and regal way of moving. Both sexes are vain and both will go to a lot of trouble to look good. You worry about your hair, which is probably thick, wavy and abundant. Leo men are terrified they might lose their hair, and may spend hours worrying about this. You like to dress fashionably, even glamourously, and to surround yourself with quality goods. A good car is an essential addition to your turnout.

Outer Manner

You are genuinely interested in people and you try to present a kindly, non-hostile personality to the world. Although you can appear arrogant, demanding and unrealistic at times, for the most part, you are liked and admired. Leo rising people have presence, graciousness and inborn public relations skills. You are a good listener and an interesting talker, which makes you popular in social situations. You are quite fussy about your choice of friends, and this is where a touch of the Leo snobbery can often be seen.

The Midheaven

The midheaven shows the subject's aims and ambitions, public standing and attitude to work outside the home. It can often throw light on strange or unexpected behaviour in a way that even the Sun, Moon and Ascendant don't always address. Some rising signs usually have only one possible MC, while others can have two or even three possible MCs, depending on the time of year in which a person was born, along with the hemisphere and latitude of birth.

If Leo is rising, you could have either Aries or Taurus on the MC. The Leo/Aries combination adds sparkle to the chart, as both are fire signs. The fixed/fire quality of Leo together with the cardinal/fire quality of Aries make for an ambitious, determined and capable person who attacks his goals with considerable enthusiasm. The Leo/Taurus combination is very fixed, so the individual is less ambitious but more stubborn, determined and practical. All Leo rising people seem to enjoy information technology and most can manage machinery of various kinds.

Leo/Aries

This combination inclines you towards self-employment, management positions and team leadership. Being a faceless member of a team is not really your scene and therefore, even when joining an organisation as a junior member, you stand out from the others and very soon begin to climb up the promotion ladder. You may not appear ambitious in the normal sense of the word, but you seem to drift towards the top, as if it were your rightful place in life. You enjoy success, status symbols and the feeling of being looked up to. Careers that may attract you are engineering, building and the driving of trains, planes and road vehicles. You could be an actor, teacher or jeweller - or a combination of these, while anything to do with politics would definitely attract you. You work at a steady pace, but with periods of sheer idleness in between. Needless to say, most of the time, you manage to achieve a great deal. It's possible that you give up the effort at some point, taking early retirement and doing what makes you happy, but you must ensure beforehand that you can afford to do this.

Leo/Taurus

This makes for success, just as long as you don't give in to your tendency for laziness. Both signs dislike change and prefer the continuity of a settled job. Both are quite ambitious, even if this is not obvious. You can work at a job purely for the money it brings in, or for the power and influence you might obtain from it; however, you are happiest when your work contains a creative element. Both signs are creative and musical, so you could find work in the fields of fashion, art, music, engineering design, landscape gardening or catering. Your creativity could lead you to start a business of your own or, if you are not career minded, to create a lovely home of your own. If your job doesn't give you an opportunity for creativity, you will look for a creative hobby.

Some people are attracted to those whose Sun sign is the same as their MC sign. This would suggest that the partner is in tune with the subject's aims and ambitions. In your case, you get on well, both at work and in your personal life, with Aries or Taurus people.

The Descendant

When the ascendant is in Leo, the opposite point or descendant is in Aquarius, so you may be attracted to Aquarian qualities in a partner. These qualities are independence; humanitarianism and an individual outlook on life, and you may treat your partners in a slightly Aquarian manner by giving them space. You are incredibly difficult to please, because you choose a partner who is capable, independent and intrinsically fascinating, but then you become uncomfortable and possibly unpleasant because you can't stand the competition.

This Aquarian descendant can cause problems due to the unstable and revolutionary nature of the sign. In terms of relationships, this means that you are likely to be married more than once, and your partners may be rather unusual. In some cases, your partners start out normal and become odd later!

Love and Relating

You want to be loved, but you have to take great care not to destroy a relationship before it even gets off the ground. You are a family person, but you cannot subordinate yourself too far to the wishes of a partner, because you need to be treated with respect. If you feel that your role is important, as either wage earner or homemaker and that your decisions count for something within the home, all is well. The love that you seek takes every form, including the love of your children, genuine care and affection for your mate and of course, sex. Sexually, you are warm, caring, gentle and at the same time, demanding. You have a well-developed sense of touch and you are a generous lover. Any form of ridicule on the part of your partner would spell out the death of the relationship. When things work out well, you can make very successful relationships.

Health
Leo is traditionally associated with the back and the heart, but this rising sign doesn't seem to have an effect on health, so one must look elsewhere on the chart to find the danger points.

Additional Information
* Many Leo rising people have golden coloured eyes and a reddish tinge to the hair.
* You are very hospitable and a wonderful host, and you can be very kind.
* You can also be prey to snobbery, arrogance, a superior attitude and you may be a bully. Try to control such behaviour, as it will ensure that you end up lonely and unhappy.
* You may be fussy about your car, so that you spend a lot of money on it and never allow anyone else to drive it. Alternatively, you may never bother to own a car at all.
* You will always feel different in some way, but you enjoy this.

LEO RISING CELEBRITIES	
Elton John	Piers Morgan
Edwina Currie	Simon Cowell
Meryl Streep	Tina Turner

Virgo Rising

Ruled by Mercury
Men of England wherefore plough
For the lords who lay ye low?
Wherefore weave with toil and care
The rich robes your tyrants wear?
PERCY BYSSHE SHELLEY, SONG TO THE MEN OF ENGLAND

This sign is mutable, which implies flexibility of mind, and it's an earth sign, which suggests practicality, while also being feminine/negative in nature, denoting introversion. Virgo rising is a sign of long ascension, which means that there are plenty of you around.

Early Experiences

One of the questions on my research questionnaire asked, "would you like to have your childhood over again?" All but one of the Virgo rising respondents replied, "No, definitely not!" The only one who gave a "yes" answer had the rising sign on the Virgo/Libra cusp, so that the entire first house was actually Libra. This is such a difficult ascendant to be born with that, if your childhood was abnormally happy, I'd suggest that you re-check your birth time!

Your parental home may have been comfortable or downmarket, but whether your family was rich or poor, their attitude to money was probably frugal. This is assuming that you were brought up in a normal nuclear family, but it's possible that you spent time being looked after by other people.

Sometimes the Virgo rising subject has a reasonable relationship with the mother but a difficult one with the father, and in some cases, the father takes delight in tormenting or bullying the Virgo rising child. In other cases, the father loves the child, but the mother cannot see any good in the child and subjects it to a barrage of criticism and disapproval. Not every case is as extreme as this, but there will be some unfair and undeserved ill treatment at the hands of others at home, at school or both.

Your parents were probably dutiful in their attitude towards you, making sure that you had your practical needs catered for. If they did this out of a sense of obligation rather than genuine affection, you would have been aware of this and you may even have felt guilty for putting them to the trouble of looking after you! You were expected to conform to a set of rules and regulations and to be clean and tidy at all times with polished shoes and straight, unwrinkled socks. Your school may also have been over-disciplined with too much emphasis on stuffy rules.

Your parents expected you to do well at school, to behave perfectly and to maintain a position at the top of the class at all times. This constant pressure and the unremitting requirement for you to be perfect at everything (except maybe for those subjects they themselves felt were unnecessary) could have left you rigid with nerves and prey to all kinds of nervous ailments. On the positive side, you had access to books, educational aids and extra-curricular activities. You were encouraged to read and to learn, and you probably got the hang of this quite early on. Some Virgo rising children don't make friends easily, while others make such good friends, that they become a kind of substitute family. Some of you are happiest in your own company or with your pets. You didn't take much interest in any of the contemporary fads and fancies in which the other children were involved.

You have a surprisingly stubborn and uncompromisingly selfish streak that may not be immediately obvious to others. Your survival instincts are strong, endowing you with a knack of appearing to be accommodating while actually pleasing yourself. Some Virgo rising children actually resist love and affection, behaving so oddly and in such an offensive manner that nobody can really take to them.

Some Virgo rising subjects grow up in an overbearing religious atmosphere where the fear of God is added to the fear of what the neighbours might think. (This is especially so when the IC is in Sagittarius.)

Appearance
Remember to make allowances for racial differences, family tendencies and the influence of the rest of your birthchart when looking at astrological appearances.

Virgo rising subjects are good looking as a rule, especially if they are born with a fairly late degree of the sign rising. You are probably a little taller than average, with a long, slim, well-defined face, thin nose and arresting eyes. All this has to be considered alongside racial differences and the influence of the rest of the chart. Typical subjects have a cheery smile and an intelligent sense of humour that shines out of the eyes. Your complexion is pale, even in the summer, because you haven't the patience to waste time lolling around in the sun. You may be a little overweight or even quite thin with a bit of a potbelly, but your above-average height and your good posture allow you to get away with this.

Outer Manner

Your outer manner is polite, formal and a little guarded. You can hang back and be shy on first meeting, especially in new social circumstances, but you soon warm up when you relax. Your mind is very sharp and you can be surprisingly intuitive. You always appear confident and capable, the very image of the perfect purchasing officer, secretary or nurse. Being shy, you may also appear to be a little standoffish on first acquaintance, and you prefer to let others do the talking, while you assess the people and the situation around you. When you're at ease, of course, you can talk the hind legs off a donkey. You are usually very smartly dressed, in an up-to-date manner with stylish and slightly unconventional clothing.

The Midheaven

The midheaven shows the subject's aims and ambitions, his public standing and his attitude to work outside the home. It can often throw light on strange or unexpected behaviour in a way that even the Sun, Moon and Ascendant don't always address. Some rising signs usually have only one possible MC, while others can have two or even three possible MCs, depending on the time of year in which a person was born, along with the hemisphere and latitude of birth.

In the case of Virgo rising in UK latitudes, the mid-heaven covers the latter part of Taurus and a good deal of Gemini. In southern Europe and the United States, you will only have a Taurus midheaven if your ascendant is in the first couple of degrees of Virgo. The vast majority of people born with Virgo rising have the MC in Gemini.

Virgo/Taurus

The effect of having earth signs on both the ascendant and the MC makes you practical, sensible, obstinate and probably rather materialistic, and this need for security leads you to find work in a safe and established trade. Both Virgo and Taurus are interested in the growth and production of food, therefore you could work as a farmer, market gardener, dietician or cook. The building trade is another possibility, as is work connected with buildings, such as fitting out, furnishing or dealing with property. The insurance business is also possible. Too much change, challenge and excitement would unnerve you, but a steady, ordinary and reasonable job would suit you well. Virgo is concerned with health and healing, but Taurus can't stand blood and mess, so the prevention of illness by diet and exercise might appeal more than dealing directly with sick people. This combination suggests a need for comfort at home and a good standard of living, and you would strive to provide this for yourself and your family. Taurus is associated with music and Virgo with words, so if your birthchart has a creative slant, you could be drawn to music production.

Virgo/Gemini
This is the sign of the competent secretary, media researcher, nurse or teacher. Mercury rules both signs, so you are very interested in all forms of communication, which includes teaching and studying, writing and publishing, journalism or driving. Your mind is active and you need to express yourself, but your shyness suggests that you are happier as a backroom boy or girl than out in front of the public. You might be interested in nutrition, medical research, methods of plant cultivation, or writing about these things. Oddly enough, acting or singing may appeal.

You look deeply at whatever you are working on rather than taking anything on face value. Your strong desire to help others can lead you into the counselling or medical fields, especially medical research. Communication in the form of travel and transport might attract you, therefore the travel trades and driving or vehicle maintenance could be good careers. Your meticulous and orderly mind could attract you to computer aided design, systems analysis or accountancy. Other possibilities are electrical work or maintenance, electronics, radar, telecommunications or television and video engineering. Any kind of statistical work might appeal, as might research and analysis. Some Virgo rising subjects make very good historians.

The MC can sometimes denote the kind of person who attracts us or with whom we feel comfortable in day-to-day life. Therefore, you might find that you get on well, both at work and in your private life, with Taurus or Gemini types.

The Descendant
When Virgo is rising, the descendant is in Pisces and this may bring difficulties in relationships. You may attract people who are out of the ordinary or even peculiar. It seems as if this descendant is trying to compensate for your down-to-earth attitude to life by throwing a spanner in the works just where you least need one. You may find yourself attached to a partner who drinks, uses drugs or who is mentally unstable.

To some extent, it's your desire to help and to reform others that may land you in this pickle. You may fall for someone who looks all right at first, but who is cruel or unable to relate to others. Some of you take on people with disabilities.

On the plus side, you also attract gentle, rather mystical types who want to care for and serve the needs of the family, just as you do. You seek kindness in a partner and will act kindly and charitably towards them in your turn. You can be happy with a partner who is musical, artistic and caring as long as they also pull their weight at work and at home. You can put up with a lot, just as long as your partner is basically decent and honest. You, yourself, can be decent and totally reliable in practical matters, but potentially unfaithful sexually. Here we go again with those Virgo contradictions.

Love and Relating
This area of your life, as you have probably guessed, has all the appearance of a first-class minefield, especially when one looks at the contradictions in your own nature. You are shy, modest, yet you marry or have sex at an early age, possibly due to a need for love and approval. Some Virgo risers trade sex for company, comfort and companionship. Oddly enough, considering the modesty and fastidiousness of this sign, you have a strong, needy and inventive sex-drive that, coupled with your curiosity, can lead you into all kinds of adventures. In short, despite all the repression, guilt and fear of making a fool of yourself, the enjoyment of lunch, love and lust creates a surprising metamorphosis in you.

Oddly enough, for such a responsible and family-minded sign, you are quite likely to be unfaithful in marriage. Possibly the need to experiment, compare and to analyse is at the back of this, or maybe a need for freedom even within a committed relationship. Maybe it's your way of getting back at a repressive partner or coping with a bad marriage. Your quiet, humourous and laid-back manner is charming and attractive, as is your quite genuine desire to please and above all, to communicate.

Health
Your health is probably lousy. If it isn't, then you may suffer from hypochondria! Traditionally, your skin, bowels and nerves are weak spots, but you could have any ailment you desire. Like your Gemini rising cousins, your nerves will let you down and plunge you into an illness whenever the going gets tough. Toothache, backache and inexplicable stomach pains are all possibilities, as are chronic ailments of all kinds. Yet, you are strong and able to overcome horrifying ailments in a way that

others cannot.

Additional Information

- You are your own worst enemy and you are the first to shoot yourself in the foot. Some of you are too self-critical, others are too ready to open your mouths and criticise others. You can be cutting, sarcastic and hurtful – yet also kind and thoughtful when in the mood.
- You may have a loud and piercing voice. As a child, you screamed and shouted a lot, which probably got on the nerves of your parents and teachers. Later in life, you may have screaming rows with your partner and you may shout at your children a lot. If you could curb this one aspect of your personality, you would do yourself a big favour.
- You dress well and you tend to look fairly "cool".
- You make friends easily and keep them for years, and you are popular. This is just as well, as you like to get out and about and be involved in local matters.
- You won't start on anything until you are sure that you can do it perfectly and that you are in no danger of attracting criticism. Sadly, this can lead to you doing nothing and achieving nothing.

VIRGO RISING CELEBRITIES	
Franklin D Roosevelt	Derek Jacobi
Winston Churchill	John Cleese
Oprah Winfrey	Madonna

Libra Rising

Ruled by Venus
We don't bother much about dress and
Manners in England, because as a
Nation we don't dress well and we've
No manners.
GEORGE BERNARD SHAW, YOU NEVER CAN TELL

Libra is a cardinal sign, which means that you like your own way. It's also masculine, positive and airy in character, which suggests an outgoing and enterprising nature. The weird thing is that the ruling planet is Venus, and that causes confusion.

This is a sign of long Ascension, so there are many of you around.

Early Experiences
This sign on the ascendant denotes a good start in life, but there can be some drawbacks even when this most pleasant sign is rising. Your parental home was probably comfortable, your parents kind and your relationship with childhood friends reasonable. As a small child, you were good looking, popular and charming and you managed to keep out of any real trouble, both at home and at school. All in all, your childhood experiences were better than most, so what's the problem?

The problem is subtle and it varies a little from one Libra rising subject to the next. Your parents may have left you to your own devices because they were busy. In some cases, the father was a distant figure; he may have travelled away from home in connection with work or he may have walked away from the marriage and left the family. In many cases, he actually died when the subject was very young. Sometimes the relationship with the father is quite good, but the mother nags, ignores the child or makes unreasonable demands. There is not enough respect by the child towards the parents and by the parents towards the child. There may be distance and neglect.

It may be that the subject and her parents have different value systems, or natures that clash, although any clashing will be done quietly when this sign is rising. There are many Libra rising subjects who are lavished with guilt-induced presents by parents who neglect them.

In less difficult circumstances, your parents are good and they understand you, but your sisters and brothers may be less than impressed by your charm, and could have behaved in a jealous and spiteful manner towards you.

You were probably lazy, slow moving, quiet and well behaved. If your parents were not too neglectful, they would have given you every opportunity to stretch your mind and they would have encouraged you to do well at school. It's unlikely that a great deal of pressure was put on you to succeed, but there was pressure to conform and not to make waves.

Being independent, even as a child, it's possible that your religious beliefs and political opinions developed differently from those of your parents. Libra rising subjects don't usually come from a highly religious background, but oddly enough, their parents seem to have strong political views. Belonging as you do to an independent-minded air sign, you would have listened to their opinions and then formed your own at a later stage in life. Although slow to do anything, and very slow to come to any kind of decision, you were able to think things out for yourself and work out what you wanted to believe in.

Even when young, you loved beauty, had taste, and style, and it's unlikely that you grew up in an atmosphere of mess, dirt and disorder. You are not slovenly yourself, and neither were your parents.

You appreciate the arts, music and anything that's attractive and well thought out. You could have been artistically creative, especially if there are other forces on your birthchart to back this up. Libra risers have a natural kind of refinement.

It's possible, even as a small child, that you assisted your parents in planning and working on a garden or in choosing the colour schemes for the house.

Appearance

Remember to make allowances for racial differences, family tendencies and the influence of the rest of your birthchart when looking at astrological appearances.

You are good looking, although not necessarily beautiful. Your features are refined, delicate and attractive. Even if plump, you have a clear skin, beautiful eyes and a lovely smile. In white races, the skin is very fair and the eyes are large, widely set and often a pale luminous grey.

You are probably a little below average height with a body which is long in proportion to your legs. Your posture is good and you move with a kind of liquid grace. Your choice of clothing may be conventional or outrageous, but it will always be classy, expensive and in keeping with your personality. You like to keep your clothes for a long time and are prepared to spend money on dry-cleaning.

Outer Manner

You are charm personified. People take to you at once, because of your friendly approach and your genuine interest in what they have to say. Pleasant, humourous and gentle, you are easy to talk to and to get along with, at least on the surface. Your manner of dealing with the world is reasonable, respectful, calm and businesslike; it's rarely brisk or officious. At work you appear to be capable, with an unhurried style that belies your ambition. Friends drift in and out of your life and though you may forget them for a while, you are always pleased to see them again when they reappear. Unfortunately, you may lack sincerity, and intuitive people spot this immediately. In private and to work colleagues, you may be extremely confrontational and unpleasant, and you never give an inch in any dispute.

Midheaven

The midheaven shows the subject's aims and ambitions, his public standing and his attitude to work outside the home. It can often throw light on strange or unexpected behaviour in a way that even the Sun, Moon and Ascendant don't always address. Some rising signs usually have only one possible MC, while others can have two or even three possible MCs, depending on the time of year in which a person was born, along with the hemisphere and latitude of birth.

In the UK and Europe, most Libra rising subjects have their midheaven in Cancer. However, those whose ascendant is in the latter part of the sign will have their MC in Leo. For births in the south of Europe and in the United States, almost the whole of this rising sign will have the MC in Cancer and only those with the ascendant in the last few degrees in Libra will have their MC in Leo.

Libra/Cancer

This combination can make for a shrewd businessperson, and you take your time before committing yourself to anything, carefully weighing up the pros and cons. You may be interested in antiques, coin collecting or Egyptology. Libra, being an air sign, is interested in communicating, keeping up-to-date and being out among people, while Cancer likes to work quietly for himself.

This apparent contradiction can be overcome by either doing your own thing inside a large organisation or by doing your own thing in some kind of loose association with others. Cancer, being a caring sign, can suggest a nursing or counselling career, so you may enjoy teaching very young children either in a school or in a Sunday school. This combination is an excellent one for a career in politics, or a quasi-political career such as Trades Union negotiator.

Oddly enough, I've come across a number of electricians and electrical engineers with this rising sign. Maybe the Cancerian MC makes you want to improve people's home and business premises, or maybe it's the presence of air on the ascendant which gives you an affinity to electrical or magnetic forces. Libra is associated with the planet Venus, and this gives you a strong interest in beauty in all its forms, so you may consider working in the field of fashion, cosmetics and design. You may exploit your flair for interior design as a career.

Libra/Leo

This combination suggests a need to leave your mark on the world, and being a big spender, you also need to be a big earner. You may be attracted to a job that offers you a chance to shine or to use your dramatic flair in some way, such as theatrical agent, recruitment consultant or an agony aunt. Both Leo and Libra are creative signs, so you may choose to work in the fields of fashion, jewellery, cosmetics or interior design. Your ability to listen and advise could lead you to work as a solicitor, counsellor, consultant, doctor or hypnotherapist. Medical and healing work often appeals to people with this combination. You may have an affinity with Cancer or Leo types, for business or love partnerships.

The Descendant

When Libra is rising, the descendant is in Aries, therefore the enthusiasm and enterprise of Aries types may well attract you. Libra needs a partner who enjoys work, and you are happy to have them work alongside you, as long as they don't try to make your decisions for you. The cardinal quality of the signs on your ascendant and descendant suggest that you must lead, albeit slowly, rather than follow.

You require a fairly calm partner who has a strongly confident centre to his or her personality, because you have a habit of taking your everyday frustrations out on your nearest and dearest, or ignoring them when you're in a bad mood. A clingy, unreasonable or jealous partner is no good for you, as you detest being pinned down or having to account for your movements.

Oddly enough, you succeed in one situation where many others fail, and that's in the area of second marriages, as you don't trouble yourself to argue with step-children or ex-wives or husbands, preferring to keep the peace if at all possible. Inside your own one-to-one relationship, you may be far from peaceful, but to those on the periphery, you appear to be decent and reasonable. If you find yourself drawn into a wider family group, you manage very well, because you enjoy the fun of family life and all the extra opportunities for conversation and advice giving. You like to experiment with relationships, so you may find commitment and faithfulness impossible.

Love and Relating
Despite your cool outer image, relating is never a cool business for you. Somewhere along the line, you will fall in love, and when this happens you will fall hard. You may not show your feelings to the world, but they are strong and deep nevertheless. If you are let down and hurt by this experience, you hide your feelings, but they go down deeper than anyone can guess, and it's unlikely that you will ever allow yourself to be placed in that situation again. This is a shame, because the next person who comes along may be far more worthy of your love, but by then, it's too late. Once you have been burned, you never place your hand in the fire again.

When you do feel intensely about your partner, your lovemaking can reach magical proportions and even when this is not the case, you are a notably good lover. Libra is a hedonistic sign that enjoys any kind of sensual experience, good food and good music and, of course, good sex. You take the trouble to make sure your partner enjoys the experience as much as you yourself, and your sensual laziness ensures that you take your time over the process, and you hate to make love in scruffy surroundings.

Health
Traditionally, the Libran problem areas are the bladder and the soft organs. Your liver and pancreas may be weak, so you should limit your alcohol intake and avoid too much sweet food, as diabetes is a possibility. You could have a weight problem, but your natural vanity will urge you to take action about this. Libra rules the motor development of the nervous system and, therefore, can be involved with rheumatic or nervous problems, particularly in the spinal column.

Additional Information
- You may look soft, but you have a strong and determined backbone.
- You may be very artistic and musical with a good singing voice, and many Libra rising subjects work as musicians.
- You have a really lovely outer manner, and often a lovely inner nature as well.

LIBRA RISING CELEBRITIES	
John McCain	Mohandas K Gandhi
Monica Lewinsky	Diana Dors
Jose Maria Carreras	Denzel Washington

Scorpio Rising

Ruled by Pluto

Give me more Love, or more Disdain;
the Torrid, or the Frozen Zone
Bring equal ease unto my paine:
The Temperate affords me none:
Either extreme, of Love or Hate,
Is sweeter than a calme estate.
THOMAS CAREW MEDIOCRITY IN LOVE REJECTED

This is a fixed sign, which implies the ability to stay with a situation and see it through, and it's a water sign, which suggests deep emotions. This is also a sign of long ascension, so there should be plenty of you around.

Early Experiences

Many Scorpio rising children are shy, cautious and rather withdrawn, so they hide their emotions behind a poker face or a blank stare. This makes them hard to read and hard to get close to, which in turn may cut them off from others. If you felt ignored when you were young, think back to the way you behaved towards others. Did you attempt to reach out to people? Did you take any interest in their needs or did you simply hide behind your mask, living inside your own head, interested only in your own dreams and desires?

This is not an easy rising sign, and there will always be residual resentment and even hatred towards those who hurt you when you were younger. There may also be a fear of abandonment or loss through people dying around you. Many scenarios can cause this underlying anxiety, but here are a few that people have told me about. Some subjects were born during a war or within a couple of years of a death in the family. Some were afraid of one or both parents or others who looked after them. Some were abused, talked down to, battered or sexually mistreated. Many had at least one drunken parent, or one who had a weak character or poor health. Whatever the circumstances, you learned early to keep your feelings under control and never allow your face to betray the thoughts inside. This retreat behind the mask, the closed-face withdrawal, is the classic benchmark of this rising sign. One subject told me that, when nine years old, the drunken bully of a father died, and they had to pretend to be sad and upset. Then they continued to keep feelings about their father away from other family members. In some cases, a nice parent dies and another adult comes along and causes problems.

You may have different values and priorities from the rest of your family, and these differing values could have consisted of almost anything. Perhaps your parents wanted a humdrum existence, while you yearned for something more exciting and more meaningful. I've come across Scorpio rising subjects who left their parental home at the first opportunity because it was boring and stultifying, mentally and physically cramped, or financially or academically impoverished. Girls with this rising sign often escape into an early relationship and motherhood.

There are individuals who got on famously with their families while they were small, only to experience difficulties as they began to grow up, at which point they left home or were thrown out. Some are happy at home but experience problems at school, while others loved school and used it as an escape from home life. One child's family moved from country to country, so it was always a stranger in school, and unable to speak the language or understand what was going on. This business of moving from one country to another and having to start again in an environment where you don't know the rules is not unusual for this sign.

The key to this sign is resentment about something that didn't work properly. Another child had a useless agoraphobic mother and a father who never spoke to them. Another was the only person in the household who spoke English, therefore being expected to deal with the feckless father's legal problems.

Some have a sibling who is favoured while they themselves can do nothing right. Understandably, many people with this rising sign prefer animals to human beings.

This rising sign is frequently involved with handicaps of one kind or another. I've come across too many instances for it to be just coincidence. There are Scorpio rising subjects who are mentally or physically handicapped from birth, and others who start out normal, but by dint of accident, disease or even by their choice of lifestyle, become restricted in some way later. Others bring up handicapped children themselves. Your weird childhood leads to you developing a powerful level of intuition, which serves you well throughout life.

Appearance

Remember to make allowances for racial differences, family tendencies and the influence of the rest of your birthchart when looking at astrological appearances.

You have good features and great hair and you look wonderful in photographs. You have a lovely smile that lights up your whole face, but you have to know someone a little before you favour them with one of your lovely grins. You are light on your feet and a naturally good dancer, but as you get older, you have to guard against too much sitting about, as you can gain weight. Your best feature is your voice, as it's low and oddly captivating. It commands respect and it sounds sexy. You may have a hawk-like face with a penetrating gaze, or a flat, slightly oriental look and a vaguely puzzled expression that gives little away.

Outer Manner

You have some special ability or interest which makes you stand out from other people. This slight studiousness, coupled with your diffidence, makes you appear clever and mysterious. You don't push yourself forward in social situations, and you are at your most relaxed when working on your own particular hobbies.

It's always a joy to sit quietly and listen to you when you relax and open out and you have a wonderful sense of humour. Your company is so good that time spent with you goes by quickly. You are curious about the motives and behaviour of other people and you may tend to put total strangers under interrogation; some Scorpio rising subjects can appear abrupt and forbidding, critical, offensive and rather frightening.

The Midheaven

The midheaven shows the subject's aims and ambitions, his public standing and his attitude to work outside the home. It can often throw light on strange or unexpected behaviour in a way that even the Sun, Moon and Ascendant don't always address. Some rising signs usually have only one possible MC, while others can have two or even three possible MCs, depending on the time of year in which a person was born, along with the hemisphere and latitude of birth.

In the UK and similar northerly latitudes, the MC is almost equally split between Leo and Virgo. In the USA and southern Europe about two thirds will be in Leo, with the remainder in Virgo. Either MC will make the subject cautiously ambitious, but the drive to achieve will be directed differently.

Scorpio/Leo

If you lose your job or suffer a setback that calls for a close look at your situation and your potential, you can view it as a tragedy, and you harbour a deep and abiding resentment for the person or organisation that cost you your career. However, your tremendous reserves of courage and energy ensure that you don't wallow in misery for long, but soon get up and make a fresh start.

The fixed nature of this sign makes you reliable and efficient, and the Scorpio motto is, "if you are going to do a job, do it properly". You are thorough and painstaking and you hate to be rushed and hassled. The Leo MC gives you a desire for status and glamour, while the Scorpio ascendant adds caution, tenacity and independence, therefore you head slowly towards the top, stamping your personal style upon your surroundings as you go. This combination can also denote a winning athlete or a top psychiatrist. Many of you opt for a career in connection with music. You could go into teaching, banking, coal or diamond mining.

Many of you spend some of your spare time scouting, guiding or something similar, while others are drawn to a military career, which offers you a pseudo family or clan atmosphere. The services provide opportunities for travel and sport, plus the opportunity to develop your natural interest in the vehicles and weapons of war. One Scorpio rising subject of my acquaintance left her awful childhood behind by taking a job on a cruise liner.

Some of you find your way into the police force, because you work well within a team and can command the respect of your comrades. Your investigative powers and natural mistrust of fellow humans stands you in good stead here, while your physical strength and well-trained body enable you to enjoy exercise and combat. Similarly, you may go into medicine or become a paramedic. These careers are useful to the community at large, offering aid and protection to the weak, and thus allowing you to express the powerful "knight in shining armour" aspect of your personality.

Scorpio/Virgo

This combination should lead you towards a medical career, or at least towards a strong interest in all aspects of mental and physical healing.

The Scorpio/Virgo combination includes surgeons, doctors, herbalists, spiritual healers and psychiatrists. There is a desire to help humanity and at the same time a fascination with human and animal biology and perhaps even with mental and physical pain. You may prefer a career in the background, as a civil servant, secretary or social worker. You could choose to work in the food or the clothing industry or even in the meat trade. These jobs supply basic needs to the public. Other choices can include acting, spiritual healing, alternative therapies and hypnotherapy. You need a career that matters and that allows you to feel as if you count for something. It's also worth remembering that Scorpio is associated with sex, therefore, rape crisis counselling may appeal to you, as might gynaecology.

The midheaven can sometimes indicate the type of person to whom you are attracted both as working partners and as lovers, so you might find yourself most comfortable alongside Leo and Virgo people.

The Descendant
In this case, the seventh house cusp is in Taurus. When you find the right partner, you settle down to a long-lived and very affectionate relationship, but even this relationship is not without fireworks. It's also worth noting that your most successful relationship is likely to be a second or subsequent marriage, after you have learned a bit about living with others. You may experiment with a sexy firebrand on one occasion and a gentle, uncritical homemaker the next.

You enjoy becoming a parent, although you may have some unrealistic ideas of what it means to bring up children. It's worth remembering that the fifth house is concerned with children, and yours is in the illusory and delusory sign of Pisces.

If your partner were the Taurean type, you share a love of music and the sensual joys of good food and good sex, but you both have powerful and destructive tempers. If you are not too uncompromising in outlook and the rest of your chart includes some lighter factors, they can work out very well. You take commitments seriously, and that's an advantage.

Love and Relating
Scorpio on the chart has a reputation for sexiness, but while some Scorpio risers are sexy, others aren't particularly interested. You may be very keen on sex at some times of your life and uninterested at others. You may choose to remain celibate for religious reasons, or because you wish to save your strength for the athletic field or the boxing ring. Some of you will do anything where sex is concerned,

while others are fastidious and inhibited.

Some of you really get off on fights and nasty atmospheres, and the casual violence of your marriages can destroy your children. If you feel threatened or maltreated, you enter into a war of attrition for years until one of you suddenly decides enough is enough and walks out. You take offence even at the most helpful, well-meant and constructive criticism, but you can be an expert at dishing it out. You soon learn just which of your partner's buttons to push. Scorpio risers need a partner who stands up to them or who lets their drama and attitude go in one ear and out the other. Having said all the above, many of you are the most loving, caring and sensitive of partners. There's just no middle road where you are concerned.

Many male Scorpio risers marry large, motherly women. You need affection, reassurance and a feeling of continuity. You appreciate acceptance, even by your spouse's family and you benefit greatly from a wise partner who encourages you to open out and express yourself. If you have the kind of partner who includes you in the mainstream of their life, who genuinely respects your opinions and wants your company, you are the best, the most loyal and hardworking mate in the whole zodiac.

There may be something odd where children are concerned, because you may have children that you don't want or you may not be able to have ones that you do want. You may leave parenthood until late in life, or take on someone else's children.

Health

The uterus and related areas can present problems, while the male organs may suffer hernias and prostate gland difficulties. Vasectomies can go wrong and there may be something wrong with the sperm count. Scorpio risers can become ill very quickly and very dramatically from time to time. When this happens you instantly become an excellent patient (at least as far as the doctors and hospital are concerned). You respond well to treatment and soon forget that you were ever very ill. Heart trouble is surprisingly common, as are stomach ulcers as result of unreleased stress and tension. Many of you suffer from time to time with problems related to the ears, sinuses, teeth and throat. Many of you also suffer from back problems.

Additional Information

- You think and feel deeply, and you are a good person with whom to talk things over.
- Many of you love animals, so you might make a career in that area.

- You may also be into conservation and alternative forms of energy or alternative lifestyles.
- You hold a grudge forever.
- You aren't good in an emergency; unless you are specifically trained to deal with sudden, unexpected problems, you can get into a flap and lose your temper.

SCORPIO RISING CELEBRITIES	
Clint Eastwood	Patrick MacNee
Claudia Schiffer	Margaret Thatcher
Edith Piaf	Johnny Carson

Sagittarius Rising

Ruled by Jupiter
Slav, Teuton, Kelt, I count them all
My friends and brother souls,
With all the peoples, great and small,
That wheel between the poles
You, Canadian, Indian,
Australasian, African,
All your hearts be in harmony!
ALFRED LORD TENNYSON

Sagittarius is a mutable sign, which implies the ability to adapt to changing circumstances. It's also a fire sign, which suggests that you catch on quickly and you do things quickly. This is a sign of medium-to-long ascension, which means that there are plenty of you around.

Early Experiences
You appear to have been born easily and to have been a wanted child, but your childhood was patchy, with parts of it being good and some parts being poor. You learned early in life to switch off and avoid things you dislike. Your parents may have separated from each other, or there could have been problems that were beyond your control, such as a deteriorating relationship between your parents. There may have been conflict between you and your parents. The chances are that even now, you love your family but prefer to live at a distance from them.

You could have found your father too fussy, disciplinarian or prejudiced for your freewheeling taste. There may have been regular rows about the state of your room, your performance at school or your lack of application to some special interest that consumed your parents. Your parents may have objected to your tendency to disappear whenever some boring chore loomed up on the horizon, or they may have felt relieved when you did disappear, because it offered them a welcome respite from arguments. Your relationship with your father is ambivalent, because you may have hated him while you were young, but developed respect for him later on. You may have loved and understood him, but never learned to communicate with him except by getting into yet another shouting match.

You may have seen your mother as the servant of the family who lived her life in a particularly old-fashioned and limited manner. You may have considered her stupid, useless or powerless. The view of your mother as a person who was incapable of making a decision would inevitably reinforce your natural desire for self-determination and independence. Later in life, you may have come to understand the difficulties under which she lived and the compromises that she had to make, but even now, you may lack any real respect for her. Whatever the circumstances, you felt cramped, restricted and even immobilised. It's possible that you were disadvantageously compared to a brother or sister and maybe you felt that you were growing up in a town or an area that was small, dull and far from the action. Maybe you were expected to follow a strict religious regime in which you had no personal belief, or to conform to a restrictive set of values. Maybe your home life was great, but financial or cultural impoverishment irritated you.

Somewhere along the line, you switched off, tuned out and began to look outside the home for some kind of escape route. Many of you realised that education could offer you a useful way out, so you were quick to latch on at school, which earned you the praise of your teachers and the admiration of your peers. You were unlikely to be the victim of bullying, due to your strong wiry frame and your natural aggression. For some of you therefore, school gave you the precious gift of early success and the opportunity to develop a sense of self-esteem. As you passed the point of puberty, your eyes and thoughts were drawn ever more outward to the wider world, and sooner or later, you left home – and may even have left the country.

You have a real knack for do-it-yourself and building work, so you might go into this kind of field.

Appearance
Remember to make allowances for racial differences, family tendencies and the influence of the rest of your birthchart when looking at astrological appearances.

If you are typical, you are medium height, slim and raw-boned, with the characteristically long jaw and brilliant smile. Some chubby and round-faced Sagittarius rising subjects have unusually attractive hair and eyes. Sagittarius rising women are often top-heavy, with rounded shoulders and a large bust. White races often have golden or reddish hair.

Outer Manner

You are friendly, cheerful and outgoing, and you lack caution or fear when meeting new people. Some of you are in a permanent whirl, chasing around like a demented white rabbit, while others affect a superior, know-it-all attitude. Some of you have a slow-moving, leisurely manner that belies the quickness of your mind. You are curious about people and therefore may subject perfect strangers to the third degree. This is usually done quite innocently, because you do not intend to hurt anybody. Every new person or situation offers you delightful opportunities to further your knowledge. You try to fit in with any company in which you find yourself, whilst actually remaining a distinct individual. You may appear eccentric to strangers, especially conventional ones, but the messages you transmit on first acquaintance are usually cheerful and friendly. You may have a knack for making tactless remarks, but you are also very funny and you love to make people laugh.

The Midheaven

The midheaven shows the subject's aims and ambitions, his public standing and his attitude to work outside the home. It can often throw light on strange or unexpected behaviour in a way that even the Sun, Moon and Ascendant don't always address. Some rising signs usually have only one possible MC, while others can have two or even three possible MCs, depending on the time of year in which a person was born, along with the hemisphere and latitude of birth.

In the UK, and similar northerly latitudes, those of you whose ascendant is in a very early degree of Sagittarius will have a Virgo midheaven, while those of you whose ascendant is in the very last degrees of the sign will have a Scorpio MC. In fact, the majority of you have a Libran MC. In the USA and southern Europe, about one third of you have Virgo on the mid-heaven, while the remainder have Libra on the MC.

Many of us are attracted to people whose Sun sign is the same as our MC.

Sagittarius/Virgo

This combination produces an adaptable person who is also very idealistic. You have a strong need to serve mankind, either on an individual basis by caring for an elderly or handicapped relative, or on a group basis by working in one of the caring professions. Some of you work for a charity or for some other idealistic movement. Subjects with this MC may choose to work as teachers, social workers and probation officers or in some aspect of the medical profession. The travel and transport industries are popular (remember, Virgo is ruled by restless Mercury), but you may also be drawn to farming, veterinary work or anything connected with animal welfare. You could help people to keep on looking good by working in the cosmetics or clothing industries. You may be into vegetarianism or good nutrition. This combination makes for a nervy and restless personality, but the attention to details that is Virgo coupled with the Sagittarian imagination and optimism can create outstanding success in any profession.

Sagittarius/Libra

By far the bulk of Sagittarius rising subjects come into this category. You are drawn to ambitious projects and large-scale ideas that can be extremely successful. Both Sagittarius and Libra are concerned with advocacy and both signs like to see justice done, so a legal career is a possibility. You could be equally drawn to spiritual ideas that lead you into a religious or philosophical way of life. Even if you don't become directly involved in the spiritual world, an element of this will enter your everyday life. The worlds of astrology or psychic matters might appeal to you. Sagittarius rising subjects are highly intuitive and often very psychic. The desire to help humanity in a more practical way could lead you into politics.

Many teachers have this combination on their charts, as it's naturally Libran to give advice, and another traditionally Sagittarian interest is long distance travel; there are many of you working as couriers, travel agents, translators and airline pilots. You get on well with most people and have no prejudice towards foreigners. In fact, you enjoy meeting people from different cultures and looking into different ways of life. Last but not least, many of you find your way into show business. You are a natural actor and comedian, and probably a good singer or dancer too, so you could spend your life actually working in the business, or you could spend a few years on the stage before settling down to a normal career. Many of you retain your interest in stage work and may even return to it later in life.

You may be good at, and very interested in competitive sports, particularly golf, tennis, yachting and motor racing. Another interest could be the care of animals, especially horses. You may like the horseracing scene.

Sagittarius/Scorpio

Very few people have this combination. Such a combination stresses the idealistic side of Scorpio, which expresses itself in a need to heal. You may work in the medical, psychiatric or veterinary fields and you may be a gifted spiritual healer. Your powerful intuition and psychic ability lead you to take an interest in spiritual and psychic matters. The legal interests that are common in Sagittarians might be used directly in forensic work of some kind. You have more patience and determination than the other two types, which suggests that you could haul yourself slowly up to a position of great authority and responsibility. You would use your powerful gifts both wisely and firmly.

You are an excellent communicator, so you could find work in journalism, radio or television. You like advising and helping the public, so a media career could well be a very good idea for you. A sporting career is also possible, as many of you are excellent sportsmen and women who can make the grade professionally.

The Descendant

The opposite point to the ascendant is the descendant, which traditionally shows the type of person to whom we are attracted. In the case of a Sagittarian ascendant, the descendant is in Gemini. These two signs have even more in common with each other than most ascendant / descendant combinations, so you either get on well with Geminis, or find them extremely irritating. Being idealistic and highly-strung, you need a placid and practical partner to create a balanced relationship. Geminis can be practical when making or fixing things, but they are far too nervous, critical, restrictive and whiny for you to cope with. You desperately need the support of a stable home and family environment, but you may have the awkward habit of keeping two relationships on the go at once, which could make life just a little bit too crowded for comfort.

You need freedom in any relationship, and are also prepared to allow your partner to have the opportunity to be a person in his or her own right. You can be cold hearted at times, even to the point of cutting off completely from other people and disappearing inside yourself. As long as you have a measure of friendship in any relationship, you can usually make a success of it.

Love and Relating

You are a relater and you need company, so you marry young, but you may be too unsettled and unstable to stay married for long the first time round. Later on, you can form a surprisingly stable marriage, due to your ability to choose a fairly self-reliant partner, although I suspect that male Sagittarius rising subjects are luckier in this respect than female ones.

Sexually, you like to experiment, and curiosity could be the main reason for your numerous sexual partners. Later in life, when some of your curiosity has been satisfied, you settle down more easily to family life. You are one of those people who can actually live quite happily without sex, as long as your creative urges are being satisfied, although you do need attention and affection. You were not cuddled enough as a child and you really do enjoy the sensation of being held and cared for by another. You can also offset any missing sex by pouring out your energies into sports, hobbies and even the Church. To be honest, sex isn't your biggest problem: your worst enemy is boredom.

As far as friendship is concerned, you can be here today and gone tomorrow. Your friendly, open nature ensures that you make friends easily enough, but you tend to drift away and forget them when you move on to other things.

Health
You are either extremely healthy or extremely unfit. To be honest, the chances are that you are rarely ill, but if you do go through a bad patch, it can last for quite a few years before you return to full health. You suffer from sporting injuries and silly accidents due to the speed at which you move. Your vulnerable spots are your hips, pelvic area and your thighs, so arthritis, accidents to the legs, and problems related to the femoral artery are possible, while women may suffer from womb troubles. Your nerves can let you down, giving you sleepless nights, skin and stomach problems, if your ascendant is late in Sagittarius, you could have allergies to certain kinds of food and drink.

Additional Information
- You may have a reasonable home life but a poor experience of school life. However, you enjoy learning and you are bound to take courses or learn things for fun later in life.
- You are extremely capable and talented. You could practically build a house with your own hands, learn anything and do anything. Indeed, you are better at solving practical problems than emotional ones.
- One unforgivable fault that I've discovered in those with Sagittarius either as a Sun sign or a rising sign is the way you lash out in a particularly hurtful and thoughtless manner if you feel inadequate, and

sadly, you can do this when nobody has any intention of criticising or harming you.

- Truly, your cheerful outer nature and great sense of humour draw people to you very easily, but one can't help wondering how long they stay enamoured of you, once they experience your sharp tongue.

SAGITTARIUS RISING CELEBRITIES	
John Galsworthy	Sylvester Stallone
Bob Dylan	Elvis Presley
Elizabeth Taylor	Marlon Brando

Capricorn Rising

Ruled by Saturn
Nothing to do but work,
Nothing to eat but food,
Nothing to wear but clothes
To keep one from going nude.
BENJAMIN FRANKLIN KING, THE PESSIMIST

This is an earth sign that's also cardinal in nature, which implies the desire to make things happen, along with the patience and determination to make sure that they do. Capricorn is also feminine/negative in nature, implying introversion and shyness. This is a sign of short ascension, which means that, as far as births in northern latitudes are concerned, there are not many of you about.

Early Experiences

Capricorn rising denotes a difficult birth or a difficult situation surrounding your entry into the world. One could theorise that, because Capricorn is associated with old age, you will have been through a number of previous incarnations, and knowing what is ahead, you don't really want to go through it all over again! Whatever the theory, your mother's labour may have been protracted, painful and dangerous, or difficult in some other way. One such subject told me that she had been born fairly easily, but the birth took place in an ambulance halfway across Ealing Common, in the middle of one of the worst bombing raids of World War Two!

Many Capricorn rising subjects are born to older parents who didn't expect to have a child at that stage of their lives. The sign of Capricorn is traditionally assumed to be a sad one, indicative of a life filled with limitations and hard lessons. There is some truth in this idea, particularly during childhood and youth, but the problems are more likely to stem from difficult circumstances than from cruel or unloving parents. This emphasis on hard circumstances is the benchmark of this rising sign.

One of your parents, probably your father, may have been a distant figure, either because he was naturally reserved or withdrawn, or because his work took up a lot of his time. Your mother might have been strict but not unreasonable or uncaring towards you. Circumstances dictated that you remain quietly in the background, making very few demands and behaving in an adult manner while you were still very young. I always think of this as an old-fashioned sign, because it's associated with the kind of childhoods that were far more common in years gone by. This ascendant is probably found more often in third world societies where opportunities for happiness or for creativity in childhood are still unobtainable luxuries. During your childhood, your parents may have been short of time and money. There may have been too many mouths for them to feed, financial setbacks or family illness. You may have had a parent or a sibling who had some physical or mental handicap. You could have had an early introduction to the sadder side of life by losing a family member in a particularly tragic manner, and it's very likely that you spent a lot of time with grandparents or other older people.

It's possible that your parents themselves had risen from obscurity to wealth, and if one or even both of your parents were especially successful, courageous or outstanding, you may have found this too hard an act to follow. The effects of this childhood could have led to a number of different reactions on your part, depending upon your basic nature. One possibility is that you followed in their footsteps; another is that you gave up the unequal battle and dropped out. A third possibility is that you followed a completely different path, finding values that are very different from those of your parents. Your worst fault would be penny-pinching stinginess.

You were shy and withdrawn and inclined to hang back and let others step forward and take all the glory. You had little confidence in yourself and you may have been afraid of one or more of the adults around you, either because there was a genuine threat to your safety, or because of vague fears and phobias. You were finely built and small for your age, and thus unable to compete with larger, tougher children, either on the sports field or in any kind of physical violence. You were a delicate and timid child, and your health may have been poor. You were not easy to bring up. The fact that you survived at all says a lot about your inner resources of courage and determination. You didn't give up on life, and you learned the value of self-control. Despite this inauspicious start, you are friendly, sociable and cheerful. You are not flamboyant, but you are chatty and even a bit flirty when it's appropriate to be so.

Appearance

Remember to make allowances for racial differences, family tendencies and the influence of the rest of your birthchart when looking at astrological appearances.

The chances are that if you have Capricorn rising, you will have rather bony features, with high cheekbones, large eyes and a nice, if slightly toothy smile. You may smile with the corners of your mouth turned downwards rather than upwards, whilst at the same time lighting up your eyes. Your hair is your worst feature, because it's sparse, fine and nondescript. Men with this rising sign become thin on top. Women spend a fortune in the hairdresser. Your height and physique are small to medium. You could put on a little weight as you get older, but generally speaking, you will remain perhaps just a little below average in height and weight. You choose conservative clothes - either city-smart outfits or cheap and cheerful, according to your lifestyle and your pocket. To be honest, you don't give much attention to your clothing unless there is a special occasion.

Outer Manner

You are the last person to push yourself to the forefront in any kind of new situation. You appear calm, quiet, gentle and modest in social situations, whilst in business situations you are formal and businesslike. The signals you send out to new acquaintances are gentle, kind and practical. You rarely express your feelings publicly, and you are a past master at the art of being non-committal. You go out of your way to make others feel comfortable, but you are reserved. Your dry sense of humour is always a delightful discovery to any new acquaintance, and your genuinely non-hostile approach to the world ensures that you are surprisingly popular. You are a good conversationalist; partly because you usually have something interesting to talk about, but mainly because you are a good listener.

The Midheaven

The midheaven shows the subject's aims and ambitions, his public standing and his attitude to work outside the home. It can often throw light on strange or unexpected behaviour in a way that even the Sun, Moon and Ascendant don't always address. Some rising signs usually have only one possible MC, while others can have two or even three possible MCs, depending on the time of year in which a person was born, along with the hemisphere and latitude of birth.

In northern latitudes such as the UK, the majority of you will have your midheaven in Scorpio, while those of you whose ascendant is in the last couple of degrees of Capricorn will have Sagittarius on the midheaven. In the case of births in the USA and southern areas of Europe, those who have the first few degrees of Capricorn rising will have the midheaven in Libra, whilst the rest will have the MC in Scorpio.

The sign on the MC can sometimes denote the type of person whom you enjoy either working or living alongside.

Capricorn/Libra

Both of these signs are cardinal in nature, which suggests that you prefer to make your own decisions, although you are fairly co-operative in working partnerships. The Libran MC modifies your Capricorn rising shyness. You could become a capable travel agent, personnel officer or financial adviser. You have a natural affinity for figures, which is useful, whatever your line of work. The Libran midheaven gives you an artistic outlook, good looks and good dress sense, so you shine in situations that require good presentation. You may not excel as a creative innovator, but you are excellent at judging the work of others. You can see at a glance what will work and what will not, and it's this critical faculty that could successfully take you into the world of fashion or publishing. You have some sales ability, but not the pushy kind.

Capricorn/Scorpio

It's possible that you would be drawn to the Scorpio interests of medicine or police work, where your careful, methodical mind would come in handy, but if you decide to eschew these careers in favour of an ordinary job, you would do it with energy and diligence. You can be relied upon to do a job thoroughly, so long as nobody rushes or pressurises you. Your best bet is to tackle one job at a time and do it properly. The Scorpio MC could take you into some kind of research work, and you could also make a good investigative journalist or scientific author. You may become interested in coins, stamps and antique silver, where your memory for details and hallmarks come to your aid. You have to take care that your outer manner doesn't offend others, especially at an interview or when trying to get information out of others. You may put on an aggressive or hostile front in order to hide your vulnerability, but remember that others will take you at face value, and thereby miss your finer qualities. The Scorpio affinity with liquids could take you into the oil industry or shipping. I've known one such subject work worked as a cleaner at a public swimming baths.

Capricorn/Sagittarius

This rare combination really doesn't fit comfortably, because the two signs have little in common, but it could make you a pretty powerful character. You may be drawn into teaching or caring for others, possibly by going into the world of probation, prisons and the law. Your practical idealism might lead you into alternative forms of medicine, counselling or even astrology. Your interest in travel and business could lead you to work for an airline or to set up a postal courier service. Alternatively, you could go into some kind of religious occupation or even become a professional mystic or a kind of businesslike Yogi.

The Descendant

The opposite point to the ascendant is the descendant. This is traditionally supposed to show the type of person to whom we are attracted. In the case of Capricorn rising, the descendant is in Cancer, which goes a long way towards accounting for the Capricorn love of family life. I have no evidence to suggest that you would go out of your way to choose a Cancerian partner, but I guess that if you did, all else being equal, the match would work well; the signs have a great deal in common, both being interested in families and also in business. However, the emotionalism and moodiness of the Cancerian might irritate you after a while and the combination of these two signs might lead to too much negativity and gloom in the relationship.

Love and Relating

This is where contradictions enter the scene. You are able to live without sex when it's not available, and you may do so due to shyness, fastidiousness or a quite reasonable fear of jumping into bed with someone to whom you haven't been properly introduced! When you are with someone you love, you can really let your hair down. Remember, this is an earth sign, so it implies sensuousness. You may be flirtatious, but your strong sense of propriety, not to mention self-preservation, will probably prevent too much actual tomfoolery.

Health

You may suffer from rheumatism, especially in your knees. Other typical problems are tinnitus or deafness, possibly associated with some kind of bone problem in the ears. Your difficult childhood may leave you with nervous ailments, such as asthma, eczema and psoriasis, together with chesty ailments such as bronchitis. Despite these annoying problems, Capricorns traditionally live to a ripe old age.

Additional Information

- You can be surprisingly talkative when with people you trust. You read a lot and love books, and because of this, you have a lot of knowledge and information inside your head.
- You are sensible with money and good in business, but you are not a risk taker.
- Some Capricorn rising subjects come from very poor or deprived backgrounds, but then pull themselves upwards by sheer hard work.

Capricorn Rising Celebrities	
Liberace	Jan Fonda
Sean Connery	Lucille Ball
John Belushi	Candice Bergen

Aquarius Rising

Ruled by Uranus
*These things shall be! A loftier race
Than e'er the world hath known, shall rise,
With flame of knowledge in their souls
And light of knowledge in their eyes.*

JOHN ADDINGTON SYMONDS (ENGLISH CRITIC), NEW AND OLD. A VISTA

This is an air sign that's also fixed in nature, so you are clever and tenacious. If you become attached to an idea, or accustomed to a particular way of life, you will not willingly change your mind. Aquarius is masculine and positive in nature, which denotes extroversion and courage. This is a sign of short ascension, which means that in northern latitudes, there are not many of you around.

Early Experiences

Aquarius is the least predictable sign of the zodiac, so it's almost impossible to generalise about any aspect of your life. There may have been some kind of dramatic or unexpected event that disrupted your life, possibly due to war or some other outside circumstance, but this may have turned out for the best in some way. One Aquarius rising subject told me that, as a result of wartime evacuation, he received a far better education and indeed, a far better childhood than he would otherwise have had. This element of unpredictability is the hallmark of this rising sign.

You were a clever child, but you may not have made much effort at school, yet you catch up later in life and you do very well in your chosen sphere of work. Despite your inability to be cajoled or coerced, you longed for parental approval, especially from your father. You may have had an excellent relationship with one parent and a prickly, uncomfortable one with the other. Either parent might have been moody, resentful, childish and unpredictable. In a normal childhood, you could have been subject to periods of unexplained withdrawal of parental affection. If your home situation was pleasant, you would have been aware of events within the family circle that appeared to be beyond anyone's control. Your school life could have been disrupted, probably due to your family moving around a good deal. Some subjects don't do well at school, but take up an interest later at which they excel. Some find it hard to concentrate on anything for long, or grasp new concepts quickly, and then lose interest again just as quickly.

Even as a small child, you needed freedom, space, and you also needed to be on the move, so you were rarely indoors for long. You had friends all over the place, and couldn't wait to shoot off out of the house to see them. Yet, you needed to know that everything was all right at home and in your own private world before you could go exploring.

There may have been very little pattern to your life. Your parents might have changed their attitude to you from one day to another or they may have handed out confusing psychological messages. For example they may have told you that they believed in total honesty, whilst fiddling the taxman and pinching stuff from their place of work. If your parents were reasonable, they may have been thoroughly unconventional. Perhaps one of your parents was particularly successful or gifted. Maybe one of them was a total failure or even a drunken wreck. You yourself were a jumpy, nervy child, being prone to nervous ailments and bouts of peculiar behaviour. If your parents were all right, they would have found you difficult to bring up, and if they were not, it's a miracle that you survived at all!

Appearance
Remember to make allowances for racial differences, family tendencies and the influence of the rest of your birthchart when looking at astrological appearances.

You are good looking. Aquarian women learn to use cosmetics well, the bone structure of your face is strong, and you have a big smile, so you photograph well. Your eyes are probably quite ordinary, plain brown and slightly prominent, but not especially large. However, your highly arched eyebrows draw attention to your eyes, making them look larger than they actually are. Your nose is prominent (maybe bent or twisted) and your teeth regular and very white, so your smile is great.

The effect of these well-developed features, with your humourous expression, gives you a strong and effective appearance. Your hair may be your worst feature, being a dull brown or turning grey when you are still very young. You may be only of average height, or on the tall side.

Your choice of clothes is totally individual and possibly even totally outrageous! You may be the very picture of the smartly dressed businessperson or a complete slob. You may restrict yourself to one colour, for example, never wearing anything but mauve, or you may choose to wear clothes of a bygone age. Most of you prefer casual clothes such as jeans and sweaters. You hate frills, patterns and bunches of flowers on your clothing, and you are far happier wearing strong plain colours. However, you could easily turn up at a formal function in a frockcoat and Red Indian headdress!

Outer Manner

Your manner is friendly, open and non-hostile, unless you are faced with someone who is offensive or unpleasant, in which case, you give him or her absolutely no quarter. You speak your mind and don't fear the consequences. You may be a little shy when you are in an unfamiliar social setting, but once you feel at home, you join in with whatever is going on.

You are a real asset to a village fete! You love meeting new people, and are not at all put off by unusual ones. Your judgement of people is excellent, and you seem to be able to see through surface impressions to the reality that lies underneath. You don't judge people by outer appearances and you cannot be taken in by anyone who puts on airs and graces. Your own approach, apart from being friendly, is businesslike and humourous, but not pushy. In some circumstances, you can appear arrogant, or you may give the impression that you class yourself above the people with whom you associate. Your most outstanding qualities are your quick wit and sense of humour. Aquarius risers are the masters of the pithy comment and the hilarious one liner.

The Midheaven

The midheaven shows the subject's aims and ambitions, his public standing and his attitude to work outside the home. It can often throw light on strange or unexpected behaviour in a way that even the Sun, Moon and Ascendant don't always address. Some rising signs usually have only one possible MC, while others can have two or even three possible MCs depending upon the time of year in which a person was born, along with the hemisphere and latitude of birth.

In Britain and other northern hemisphere areas, you will have Sagittarius on the MC, but in other parts of the world, you could have Libra or Scorpio on the MC.

Aquarius/Libra

You are broadminded and sociable. Your wonderful people skills could take you into politics, business, sales or the law, and you could become a spokesperson for a pressure group. You may go into broadcasting or the press. You like the good life, a good home, nice food, great clothes and possessions, and you learn that the only way to have these things is to overcome your natural tendency to laziness and to go for the kind of job that will bring you a good income. You are very loving and your intentions are good, but you may be too flirtatious and unsettled for marriage or long-term relationships, while your great looks and zest for life bring you many short-term lovers.

Aquarius/Scorpio

You are extremely intelligent and a deep thinker who can't accept anything on face value alone, so you will always research those things that interest you. Your working life will include some level of idealism, so you may work in an engineering or business environment, but some aspect of the work ultimately helps humanity, cares for animals, or preserves the planet. You may be attracted to medicine or alternative health, but your high level of intuition and psychic ability could take you into the world of spiritual healing or mediumship. Other areas are mining, working on oilrigs and other jobs that take you into harsh environments.

Aquarius/Sagittarius

You need freedom, and you cannot stand being restricted, dictated to or bullied. You seek out the kind of job that allows you to get out and about and meet a variety of people. Your work will involve you meeting and dealing with people from many countries and cultures, and you enjoy this diversity. You look at the world with fresh eyes and bring exciting new ideas to everything you touch, so you are very useful in solving technical problems. Your obsessive nature can be useful, because when the urge hits, you can toss aside your languor and beaver away at a problem until it is solved.

Although you can succeed in any technical field, the most obvious ones include electronics, telecommunications and computers. You are intelligent and quick on the uptake and you have a good memory, therefore you need a job that stretches your mind. Your interest in scientific research could take you into the fields of physics, medicine or even horticulture, but your balanced mind and natural arbitration skills could lead you into law. You are a skilled negotiator, which could suggest either straightforward legal work or something similar, such as Trades Union negotiations. You may be interested in becoming an agent for writers or performers, where you meet talented and interesting people. You could become an inventor or an imaginative writer, especially if the rest of your birthchart leans that way.

You look laid-back and easy-going, but this is a pose, because you are actually very ambitious and you enjoy status, so you need a good position within your job and a career that makes you an object of admiration and envy. You earn money easily but you spend it just as easily, so you enjoy it rather than pile it up for the future. There will be some attachment to religion or mysticism somewhere in your family, or you may become interested in these things yourself, although you will resist being told what to believe in.

The Descendant

The descendant, or cusp of the seventh house, is traditionally supposed to throw light on our attitudes to partnerships and may even indicate the type of person whom we choose to marry.

In the case of Aquarius rising, the descendant is in Leo. There is no evidence that you are especially attracted to Leos, but you do find them easy to understand, because you have a good deal in common with them. Your personal standards are high; you are proud, dignified, obstinate and tenacious. It's possible that you could work well together, but I doubt whether two such egocentric people could actually manage to live together for very long. In general, you seek a partner who is intelligent, independent and good-looking.

Love and Relating

You find it hard to give reassurance to others, and your detached attitude and tendency to give logical answers to emotional questions can leave your partner feeling misunderstood. You need to guard against too much tenacity in relationships, because you can hang on far too long to the wrong person.

You are very active sexually and you are an inventive and exciting lover. However, the most important ingredients in a relationship for you are intelligence, humour, shared interests and friendship. You may go through an experimental stage where you separate love from sex, having a variety of partners, but once you settle into a permanent relationship, you are the faithful type, as long as your partner treats you decently. You are completely turned off by a lack of personal hygiene. You don't fall in love easily, but when you do, that romantic child-like Leo descendant makes you very loving and romantic.

Health

The traditional weak points for this sign are the ankles, so you must guard against phlebitis, thrombosis and accidents to the feet and ankles. I've discovered that Aquarius rising subjects have a great deal of trouble with their ears, noses and throats, and many suffer from hay fever, asthma and allergies. Some are allergic to Penicillin or other antibiotics. Your teeth are either very good or very bad. You have a nice smile, so it would be wise to cultivate a good dentist. You could also be subject to backache.

Additional Information

- You probably travelled a good deal in childhood and during your youth. This would have been an interesting, beneficial and enjoyable experience for you. You probably still love to travel whenever you can afford to do so.
- Your desire to help the underdog could take you into local or national politics, and your ambitious nature could take you to the top of this field. Whatever line of work you choose, you will move upwards and your ambition and ability to work hard will serve you well.
- You can present a very unconventional image to the world, which may reflect the real person or just be part of your outer persona.

Aquarius Rising Celebrities	
Barack Obama	Larry Hagman
Janis Joplin	Tammy Wynette
Bjorn Borg	Michael J Fox

Pisces Rising

Ruled by Neptune
We are the music-makers,
And we are the dreamers of dreams,
Wandering by lone sea-breakers,
And sitting by desolate streams;
ARTHUR O'SHAUGHNESSY

Pisces is a feminine water sign, which makes you very intuitive. You may be a good sales person or a good businessperson, due to your natural understanding of people and what they want. This sign is mutable, so you will spend your working life dealing with people or with things that come into your life, pass through and move on. In northern latitudes, this is a sign of very short ascension, so there are very few of you around.

Early Experiences
When pregnant with you, your mother may have been unhappy, unhealthy, short of money and in no shape to have a baby, so your entry into the world was difficult and dangerous, and your survival over those first few weeks may have been in doubt. You seem to have entered this world with the remnants of a previous life still clinging to you. Your early life is characterised by loneliness and separation from others, possibly due to sickness. Your father may have been severely incapacitated or he may have been an ineffectual character. He may have died or deserted the family, leaving your mother to cope alone. Your mother was probably strong enough to cope with this, but she may have become tired, embittered or self-pitying.

Some Pisces rising children have very poor health, and it's probably only when your ascendant progresses from Pisces into Aries that life starts to take off for you. You may have been so ill at times that you were not expected to recover. You may have spent some time away in hospital or in a special school. Even if you were not sent away, you would have spent a good deal of time alone in bed, reading and thinking, and this enforced withdrawal from life allowed your creativity and your imagination to develop.

Your health may have been all right, but other difficulties may have arisen. For instance, Michelle told me that her father left, forcing her mother to bring up Michelle and her younger sister on her own. Her mother had to work, of course, but also enjoyed a great social life with many boyfriends, holidays and outings, leaving Michelle in charge both of the household and her younger sister from a very early age. Despite this, Michelle did well at school, learned to speak a number of languages, and eventually became a courier in the travel trade.

It's just possible that your home life was reasonable, but that you were not on the same wavelength as the rest of the family, so you eventually drifted away and made a life for yourself among like-minded people elsewhere. At school, the only subjects that interested you may have been sport, art, music and dancing. You may have been bullied at school and thus learned to be suspicious of new people. Later in life, you take courses on the subjects that interested you, and you become quite an authority on those things.

One aspect of your personality that will always set you apart from others is your incredible level of intuition. Indeed, you may be extremely psychic. You will be drawn to such things as crystals and crystal healing, or perhaps psychic art, where you draw pictures of people's spirit guides for them. It's very likely that you read Tarot cards, and perhaps tea leaves.

Another alternative is that you become religious, even to the point of joining some silent order, or getting into some weird cult. Many of you take up Spiritualism or Wicca.

On a more practical note, you are probably very sporty and you might be a very lucky gambler. You could be attracted to the world of health and healing, thus becoming a nurse, doctor or complementary therapist.

Your downfall would be escaping into fantasy or perhaps getting into drugs and alcohol, but if you avoid these pitfalls, you could become a top dancer, actor, sports person, novelist, artist, sculptor or musician.

You could reach the very heights of human existence, or fall to the lowest levels.

Appearance

Remember to make allowances for racial differences, family tendencies and the influence of the rest of your birthchart when looking at astrological appearances.

You should be of medium height and size, with a pale, translucent complexion and fine hair. Your eyes are probably very pale grey or grey-blue in colour and they may be large and lustrous. You are slim when young, but inclined to put on weight later in life. You have a quiet, gentle and humourous voice that's pleasant and relaxing to listen to. Your choice of clothes is casual and sporty, but not especially unusual, and you are not especially self-conscious about your appearance. Oddly enough, you may be fussy about the colour of your clothes, preferring to stick to one or two colours that you like.

Outer Manner

I've come across Pisces rising individuals who are friendly, helpful and pleasant, with a humourous and kindly manner, but many are unpleasant, hostile, hard and offensive. There may be a kind hearted and loving person under this crusty exterior, but I wonder whether many people are prepared to hang around long enough to find out.

The Midheaven

The midheaven can show the individual's aims and ambitions, his public standing and his attitude to work outside the home. It can often throw light on strange or unexpected behaviour in a way that even the Sun, Moon and Ascendant don't always address. Some rising signs usually have only one possible MC, while others can have two or even three possible MCs, depending upon the time of year in which a person was born, along with the hemisphere and latitude of birth.

In the northern hemisphere, Pisces rising can only have a Sagittarian MC, but in the southern hemisphere, it is just possible for those born with very early Pisces rising to have a Scorpio MC. The MC can show the signs that we get on with best.

Pisces/Scorpio

This extremely unusual combination makes you very psychic indeed, to the point where it's almost inevitable that you will become involved in spiritualism, ghost hunting, spiritual healing, crystal healing, psychic art or something similar. You long to see beyond the veil and to commune with the gods. It's possible that the same spiritual impulse could take you into the world of religion or perhaps of Wicca. You may work in the health area, either as a doctor, nurse or midwife or as a therapist - either within the establishment, as in something like osteopathy, podiatry or as a complementary therapist of some kind. If Wicca interests you, herbalism might become your route to career fulfilment. You may choose to work in a prison, a mental hospital or any place where the most disadvantaged people gather to find help. You may go abroad to work in a war zone or to help orphans in Africa or some such thing.

Pisces/Sagittarius

The northern hemisphere, and in most southern hemisphere births, the MC is in Sagittarius. In this case, you may be attracted to the Sagittarian careers of teaching and training or the Piscean ones of social and medical work. Both signs have a strong urge to belong to organisations that help people so you may be drawn to work in a prison, a hospital, a mental hospital or a home for elderly or disabled people. Your desire to help and care could take you into childcare or nursing, while the Piscean attachment to feet could lead to a career in chiropody. Many Piscean subjects make a career out of caring for animals. You may take up voluntary work, possibly attached to a hospital. Your strong sense of justice could lead you into legal work or a career in arbitration. You may be very creative and artistic, so you may take up a job in the arts or have an important artistic hobby. Its possible that you take up a career an actor, musician, singer or dancer.

Both Pisces and Sagittarius are deeply interested in religion and philosophy, so this will figure strongly in your life. You may become involved in some kind of organised religion or take an interest in spiritual and mediumistic work and spiritual healing. You could take up this kind of work on either a full or a part-time basis. Angels and other mystical matters would appeal to you.

You are restless and you may be drawn to a job that involves rivers, lakes or the sea, even working in the fishing industry. Your talent for languages, combined with your itchy feet, may take you travelling around the world, either in connection with your work or as a hobby. Your restless nature is best suited to a job that involves being on the move rather than sitting in one place. You may work from home on some kind of private project, travelling out for purposes of research or observation. You may have a peculiar kind of love/hate relationship with motorcars, so if this affects you, you may be an excellent driver or you may never bother to learn.

The Descendant

The descendant, or the cusp of the seventh house, is traditionally supposed to show the type of person to whom we are most attracted. In the case of Pisces rising, the descendant is in Virgo. You look after your partner very well, and you will put up with a good deal of restriction or even unpleasantness. You cope with this by switching off and letting your mind roam elsewhere, away from the reality of your day-to-day life. If you are lucky, you will be able to find someone reliable, competent, hard working and decent. You may marry initially for security or in order to escape from your parents, but if you make a mistake the first time around, you will then look for someone who shares your interests, and who is willing to communicate with you and also offer you a peaceful, decent home life.

Love and Relating
Pisces is a very sexy sign, so if you have the right partner, this aspect of life becomes a major joy and pleasure for both of you. However, you may live for years with a poor lover. You need to give and receive love and affection, possibly because you were deprived of it when you were a child. Some of you divert your sex-drive into a calling, such as religion or good works. Your partner must be able to cope with your moodiness though.

Health
Traditionally, you are supposed to have bad feet, and it's often the case that your feet do give you problems. They are very sensitive and are apt to swell up when you are overtired or overworked. Your lungs and heart may be weak, as may be your spine. Females tend to suffer from menstrual problems, while both sexes will have difficulty in balancing their body fluids. This may result in high blood pressure, cystitis, varicose veins and a host of other problems. You may have something serious to contend with, such as epilepsy or some form of paralysis, but despite your poor health, you usually manage to live a full and long life.

Additional Information
- You love your home and you love to spend time in it, but you also love to travel and have holidays in the sun.
- You may never be wealthy, but you always have enough money for your needs.
- Pisces anywhere on a chart can show a link to alcoholism, so this may be your problem or it may afflict someone close to you.
- Where children are concerned, you will go to great lengths to ensure their happiness and to do whatever you can to make them successful. You may not have much to give them, but you will encourage them every step of the way. You really love your children, and when it comes

to grandchildren, you simply adore them. You are very gentle and loving towards animals, babies and anything or anyone who is helpless.

- You may be a great salesperson, as your sign is associated with dreams, so you can sell the idea of a perfect holiday, a car that raises its owners status or a beauty makeover that's guaranteed to make an ordinary person look fabulous.
- You have a tendency to moodiness, a habit of taking offence when none is intended and a tendency to ridicule others, or to go out of your way to offend them. Curb these habits if you want love and companionship.

Pisces Rising Celebrities	
Bob Monkhouse	Ringo Starr
Pauline Collins	Whitney Houston
Mark Knopfler	Dean Martin

Quick Clues to the Rising Signs

Rising Sign	NATURE
Aries	Quiet voice, needs adventure, works in big organisations helping the public. Generous.
Taurus	Pleasant outer manner and good socially. Can be argumentative, obstinate, materialistic.
Gemini	Friendly, quick, clever, talkative, busy. Bad teeth, fine hair. Unhappy childhood leads to lack of confidence later.
Cancer	Slow moving, good salesperson, friendly. Either very good or very bad relationship with parents.
Leo	Great hair that looks interesting, vain, tough in business. Only really interested in self and own family.
Virgo	Unhappy childhood, much emphasis on appearing to do the right thing. Loud, can be difficult, obstinate. Own worst enemy.
Libra	Attractive, pleasant, sociable, lazy, fond of the good life. Artistic and musical. Marries when young.
Scorpio	Much resentment at things from childhood. Makes the best of difficulties and becomes a success later in life.
Sagittarius	Good looking with a nice smile. Quick, clever, but may flit from one job or person to another.
Capricorn	Hard circumstances in childhood, does quite well later, despite lingering health problem. Must guard against stinginess.
Aquarius	Had unusual parents or school experience, makes friends easily, nice smile; can be very successful once the right way is found.
Pisces	Either kind and friendly or hard and hostile. After difficult teens and twenties, does well in life. Loves children and grandchildren.

The Midheaven

The midheaven (MC) is so heavily influenced by the Asc that I think it's worth taking a deeper look at it here.

Techie Data

Briefly, the MC is the point of intersection between the ecliptic and the meridian in a person's natal chart. If you would like a more detailed explanation, an Internet search will bring up a goodly number of references for you.

At the time of the spring and autumn equinoxes (21st March and 21st September), the days and the nights are more or less of equal length everywhere in the world. For births at these times of the year, the MC/IC line is nearer to perpendicular to the Asc/Dsc line, albeit with variance according to the birth latitude.

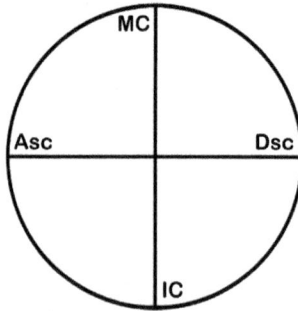

At the time of the solstices (21st June and 21st December), the MC/IC line can be at a steep angle to the Asc/Dsc line, as per the following illustrations.

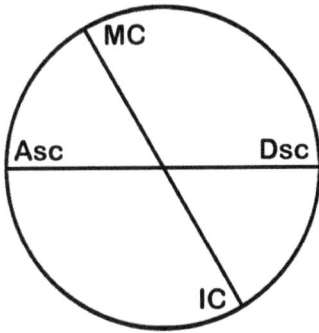

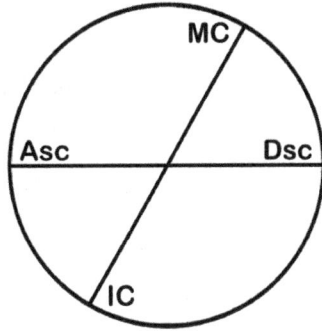

While the Asc tracks its way through a particular sign, the MC will also move along, but at some times of the year and in some latitudes, the angle that you can see in the illustrations can change rapidly.

Some rising signs take longer to rise than others, depending on the latitude and the time of year. In some cases, therefore, the sign takes so long to rise that the MC passes through two signs, and it may even touch a third. For example, Cancer rising can just touch on three MC signs. Southern hemisphere births can show the same effect, but in reverse, with Capricorn rising having three possible MCs.

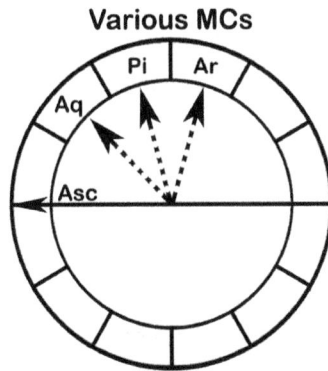

Various MCs

The Astrology of the MC

The MC is much underrated by astrologers. It has a more profound influence on the personality than we give it credit for, and it modifies the action of the rising sign far more than we realise. The MC and the tenth house represent our reputation, the role we wish to play, what we want to become, and what we want to do with our lives. For instance, do we want to be seen as a respectable member of society, a doctor, teacher, writer, good mother, great gardener or what? This part of the horoscope operates on a surprisingly deep psychological level.

The MC is usually more concerned with activities and interests outside the home and family than within it, so astrologers often use it as a career indicator. It is certainly that, but it really relates to the person's true interests, which may have nothing to do with the way he earns his living. An example would be of a bus driver who is a keen ballroom dancer. He invests most of his time, attention, thought, energy and money into dancing, and only puts the minimum amount of thought into moving his bus around the neighbourhood.

While one can say that the MC is usually more interested in creating a possible future than delving into the past, even that isn't always the case. Take a Cancerian MC and Capricorn IC. This person may be the child of a real captain of industry, but he could well decide to turn away from his father's achievements and become a good family man instead. He may also be interested in history, the past, patriotism and things of the past, such as antiques, old clothes and old coins. This is a good illustration of where one comes from (the IC) and where one strives to get to (the MC). Moreover, when looking at the MC, you need to look at the houses nearby and the planets therein.

Although there is no hard and fast rule, the Asc often rules the way we present ourselves to others, especially those who we meet for the first time, while the MC (along with the Moon and other things) shows what we want to achieve or become. This means that two or three people with the same rising sign may have very different inner motivations if their MCs are in different signs. For example, a subject with Taurus rising should be extremely practical - so much so, that the subject may have no use for astrology, religion or any kind of philosophical or abstract concept. When this fixed/earth ascendant is accompanied by the equally practical and hard-headed cardinal/earth Capricorn MC, we are looking at a strong will, ambition, and a desire for a nice job in banking, complete with fat bonuses.

In a few cases, Taurus rising can be accompanied by an Aquarius MC, and that's a very different kettle of fish. While still practical and capable, this subject has values and interests in things that don't necessarily make money. They may be interested in saving the planet, saving animals or doing something for humanity. They may have a job that pays the mortgage alongside personal interests that are very different, and they may not advertise these to their4 work colleagues. Taurus rising folk look conservative, but one may be a member of the Conservative party, while the other works for Greenpeace.

There are people whose Sun sign and planetary positions make them appear extremely stable and sensible on the outside, but who are actually extremely moody and difficult. These subjects can switch from one thing to another in the blink of an eye. Look for water signs on both the Asc and MC. A classic example would be Cancer rising and Pisces on the MC. These people have moods that change with the tides, as they can be kind-hearted, humourous and friendly when they are in the right mood, and sharp tongued and hurtful when their mood changes.

Look at the element and quality of both the Asc and MC. If there is something in common, the outside manner and inner drives will have some similarity. A Scorpio Asc and Leo MC is made up of water and fire elements, but these are both fixed signs, and Leo is less emotional than Scorpio. Now look at Scorpio rising with a Virgo MC. Scorpio is fixed/water and Virgo is mutable/earth, and somehow this combination finds it hard to keep its feet on the ground. I've known several people with this combination, and while they were all intelligent and charming, a number of them had problems with drugs and alcohol. It appears that the mutable Virgo MC and the escapist Pisces IC can't give the determined, obstinate, moody and emotional Scorpio Asc the strength it needs. To quote my late friend Jon Dee, the situation is like a tree that looks good but whose roots and trunk aren't strong enough to support the canopy. Needless to say, if other planets in the chart offer strength, then the situation is much improved, and the problems can be overcome.

The double cardinal Libra Asc with Cancer MC emphasises cardinality. Cardinality wants its own way at all costs, and with the addition of moody, emotional Cancer, the famous Libran logic turns into arguments and scenes. A Libra Asc and Leo MC combo is less hysterical, partly because Leo is less emotional than Cancer. In addition, this subject will find an outlet for his or her talent and determination in music, the arts, show business or arbitration. The stress in the chart is relieved because the subject finds something to get his teeth into.

One final point worth mentioning is that marriages and partnerships where one person has the Sun on the other's MC tend to work well. If both parties have this connection, the marriage should be extremely successful.

If all this isn't enough, look into the Decans and Dwaads of the MC as well. These have only a short chapter here, because they are beyond the scope of this book, but as usual, an Internet search will find a number of references.

Quick Guide to the Midheaven

Here is a short guide for easy reference.

Aries MC

These individuals are imbued with a powerful instinct for self-preservation and a strong urge to serve their own interests. They are independent folk who don't allow others to take advantage of them, but while they make very pleasant and amusing acquaintances, they are not easy to live or work with. They work best when self-employed or in the tough world of high-level politics. They are competitive.

Taurus MC

These people seek stability, wealth and comfort, looking forward to the day when their mortgage is paid up and when they can own a farm or have nice things. These individuals have strong wills, and they can carry things through to a conclusion. They find a job that they like and stick with it. They know how to relax and enjoy life so they don't get too stressed out.

Gemini MC

It can be hard for these folk to stick to one job, because they get bored very quickly, so they need variety, changes of scene and new faces at intervals. Teaching is a good option for these people, but they are unlikely to stay in one job for more than a couple of years at a time. These subjects are probably the most caring and protective of their families of any astrological type.

Cancer MC

These subjects can make a career out of household tasks, such as catering, selling furniture, estate agency work, painting and decorating or perhaps something linked to the past, such as antique and stamp collecting. They remain close to their families throughout life and they may work from home or have a small business where family members to join in and take part in the work.

Leo MC

There is a touch of show-business about these people, so they may spend some of their time engaged in music, dancing or the world of art, either as a job or as a sideline. They like to work in glamourous or highly respected fields and they usually reach the top of the ladder. When they fall in love, it is deep and very real, but they may love their children and pets more than their partners.

Virgo MC

Many of these people work in the fields of health, healing or psychology. Some love new technology while others hate it, and some are good at detailed work, such as design and dressmaking. They all seem to dislike doing accounts and figure work. These folk are close to their families, especially their fathers, even though they argue with them from time to time.

Libra MC

This MC leads to an interest in arbitration, trades union or legal work, and it can also lead to a successful career in teaching. These folk are friendly, sociable, sometimes very sophisticated, elegant, attractive and well travelled. Many of them are somewhat interested in astrology and spiritual matters. While too restless and argumentative for family life, they love their children.

Scorpio MC

These people are keen on business, and their ability to persuade others can make them good salespeople. They need to have a house that is paid for, a bit of land and nice things. While they value family life, they also need freedom to come and go, as they travel for fun and on business. They are either very generous or extremely stingy. There are no half measures with these folk.

Sagittarius MC

This is a lucky MC, so these people get themselves out of difficulties and fall on their feet even in times of trouble. They are likely to travel in connection with work or for pleasure. They may be eccentric and exotic or ultra conservative, but they like to be stylish and modern. Their quick minds can take them to the pinnacle of power and influence, as long as they don't get distracted by family demands.

Capricorn MC

This MC confers executive ability and ambition but it can make these people too devoted to money and success for a balanced life, so they may be too serious. They may not be quick at what they do but they are very thorough. On the plus side, they love music, singing, dancing and art, and they enjoy hobbies in these areas. They also enjoy socialising either as part of their work or as a change from it.

Aquarius MC

These people are hard to influence but they love to explore ideas and they will accept something when they can prove to themselves that it works. They need an interesting career but they may have two part time jobs on the go at once to give them variety. Money is less important than new ideas, especially idealistic ones. They love new technology and will use any excuse to buy a new gadget. These people may be too cool to adapt well to family life.

Pisces MC

These people take jobs with travel or where they deal with the general public. They are excellent salespeople, and reliable workers who are clever at solving problems. At home, they are less pleasant, as they are apt to be moody - sometimes kind and loving, but then spiteful and hurtful, or silent and sulky. They may suffer from health problems or have family members who are ill.

The Imum Coeli

The IC is at the bottom of the birthchart, directly opposite to the midheaven, and it concerns the private side of life, including the home and the family. Traditionally, the IC also refers to the beginning and ending of one's life, the mother or mother figure, the background to anything, and any kind of ancestral memory.

The IC is traditionally associated with the mother, but it can relate to any person or any circumstance that influenced the person's past.

Aries IC

There may have been a conflict going on in the family at the time you were born. However, your childhood environment was cheerful and your parents helpful and encouraging. Your adult home is an open and friendly place with many visitors and a lot of fun and noise. You could fill your home with gadgets or sports equipment.

Taurus IC

Your birth should have been comfortable and well arranged, and if your early environment was lacking in either material or emotional comforts, you can rest assured that your later life will make up for this. Your own adult home will be full of music and beauty, and probably over-furnished and full of souvenirs.

Gemini IC

This sign suggests a strange start in life, possibly due to some kind of disruption in your family or in your schooling. You will probably be active and working right up to the end of your days. You will have either exceptionally good or exceptionally bad relationships with your brothers and sisters. Your own adult home will be full of books, music and people, and you may run some kind of business from it. You need freedom to come and go, but the home you return to will be spacious and full of expensive furniture and equipment.

Cancer IC

Your early experiences will have a strong impact on your future development. You should remain close to your parents throughout their lives. Your adult home will be very important to you and even though you frequently travel away from it, you see it as a safe haven. You may work partially or wholly from your home. You may enjoy cooking, and your kitchen should be very well equipped. You could collect odds and ends, antiques or even junk.

Leo IC

Your early days could have been very difficult, either because you were over-disciplined or because your parents lived a nomadic existence. Later on, you try to make a traditional and comfortable home, but this may become disrupted in some way. You may want a nice home, but somehow find that you are prevented from spending a lot of money on it. If you entertain, you will do so in style and if you work from home, you will make sure that you have all the latest equipment to hand.

Virgo IC

Your early life could have been difficult, either in the home or at school. However, your home environment was full of books and music. Your parents would have placed a bit too much importance on good behaviour, a proper diet and cleanliness, and too little on how you felt. Your adult home is spacious and comfortable, with a well-stocked kitchen. If you work from home, you will have all the latest communications equipment.

Libra IC

Your early life would have been calm, pleasant and loving, with nice surroundings and respectable parents. Your adult home should be large and very comfortable, full of artistic objects and music. You probably like cooking, so your kitchen will be well equipped, but any entertaining that you do will be on a small scale.

Scorpio IC

The circumstances of your birth may have been strange, and there could have been some kind of conflict raging in the family at the time you were born. The atmosphere in your childhood home may have been tense and uncomfortable. Your adult home would be far more pleasant, with an emphasis on good food and a comfortable lifestyle, but you must guard against tension creeping in even there. You may find that you spend a good deal of time alone in your home, either by choice or by circumstances.

Sagittarius IC

Your early life may have been peculiar, either because your parents were heavily involved in religious activities or because they were immigrants from another culture. You may have lived in two worlds at the same time, or moved from one country to another and possibly back to the first again. Your adult home will be pleasant and open, not over-tidy but full of interesting knick-knacks. You may work from home or use it as a base.

Capricorn IC

Your childhood home may have been happy, although lacking in material comforts, or it may have been a source of tension and stress. You would have been encouraged to work hard for material success. Your latter days will be very comfortable and you could well end up being very rich. Your adult home will be well organised and filled with valuable goods, but you may decide to keep animals in preference to having children.

Aquarius IC

During childhood, your life at home or school may have been very unsettled or even eccentric. Your adult home might be sumptuous and filled with expensive goods and gadgets or filled with an odd assortment of junk. Alternatively, your furniture and equipment could be ultra modern. You may work from your home part of the time. Your home is often filled with friends and neighbours. You may move house a lot.

Pisces IC

There may have been some mystery surrounding the circumstances of your birth or alternatively, you might have been brought up in a nomadic family. Both your childhood home and your later adult one will reflect the many interests of the people who live in it. These may include books and equipment associated with the occult, magic, religion or travel. Your surroundings may have been unconventional, perhaps arty or musical. Your children will have a good deal of freedom, but they may not actually communicate much with you.

The Descendant

The Descendant can indicate the virtues and values that we find attractive in others, and many of us are drawn to those people whose Sun or Moon is in their Dsc sign. My observations over the years show that we find more friends than lovers in this sign.

Descendant	Attributes
Aries	You seek adventurous, active, fun friends
Taurus	You choose stable, reliable and well-off friends.
Gemini	You want friends for fun and conversation.
Cancer	Perhaps you seek motherly friends.
Leo	Your choose lively, fashionable and sophisticated friends.
Virgo	You value competent, efficient colleagues.
Libra	Intelligent friends who share your mental wavelength suit you.
Scorpio	Shared interests and mutual respect are important.
Sagittarius	You need friends who enjoy a good laugh.
Capricorn	Your friends are few, but valued, and probably older.
Aquarius	You have lots of friends, and you love to chat with them.
Pisces	Your friends must share your interests.

The Angles and Their Rulerships

Each sign of the zodiac is attached to a planet that we call the ruling planet, and here is a list of the rulerships as astrologers use them today.

The trick now is to find these rulers and check out the aspects to the rulers and the signs and houses they occupy.

The Chart Ruler

The planet that rules the sign on the Asc becomes the ruler of the Asc and it is also called the chart ruler, so it is an important factor. For instance, if an individual has Libra rising, Venus rules the Asc and is therefore called the chart ruler, making it an important planet for that person. The individual then needs to check out Venus to see what sign it is in, whether it is well aspected and so on, because a well-aspected chart ruler makes for an easier early life than a badly aspected one, while it also shows something of the person's manner and way of dealing with the world.

For example, someone with Libra rising who has a well aspected Venus will be at ease in any company; they will probably be suave and sophisticated, charming, good looking and popular.

As another example, someone with Aquarius rising will have Uranus as the chart ruler. If the natal Uranus is well aspected, the subject will be happy and possibly successful, with many friends and acquaintances, but if it is not, the first thirty years of life – if not, the whole of life – could be tricky.

If the chart ruler is in the fourth house, the person would be lucky in family matters, perhaps even inheriting property or being given something old and valuable by a family member. Maybe the person would write bestselling history books or become an expert in retro fashion. In addition, a native with the chart ruler in the seventh house would have a happy, successful, prestigious and wealthy marriage or partnership.

The Ruler of the MC

The sign that the MC resides in is ruled by a planet, and that becomes the ruler of the MC. This influences what people strive to be, their reputation, and how easy it is for them to become respected and admired by others and maintain their reputation once they have got it.

For instance, if a woman wants to become the Chair of important local committees and to be able to throw her weight about in her community, the right sign on the MC and a well aspected MC ruler is essential. In this case, she would need Leo on the MC with a very well aspected Sun, as this would be the ruler of the MC, and if the Sun were in the third house, which rules local matters, this would be ideal.

A man might wish to become the owner of a major international business, in which case Sagittarius on the MC would make Jupiter the ruler of the MC, bringing him the international connection and the sheer good luck to make it happen. If his natal Jupiter were in the fifth or ninth houses, this would become even more likely.

An MC in Capricorn means that Saturn is its ruler, and there is no better planet for someone who wants to be seen as a master of their game, but this would only take the person to the very top if Saturn were well aspected. It is worth looking at the house that Saturn occupies because that could point to the route that would lead the individual to the top. For instance, the MC ruler (Saturn) in the first house could lead to a glittering career in sport, the military or politics.

The Ruler of the Dsc

The Dsc shows the kind of person the subject likes and the type that the subject may choose for a friend or a life partner. The ruling planet of the Dsc can show how lucky the individual is with the choice of friends and partners, or it can describe difficulties in making friends or finding lovers. For instance, a Scorpio Dsc would suggest that Pluto is important to this person where it comes to these matters, so that a well-aspected Pluto would be a godsend, and the house that Pluto is in would show the best place for the person to start the search for friends and lovers. Say, for instance, Pluto was in the sixth house; a hospital or a health food shop would be a good place in which to start looking for the right partner.

The Ruler of the IC

The IC points to the family background and the things that influence the start and end of life. So, if the IC is in Aries, the IC ruler is Mars. If Mars is well aspected, these areas of life would be fine, but if not, there could be poverty, criminality, loss and despair in the family, which might encourage the subject to leave home as soon as possible and make a better life elsewhere. The house that the IC ruler is in will show where repairs can be made; for instance, if the individual's Mars were in the second house, the person would be happy with a home on a farm, producing organic food, or indeed living in any world that is related to second house topics, such as the perfume and beauty industry, singing, gardening, cooking and so on.

The Cusps

A cusp is the point where one sign ends and the next begins, so if your Sun or ascendant is on a cusp, these may be the results:

Aries/Taurus cusp

This belongs to a powerful personality with the kind of vision that allows the individual to look forward while retaining strong links to the past. This person can be charming when he feels like it, but also determined, obstinate and possibly aggressive. There is a strong sexual drive that may or may not be diverted into other activities. The person is probably interested in art, music or architecture and he or she could be a powerful, visionary leader, or a complete mess.

Taurus/Gemini cusp

This person can be a creative dreamer, a self-indulgent person who wants the good life and who may even make an effort to work for it if pressed. The subject is dexterous and good at do-it-yourself or engineering. This person likes travel, and enjoys work and family life. He may move and talk slowly, but the mind is quick and shrewd.

Gemini/Cancer cusp

This person is moody and difficult to understand, but the subject is a good listener and a good talker. He could be a good accountant or business person. Although desperate for a good relationship, this confusing person is both a mixer and a loner. The subject may always be on the move, looking for the most advantageous mixture of circumstances. He is sensitive and easily hurt.

Cancer/Leo cusp

This subject wants to make a splash, to be noticed and respected, but he may be too lazy to achieve this ambition, so he may try to marry someone who has a good income instead. The native is probably quite artistic and certainly creative, with a talent for working in the financial field, and may be an excellent accountant or insurance salesman. May be an excellent sales person.

Leo/Virgo cusp

A nervy, high achiever who never thinks he has done enough. He can become ill when things go wrong or he can punish himself unnecessarily. Emotionally vulnerable, slow to grow up or accept change, he needs to gain confidence. He also needs a stable family life. He is kind hearted and good to family and friends, but he can be moody and unpleasant at times.

Virgo/Libra cusp

This subject is highly sexed and highly charged with many other kinds of energy as well. He enjoys work, especially if it gives him a chance to manage others, and he may travel extensively in connection with his work. The subject has many secrets to keep, and though fascinating, is not easy to live with. This subject may dabble at things rather than do things thoroughly.

Libra/Scorpio cusp

This person's spine and legs may be affected in some way, even to the point of semi-paralysis. Despite any disability, the subject overcomes everything and goes on to have an interesting career. Marriage and other family or close relationships are likely to be excellent, but there may be no children. The outer manner may be abrupt, so the subject needs to work on this.

Scorpio/Sagittarius cusp

Here, we have a mystical or spiritual outlook, with a strong desire to help others. This person suffers more than most and puts up with it for longer than is necessary. This is a reliable and hard worker who will stick to a job until the finish, but he likes variety in a job and is happy to travel for business. This subject can suffer from accidents to the legs, but seems to overcome everything and keep going. He may be drawn to work in the fields of medicine or religion.

Sagittarius/Capricorn cusp

This subject is fascinated by the occult and may be very psychic. This person can be businesslike one minute, but unrealistic the next. He needs to relax and have fun, as all work and no play makes him dull. Family and friends depend on the subject, but don't give much back in return. He must guard against being abrupt or offensive.

Capricorn/Aquarius cusp

Outwardly competent and often sarcastic to the point of being offensive, but at the same time idealistic and kind hearted, this person is very good to his family and close friends, but may be too involved with work to spend much time with them. This subject judges character by work or status rather than as a person. Muddle-headed and somewhat messy administratively, he is at his best when teaching or helping others. This person's ideas are often very clever and truly workable.

Aquarius/Pisces cusp

Here is a strange mixture of weirdness and shrewdness, with leanings towards astrology and psychism. These people can inspire others with vision, but daily life may be chaotic. They may be very eccentric and faddy about everything, from food to clothing and the household. They may prefer animals to people.

Pisces/Aries cusp

This person may choose to work in the astrological or psychic world. The mixture of superb intuition coupled with commercial instincts can make this subject very successful in almost any field of endeavour. However, high ideals or too many absorbing interests can make the individual hard to live with. A good sales person and a clever politician.

The Decans

Each sign of the zodiac is divided into thirty degrees, and can make three groups of ten degrees; these sub-sections are called decans. The first decan is sub-ruled by its own sign, the second is sub-ruled by the next sign of the same element, and the third decan is sub-ruled by the remaining sign in that element.

For example, the sign of Aquarius is an air sign. The first decan is sub-ruled by Aquarius itself, the second by Gemini because it's the next air sign round the zodiac system, and the third decan is sub-ruled by Libra. If you are into astrology enough to know the degree of your ascendant, you can easily work out which decan was rising. The first decan is found anywhere from 0 degrees of a sign to 9 deg 59 min of the sign; the second decan is from 10 degrees to 19 deg.59 min, and the third decan at 20 degrees to 29 deg.59 min.

The decans subtly modify the influence of the rising sign, but they can also demonstrate links to other members of the family. For instance, I've come across one mother and her children who link like this:

Mother:　Sun Cancer in the Scorpio decan, rising sign Scorpio in the Cancer decan.

Son:　Sun Scorpio in the Cancer decan, rising sign Cancer in the Scorpio decan.

Daughter: Moon Scorpio in the Cancer decan, rising sign Cancer in the Scorpio decan.

Here is a very brief introduction to the influence of the decans. It's much too large a subject to cover in this book, but if you want to know more about this fascinating subject, there are books available on Amazon.

Sign and Decan	Influence
Aries/Aries	A real go-getter, likely to lack consideration for others.
Aries/Leo	A go-getter who finishes what he starts.
Aries/Sagittarius	Many interests, good teacher.
Taurus/Taurus	Very capable, but too obstinate.
Taurus/Virgo	A good worker, good with details.
Taurus/Capricorn	An excellent banker or businessperson.
Gemini/Gemini	A flirt, very clever, a good memory.
Gemini/Libra	Good team worker, but may be argumentative.
Gemini/Aquarius	Clever, with a deep and serious mind.
Cancer/Cancer	Very attached to family, loves travel.
Cancer/Scorpio	Loves travel, chooses a weak partner to mother.
Cancer/Pisces	Intuitive, spiritual, can be moody.
Leo/Leo	Very enterprising and successful.
Leo/Sagittarius	Loves travel and philosophy.
Leo/Aries	Enterprising, will follow a hunch in business.
Virgo/Virgo	Reliable worker, but may be neurotic.
Virgo/Capricorn	Good business head, but might be cold hearted.
Virgo/Taurus	Clever at design and construction.

Sign and Decan	Influence
Libra/Libra	Attractive, lazy, argumentative.
Libra/Aquarius	Good ideas, but may be impractical.
Libra/Gemini	Good in business, health may be poor.
Scorpio/Scorpio	Likes business, but emotions dominate thinking.
Scorpio/Pisces	Intuitive, psychic, may be stingy in small ways.
Scorpio/Cancer	Loves home, family, friends, work and travel.
Sagittarius/Sagittarius	Adventurous, interested in everything.
Sagittarius/Aries	Hot tempered, sometimes acts without thinking.
Sagittarius/Leo	Steady and able to achieve and reach goals.
Capricorn/Capricorn	Can be workaholic, otherwise very status conscious.
Capricorn/Taurus	Practical, sensible, good homemaker.
Capricorn/Virgo	Clever business person, good accountant.
Aquarius/Aquarius	Very clever, but impractical ideas and soapbox mentality.
Aquarius/Gemini	Bright, humourous, good with figure work.
Aquarius/Libra	Laid back, great ideas, but nothing may come of them.
Pisces/Pisces	Very dreamy, artistic, may live chaotic lifestyle.
Pisces/Cancer	Good at business, sales and with people.
Pisces/Scorpio	Can be over-emotional and act without thinking.

Rising Planets

The term rising planet refers to a planet in the first or second house that will rise above the ascendant within a few hours of a child's birth. The range has broadened a little now to include a planet in the twelfth house that has already risen, as long as it's close to the ascendant. If there is only one planet near the ascendant, it will be strongly emphasised. If there is a group of planets, then the house and the sign that it occupies will be stressed. A rising planet can be almost as important as the Sun in a birthchart.

Sun Conjunct Ascendant

If the Sun and the ascendant are in the same sign, the sign becomes an ultra important factor on the chart. If the Sun and ascendant were in adjoining signs (e.g. Sun in Libra, Virgo rising), both signs would be emphasised, but not as much. Transits and progressions over that part of the chart will be exceptionally noticeable. If the two factors are in the same sign, there is no need for the ascendant to act as a shield to the personality. The Sun's influence makes for a confident, outgoing, well-integrated person who was encouraged and loved in childhood. If the Asc is a difficult one (Virgo, Capricorn or Gemini for instance), the childhood was hard, but the subject had the inner strength to rise above the problems and achieve a good deal of success in spite of them - or maybe because of them.

These powerful personalities need to express themselves in daily life, and they put their own stamp on everything. They cannot live or work in a subservient position. They are strong and healthy, with good powers of recovery from illness, despite potential problems in connection with the back or heart. These people are initiators who are not happy to be in the hands of others or the hands of fate, and they turn all situations to their own advantage. They have sunny personalities, but they can be arrogant.

Moon Conjunct Ascendant

This placement denotes a sensitive and vulnerable nature. The feelings are close to the surface and are easily brought into play. The subject reacts in an intensely personal way to every stimulus and links easily to the feelings of others. The mother may be an extremely powerful (and possibly extraordinary) figure, and her life and emotions will have a profound effect. The subject will remain close to her, perhaps remaining involved in her life and her work for many years. It's possible that the subjects can "remember" things that happened to their mother while they were in the womb! Childhood experiences and early training remain in the subjects' unconscious throughout life. They are likely to be the eldest siblings in a family.

There is a strong need to create a home and family as well as look after others by working in one of the caring professions. These subjects want to protect the environment, preserve places, buildings and objects from the past and create a better, kinder and safer future for mankind: Psychic ability is almost always present, and there may even be vestigial memories of previous lives. All forms of intuition are well developed. These people love travel and to be on or by water. They also like to run a small business for themselves. They are interested in history and tradition and they may try to revive traditional crafts, or collect fine things from the past. They retreat from the rat race from time to time, in order to calm themselves and recharge their emotional batteries. Oddly enough, the Moon is associated with work in the public eye, or for the public good, so these people often become well-known personalities. Being sensitive, they become depressed or downhearted and they may absorb the unhappiness of others; this psychic absorption can make them ill. In a notably macho or materialistic chart, this Moon placement lends introspection and sensitivity to the needs and feelings of others.

Mercury Conjunct Ascendant

Mercury is concerned with communication and the mentality, therefore these subjects are fluent talkers and good communicators. They range from highly intelligent to bright, active, sensible and street-wise. They work in careers directly involved with people and with communications. These people have good minds, but they may never make much use of their brains. They switch off from time to time, to allow the mind to relax. They are dutiful towards parents and either very close to siblings or at odds with them. They are happiest working for themselves or in their own little department, and they need to feel that their work is appreciated.

They can be restless, easily bored, interesting to listen to, humourous and sometimes very sarcastic. Their health is not good, but they can also be hypochondriacs in some instances. In a stodgy or over-practical chart, this Mercury placement adds quickness of mind, curiosity and adaptability.

Venus Conjunct Ascendant

This confers good looks and a pleasant social manner, with a pleasant speaking voice, and possibly a good singing voice. These subjects are refined and they dislike anything ugly, dirty or vulgar. They take jobs where they can create beauty in some way, for example as a gardener, furniture designer, artist, hairdresser or dancer. Alternatively, they take up artistic or attractive hobbies. They can be good arbitrators, with a natural desire to create harmony and understanding. They can also be diplomats and ambassadors who use their charm and tact in their daily lives.

These people enjoy making money and spending it on attractive and valuable goods. They are concerned about values, both in terms of getting value for money and in terms of personal values and priorities. They won't sacrifice anything they value for the sake of others. They can be sleepy and lazy or argumentative in some cases. Venus on the ascendant can add placidity and pleasantness to an otherwise forceful, dynamic or neurotic chart.

Mars Conjunct Ascendant

This adds impulsiveness, enterprise, courage and a quick temper. These people make things happen where other less courageous souls would prefer to run away and hide. They stand out in a crowd, dominating those around them. They can become highly successful achievers, who are best suited for positions of leadership or as self-employed entrepreneurs. Successful sports people tend to have this Mars placement, because above all, it's associated with competitiveness. In an otherwise timid, stodgy or lazy chart, this can add enterprise, enthusiasm, energy and will power. The person's birth may have been fraught with danger, or the prevailing situation may have been dangerous.

Jupiter Conjunct Ascendant

These people are attractive, with sunny smiles and good teeth. This placement adds the kind of broad frame and comfortable shape that looks great on a man, but that's unfashionable nowadays for a woman. The outer manner is cheerful, optimistic and confident, and these people carry authority well and can be inspirational leaders. These subjects are unlikely to be biased against any class or colour of person and they are not the slightest bit snobbish, but they can be intolerant of wannabes and posers. This placement gives a love of travel and exploration, plus a touch of studiousness, and these people may be interested in philosophy and metaphysical subjects. They may be lucky gamblers, especially on horses. Their minds are good and they can usually see both sides of any argument, but they can also become very attached to their own opinions. I've noticed that people who have this planet rising experience quite drastic ups and downs where money is concerned.

They are invariably attractive, but the optimism which the old time astrologers associate with this planet can be dampened if there is a good deal of water on the chart. Nevertheless, this placement adds a touch of enterprise, luck and vision to an otherwise stodgy or earthbound chart. Jupiter rising subjects travel widely, often in connection with their work, and some eventually leave their country of origin altogether.

Saturn Conjunct Ascendant

These people are squashed in childhood so that they don't develop much confidence or self-worth, but they can become surprisingly successful later in life, due perhaps to their tendency to put their noses to the grindstone and keep them there. This planet brings insecurity and even fear during childhood. These subjects may have lost parents and been brought up by grandparents, or other older people who may have taken them in on sufferance. If the home life was all right, school would have been a nightmare. These types are happy to grow up, because that's when their life starts to improve.

Hiding their real needs and feelings, they may even deny themselves the right to have any needs other than those which other people consider suitable. Their natural creativity may be squashed because it doesn't fit in with the requirements of those around them. Depending upon the rest of the chart, this childhood can develop a hard and aggressive attitude to others later in life. Alternatively, these people may become doormats who avoid making even reasonable demands upon others. In a way, this is not such a bad thing, as these people are very independent and they neither lean on nor drain the energy of others. Some rise above the unpromising start and become outstanding success stories. These subjects take commitments very seriously and they finish what they start. Many of them become writers or work in publishing, where patience and attention to details are important. They also have a talent for maths and science. They may be religious, but they tend to be realistic and down-to-earth as well.

Saturn on the ascendant or in opposition or square to it at the time of birth indicates a difficult birth. Another interesting theory is that the parents worked hard while the child was young, giving him especially diligent parental role models. They may be deaf or suffer with some chronic ailment.

Uranus Conjunct Ascendant

These individuals may be idealistic, unpredictable and quite fascinating. Their interests are unusual, they are highly intuitive and able to jump to the right conclusion and they may be into astrology and psychic matters. Humanitarian and broad-minded, these people opt for an unusual way of life, either following unusual beliefs or making them up as they go along. Their lives take peculiar twists and turns, partly because they are prey to unusual circumstances and partly because they can't stand too much normality. These individuals are clever, but they can also be obstinate. They have good minds that are directed towards unusual subjects. They may be cranky, strange or visionary, whilst at the same time being stubborn and determined. Even an extremely mundane chart will be enlivened by this placement.

Neptune Conjunct Ascendant

This fascinating planet can make people into inspired artists, glamourous film stars or complete nut cases – or all three. The childhood may have been strange, and there could have been some kind of mystery surrounding birth and parentage. It's possible that one or more of the parents were absent or very peculiar, even to the extent of being mentally ill. These subjects are sensitive, vulnerable and easily hurt, and they may never have a clear idea of their own needs and feelings, trying to live to the rules of others – only discovering later that these rules were abnormal or twisted in some way. This placement can make subjects psychic, mediumistic or prone to fantasies. Loneliness or isolation in childhood will have encouraged these children to read, think, dream and listen to music, and to develop their creativity and imagination. In extreme cases, they lose track of reality altogether. Bear in mind the rest of the chart when Neptune is rising, because if it's practical and sensible, this will simply add artistry and sensitivity.

These people may work in the photography, music or the psychic fields, and they have a soft spot for animals or those who are weak and vulnerable, so some work for charity organisations, while others collect lame ducks.

Pluto Conjunct Ascendant

These people want to control, direct and guide the lives of others, so they may go into politics. This directing instinct can take them into the world of medicine, the media or teaching. The personality is so controlled that it's hard to work out just what these people are thinking or what really motivates them. They may be pleasant at work and hard at home or vice versa. Others put them down when they are young, so they can be slow to grow up. They can have deep-seated resentments due to being made to feel inadequate at home or at school when young. They seek to overcome these feelings later in life, sometimes by being economical with the truth.

These subjects have sharp minds and the kind of insight that allow them to pick up even the mildest of undercurrents, and they always know when someone doesn't like them. They may appear mild, gentle and amenable, but when challenged or hurt, they lash out. This planet adds tenacity and reliability to the chart, so they don't take time off work when feeling off colour. They finish what they start, arrive in good time for appointments, and they are alert and properly equipped to do what is required. They must be able to come and go as they please. This planet adds sexuality, and depending upon circumstances and the rest of the chart, this may be an important issue. If this aspect of life is squashed, these subjects can become embittered or depressed.

The person may have been born into a family in mourning or at a time of danger, such as during a war. In a mundane chart, this Pluto position adds depth and intelligence.

Chiron Conjunct Ascendant

Chiron rising is rather like Saturn rising, in that the person will have severe problems during childhood, perhaps through illness or through being badly treated by those around him. This can lead these people to work in the fields of healing or psychology, where they use their own understanding of pain to help others.

North or South Node Conjunct Ascendant

When either node is conjunct the Asc, fame and fortune are possible.

Predictive Techniques

The ascendant may not have the impact of planetary transits and progressions, but it does have valuable uses, particularly when looking at a year in question and when judging long-term situations. I will show you the easiest, and probably the best method of judging the changes that a progressed ascendant can bring.

Degree For a Year Progressions

There are many ways to progress your Asc, but this is the easiest, as all it requires is that you move the Asc forward by a degree for each year of your life. There are 30 degrees within each sign, running from 0 to 29.

A person with an Asc at 12 degrees of Aries will see the Asc progress into Taurus at the age of seventeen, and onwards to Gemini at 47 and Cancer at the age of 77.

When an Asc is very early in a sign, that rising sign has more impact on the personality, partly because most of the first house is in that sign, but also because it will take several years before the Asc can progress to the next sign. Conversely, when an ascendant is very late in a sign, it may have less impact, because much of the first house is in the next sign along, and also because the progressed Asc will leave the rising sign and move into the next one in early childhood.

After considering the age at which the progressed Asc changes sign, you can look for the age at which it crosses another planet, as this will set off some kind of event, the nature of which depends upon the planet in question.

Aspects also work with this system, so if you are far enough into astrology to understand them, you can look back over your life to see what happened in a year when the progressed Asc made a sextile or trine to a planet or when it squared or opposed one. Remember to consider the nature of the planet in question.

Other Forms of Progression

This section is for those of you who have some astrological knowledge.

- You can progress the MC by the rate at which it moves, and then reset the Asc appropriately.
- You can progress the Asc by the rate at which the Sun moves, thus using Solar Arc Directions.
- You can use Secondary Directions, which are also called Day-For-a-Year Progressions.
- Secondary Directions move the ascendant more slowly than the other methods, as long as you live in the same area throughout your life (say by remaining within sixty miles or so of your place of birth). It will move along slowly. If you move to another part of the country or another part of the world, the progressed Asc moves in strange ways, and it can even move back to an earlier position than it was at birth.

Progressing the Midheaven

You may find the MC even more effective than the Asc as a tool for predicting events. Either progress the MC a degree for a year or select Secondary Directions on your computer software to locate a progressed MC position.

Degree for a year MC progressions are particularly useful when rectifying a birthchart, which means finding the Asc for someone who only has a vague idea of the time of birth, as you will see in the following chapter on rectification.

Transits

This is the first kind of predictive technique that all astrologers learn, and it involves using the ephemeris (book of tables) or an astrology program to locate the position of the planets in the sky at any one time. If you can link the figures in your book or on your computer screen to what you see in the sky, you can often go out at night and watch the lunar and planetary aspects looking down on you.

Check out any planets that cross the Asc, particularly those slow moving outer planets that transform our lives, such as Pluto, Neptune, Uranus and Saturn. Look at the aspects that planets make to the Asc as they work their way round your chart. You will find that the faster moving inner planets, such as the Moon, Mercury and Venus won't make much of an impact, other than a short lived one on the day that they cross the Asc Aspects from the outer planets will make themselves felt, though.

Aspect	DISTANCE	EFFECT
Conjunction	0 degrees	Both very good and very bad, depending upon the planet.
Semi-sextile	30 degrees	Mildly pleasant or mildly irritating.
Sextile	60 degrees	Beneficial.
Square	90 degrees	Difficult.
Trine	120 degrees	Beneficial.
Inconjunct	150 degrees	Awkward, tense, irritating.
Opposition	180 degrees	Can be good, but often difficult.

The Planets by Progression or Transit

This is a brief rundown of the way each planet behaves and the impact that it might have on the Asc by progression or transit.

Planet	AREAS OF INFLUENCE
Sun	Happy time, luck, success, creative, children might become important now. If a difficult aspect, can feel like a long period of bad luck, illness, slipped discs, heart trouble.
Moon	Dealings with parents, family life, house move, renovations, starting a small business. Joy or sadness.
Mercury	Education, exams, replacing office equipment, getting job, cars, transport, travel, communications, neighbours and neighbourhood, health. Increased curiosity.
Venus	Love, relationships, harmony, social life, personal finances, personal purchases and possessions, abundance. Loss, extravagance, expense, trouble with love life, disharmony.
Mars	Drive, ambition, confidence when starting something new, sex, activity, fighting for what you want or for what is right. Attack, accidents, operations, fevers, sudden setbacks.
Jupiter	Expansion of horizons, legal matters, foreigners and travel, spiritual matters. Legal or financial trouble, over-expansion.
Saturn	Putting down roots, attention to details, a good job, a step up the ladder, a serious attitude, help from superiors or elders. Struggle, illness, setbacks, a dampening effect.
Uranus	Breakout and a fresh approach, originality, friends, groups and societies, modern ideas, astrology. Sudden setbacks, loss of friendship or loss of a group or club situation.
Neptune	Dreams come true, spiritual growth, artistry, music, the sea and pleasant interludes, kindness. Muddle, disillusion, swindles, not being able to see what's going on.
Pluto	Period of major transformation hard to live through, but leads to a better way of life. Death, birth, taxes, other people's money, shared resources, marriage and divorce, legacies, legal matters.
Chiron	Health and healing, accidents, illness, operations. Interest in healing arts and music.

Not only People...

All the above ideas can be applied to a business, a property, a pet animal, a governmental administration or a national election. It could apply to a city, a country, a reign, or anything else that has a definite time, date and place of birth.

Retrograde Progressions

There are times when planets appear to go backwards in the sky, and this effect is called retrograde motion. The Moon and Sun are the only "planets" that can never go retrograde. When a progressing planet crosses the ascendant, retrogrades back over it and then passes over it again by forward motion, matters that are symbolised by that planet become more obvious. During the retrograde period, matters may be delayed or problematical, but the final forward progression will clear away the problem and bring ultimate benefits.

Retrograde Transits

Where transiting planets are concerned, the inner planets move too quickly to be important, although an inner planet passing, retrograding and then re-passing the Asc will make its presence felt for a while. For instance, Mercury may pass the Asc, retrograde back over it a week or so later and then move forward over it again, marking a month or so of intense Mercurial activity. Venus will take a little longer to do this, and Mars will hang around in the vicinity of the Asc for several months, making its presence obvious while doing so.

Transits by outer planets are more important, so if they make this "triple conjunction" to the Asc, this will mark an extended period in which the effects of the planet can be felt. Obviously, a planet such as Saturn or Pluto can bring difficulties, but even these planets have their good sides. The outcome for a "triple conjunction" of Saturn to the Asc will be growth and consolidation, while Pluto will ultimately bring birth or rebirth, financial and business improvements and possibly an inheritance or money from a divorce settlement, after an extended period of aggravation. This planet can bring personal transformation and personal improvement, so that the person gets into shape, tosses out old clothes and buys better ones, makes new friends, gets a better job, moves to a larger/smaller home, finds a soul-mate, discovers good sex and so on.

A Uranus "triple conjunction" would bring a complete change of life and a totally new outlook. A Neptune situation would bring art, music or mystical events into the subject's life, and it might encourage a move to the seaside. Jupiter brings travel, new opportunities, a fresh outlook, perhaps also an interest in education, or success in exams.

Rectification

If you're interested in rectification, try my book, "Astrology in Focus: Find your Rising Sign", as it's helpful to those people looking for their own or someone else's time of birth.

If you have an approximate birth time, say for example between about 2:00 and 3:00, you need to make up a chart for 2:30 and then do a little fine-tuning. You do this by moving the MC. The MC moves at a degree for a year, therefore events can be pin-pointed by the aspects it makes to other planets on the natal chart as it progresses. The subject can be asked to mention any particularly memorable events in his childhood and the rectified MC can be swung backwards and forwards until it connects with one of the planets or some other feature on the chart at the relevant age.

For example, a change in one's direction in life would connect with a progression of the MC from one sign to another. An accident might be set off by an MC square to Mars or Uranus. Good exam results might be MC conjunct, sextile or trine the Sun or Mercury, while a move of house would connect with the Moon, or with a square or opposition if the subject felt it to be an unhappy event, or with a trine or sextile if it was a happy one. A conjunction could go either way. Obviously, this takes a good deal of astrological knowledge, but there are plenty of books on the market which show the effect of planets natally, by progression or when transiting.

Pre-Natal Epoch Birthcharts
A normal pregnancy takes 280 days or 40 weeks, so counting back from the date of birth will take you back to the date of conception. Look at the position of the Moon on the conception date because the theory is that this will be near an angle. I've tried this several times and it does seem to work. Incidentally, if you have decent software, it will do this for you if you select it.

Simply using this book will help you to get close to the right time of birth, as the person will recognise which Asc, MC, Dsc and IC are theirs. Then, it's only a case of fine tuning the chart by linking events to the movement of the MC or to particular transits on the chart.

"I 'ave No Ascendant!"

Just to show you how weird things can get in astrology, here is the strange tale of Olga (not her real name), the Russian artist, who Jan and I met several years ago at a gathering of astrologers and psychics in London.

- "I 'ave no ascendant" breathed the charmingly accented foreign voice in my ear.
- "What?" I replied in surprise. "What do you mean, you have no ascendant?"
- "I am Russian and my name is Olga" said the attractive young lady, "I was born way up in the north of Russia during polar night, and though I 'ave been to many Russian astrologers and even one or two 'ere, nobody has been able to find my ascendant."

This was certainly an unusual situation and it looked as though Olga might be right. In the popular astrological systems, such as Placidus and Equal House, dropping a line down from sunrise at the birth latitude to the ecliptic forms the ascendant. So, in theory, if there is no sunrise, there can be no ascendant! I said, "You'd better come and see me and I'll think of something."

NB: Olga was born on the 21st of January 1963 at 11:10 am local time in Norilsk, Northern Russia.(69 deg. 20 min North, 88 deg. 66 min. East)

Olga came for her consultation a couple of weeks later, and as luck would have it, my friend Sean Lovatt happened to phone me while she was there. I told Sean about Olga and he stayed on the line as he entered her details into his computer, while I put her details into mine. Sean and I experimented with various different house systems. Sean tried Campanus and commented that it showed an ascendant of 27 degrees of Virgo. He also muttered darkly that in theory, Olga's ascendant was also her descendant. Sean cut the connection and went off to play with Olga's chart by himself.

The phone rang again and this time my friend Jonathan Dee came on the line. Jon is another very experienced astrologer, and he immediately threw Olga's data into his machine and said that he would ring back if he came up with any bright ideas. Before he rang off, Jon said that he would give Porphyry a try. Meanwhile I got on with trying anything that I could think of.

I discovered that Porphyry only showed four astrological houses, these being the first, sixth, seventh and twelfth. Campanus was better, as it showed a few more shrivelled houses gathered at the MC and the IC. Calls came in from Jonathan and Sean, both saying that they had also discovered that Campanus gave the best results. It was interesting that Sean, Jon and I were all using different software. While none of the programs could cope with this chart, at least they all made exactly the same mess of it!

Olga understood the system, but she commented that a Virgo ascendant simply didn't fit any aspect of her life or her personality. I was just coming to the crazy conclusion that Olga's chart was upside down when Jon phoned me back to tell me that he had also come to that conclusion! Then Sean phoned to tell me that the chart was not only upside down but also back to front! A Virgo rising chart showed the sun and its close neighbours, Mercury and Venus, in the lower hemisphere, but Olga was born at 11.10 am. Even allowing for Polar night, a morning birth couldn't possibly put the sun in the lower hemisphere, i.e. below the equator!

For people like us who live in the northern hemisphere, the only way to make sense of an astrology chart is to stand facing the south. Then the midheaven points towards the sun, the ascendant is to the east and the descendant to the west. If I did this with Olga's chart, it showed that the sun was shining on the other side of the earth. Clearly, at that time of the year, it was - but this made no astrological sense.

In addition to what was clearly a wrong ascendant, Olga's computer-generated chart showed aspects that weren't actually possible. The nodes of the Moon can only be in opposition to each other, but Olga's were trine! The chart bore some resemblance to older types of European charts in which the houses stayed equal and the signs stretched to fit them, but everything on them was all so much out of alignment that it was hard to see what the aspects between the planets really were.

I gave up on the astronomical impossibilities and followed a hunch that Pisces was the probable ascendant - in other words, that the apparent Dsc was actually the Asc. I gave Olga information about the personality and the early life experiences of someone with Pisces rising, and she agreed that this described her childhood and personality. In addition, Olga is a professional artist, which fits a Pisces ascendant. I then rectified the chart to give an ascendant of 27° degrees of Pisces and used the Equal

House system. This gave me a workable chart, and it was no hardship to write in the correct position for the moon on both the natal and progressed charts by hand. I then interpreted the chart for Olga in the normal way, taking my time about it and looking at every point in detail. An ecstatic Olga went away with her newly minted ascendant!

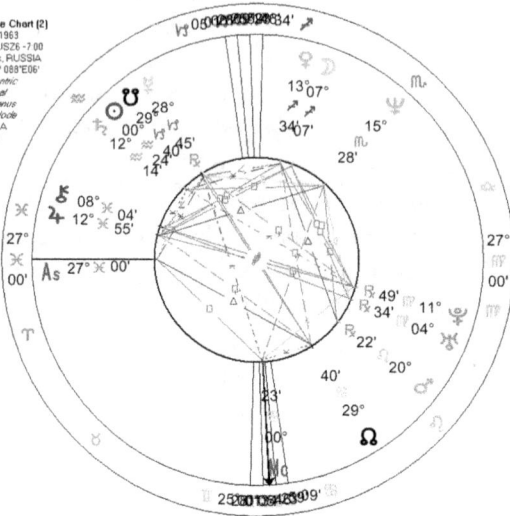

Olga -
Campanus Chart

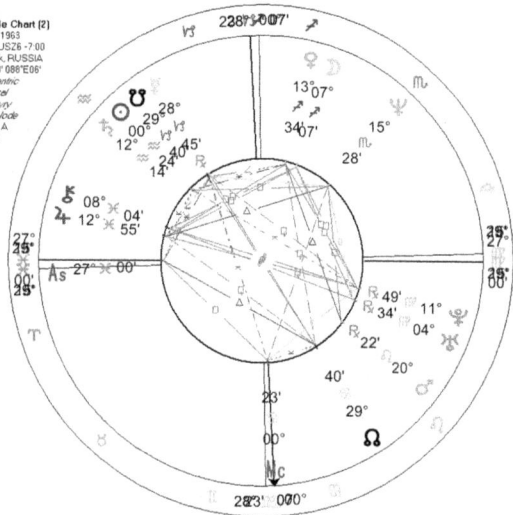

Olga -
Porphyry Chart

Additional Data

The equal house chart worked as well as anything could, but see where the MC is - it's at the bottom of the chart! Also, the Vertex is near the Asc, rather than being where it should be, which is in the fifth, sixth, seventh or eighth house.

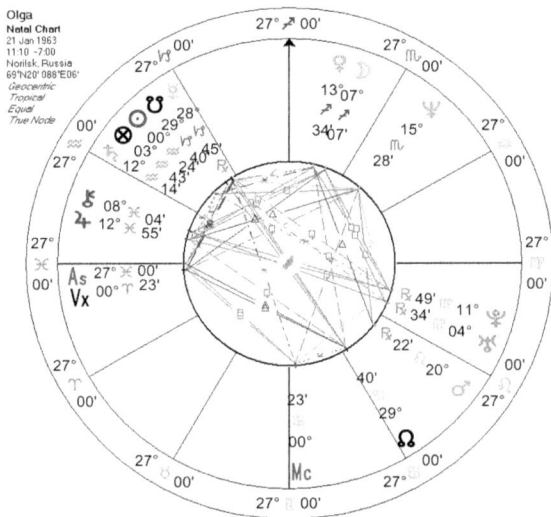

Olga - equal house Chart

Some Celebrities in More Detail

Boris Johnson

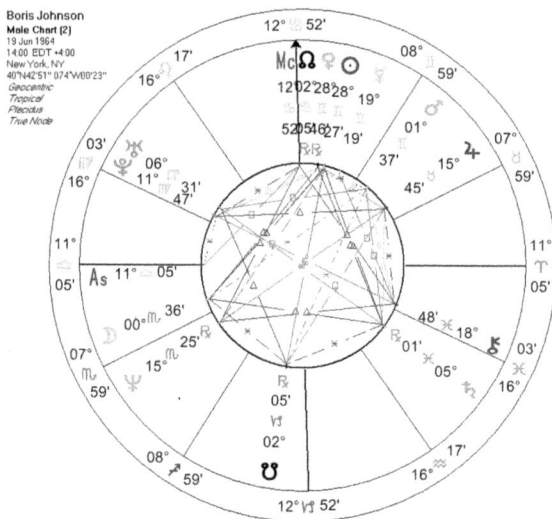

Boris Johnson
Male Chart (2)
19 Jun 1964
14:00 EDT +4:00
New York, NY
40°N42'51" 074°W00'23"
Geocentric
Tropical
Placidus
True Node

Boris has Libra rising, and this is the most charming and loveable rising sign of all, so whatever Boris may be underneath, his Asc allows him to make the most of himself, outwardly at least. In his case, he comes across as a cuddlesome, living, breathing, oversized teddy bear. There is a touch of sexiness about our Boris too, because Libra is a sexy Asc. So is his Scorpio Moon, and he has masculine Mars and lucky Jupiter in the sexy eighth house. In theory, this set-up would signify a dark and dangerous looking suave and sexy film star, but mop-haired Boris shambles along and looks a mess. However, women want to tuck his shirt in, brush his hair and mother him. Boris has the Sun, Mercury and Venus in Gemini in the ninth house, so he has a quick and clever brain. This makes him even more interesting to some of us, as we quite like our political leaders to have a bit of brain as well as personality.

Boris was born in New York, of an international background, and he is a member of the British and German Royal Families, albeit on the wrong side of someone's sheets! He says he is the original melting pot, being Turkish, European, and with Jewish, Christian and Muslim antecedents. His international background and appeal is shown by the stellium of planets in his ninth house. Wherever he happened to be born, he takes his responsibility to London and Britain very seriously, and with the Moon as rising planet, along with his Cancerian MC, he is patriotic and protective towards the UK.

He is more sensitive than he looks on the outside, and also more ambitious than he looks. He may act the bumpkin at times and he does make gaffes, but he is quick, clever, a fantastic linguist and very well educated. As one would expect with so much Cancer on his chart, he is a knowledgeable historian.

Barack Obama

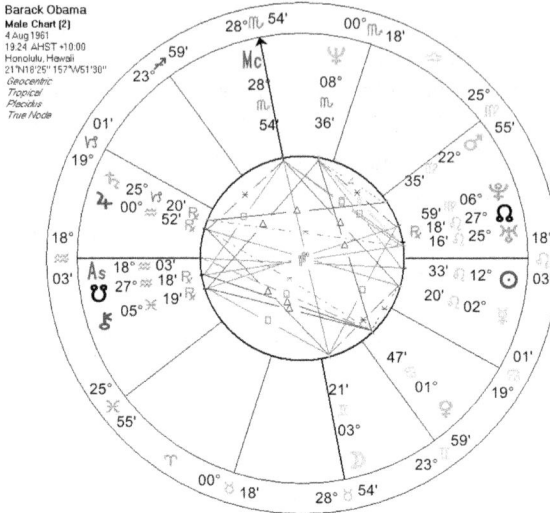

Barack Obama has an international background. He was born in the exotic city of Honolulu in the Hawaiian Islands, which were once British. His father was Kenyan and his mother mid-Western American, but her antecedents were English, Scottish, Irish and Italian. He has a sister living in Germany and other siblings in Africa and elsewhere. He has lived in Indonesia and he has an old-world dignity about him that suggests more than a whiff of the now-vanished British Empire.

Barack Obama has Aquarius rising, which makes him a force for change, a revolutionary and a man who can bring about breakthroughs where others face brick walls. The Sun in Leo and his Aquarius Asc make him a determined and stubborn (albeit charming) personality who won't let much get in his way. I am slightly worried about the Scorpio MC, as he would have more luck on his side if it was Sagittarius - but, if that were so, then perhaps he would have settled for Secretary of State for Foreign Affairs rather than go all out for President.

His Sun in the sixth house makes him a hard worker who can cope with details, while the Gemini Moon makes him intelligent and quick-minded, although apt to argue when it isn't always necessary. The friendly Aquarian Asc, Leo Sun and seventh house stellium make him a people person, while the Scorpio MC gives him a touch of much needed gravity.

Michelle Obama

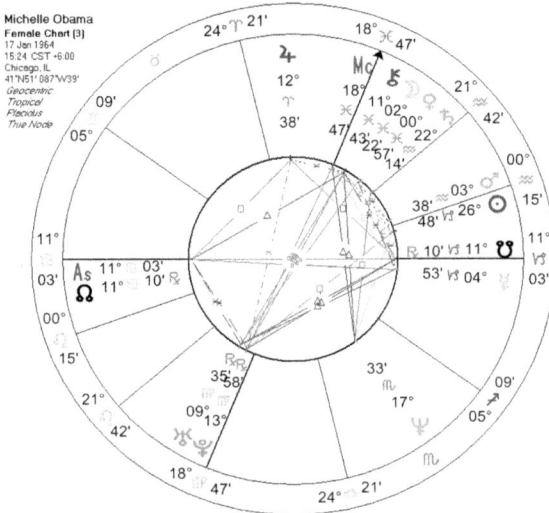

We know that a Capricorn Sun leads to ambition and a tendency to count the pennies, but Michelle's Cancer Asc makes her appear to be the perfect mother. She should have - and indeed does have - a good relationship with her own mother, and she is very close to her children. She could become a kind of "mother to the nation" in a similar way to Princess Diana and the Queen Mother in the UK. Her MC, Venus, Chiron and Moon in Pisces make her extremely sensitive, romantic and vulnerable, and this adds to her "Princess Diana" image, but it also makes her somewhat unpredictable.

My guess is that she is tough and capable on the outside, due to her cardinal sign Sun and Asc, but she is gentle, sensitive and easily hurt on the inside. Some may pip her as a future President, but I suspect there isn't enough deep-down hardness in her makeup, and she may also fantasise a little too much, so that if pushed, she could be caught out in thoughtless exaggerations or silly remarks. She would be a wonderful storyteller or writer of children's books.

Harrison Ford

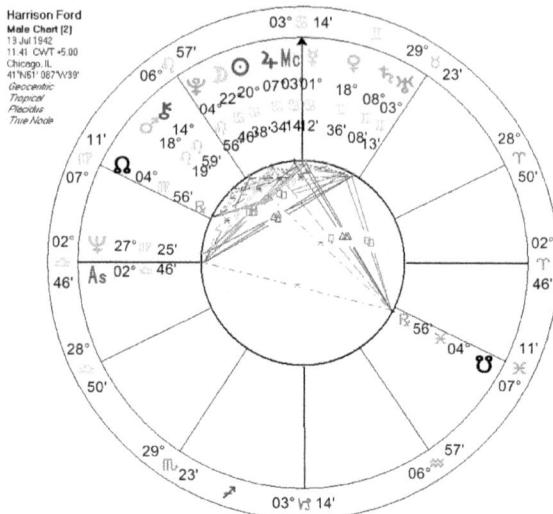

With Libra on the Asc, Harrison's charm and popularity is assured, but he is not as soft as he looks. Libra is a cardinal sign, and his Sun, Moon and MC are all in Cancer, which is also a cardinal sign, so there is no arguing with this man. We know that Harrison was a carpenter before his acting career took off, and that he still relaxes by making furniture; the Cancer stellium would fit with that scenario, as Cancer likes to make things that help to create comfy homes for people.

Cancer is a sign that can create a fantasy in its own mind and then bring it into being. Cancerians really can make the impossible happen, so they are wizard at throwing out an image that may be very different from their real natures. Neptune is close to Harrison's Asc, giving him a rich fantasy life and endowing him with acting ability. This rising planet adds to his attractiveness.

He uses his homely Cancerian image to present himself on-screen as an ordinary man who has become caught up in extra-ordinary situations. The fact that there are no planets below the horizon means that his image and public life are vital to him, but the emphasis on the "home and family" signs of Gemini, Cancer and Leo make his private life equally important to him.

Angelina Jolie

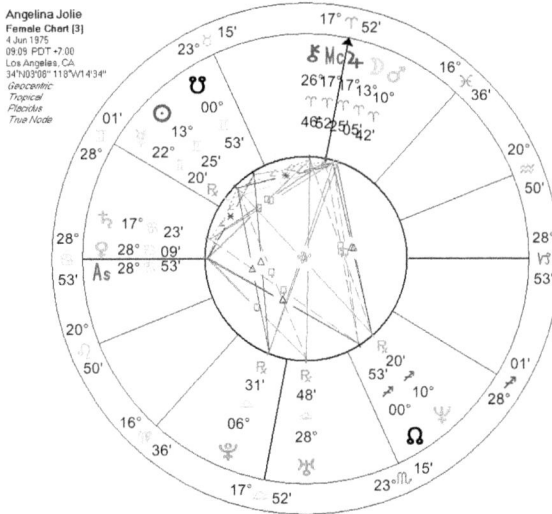

Angelina Jolie's ascendant is almost at the end of Cancer, so the need for home and family life is powerful, but so is the need for recognition. She comes from an acting family, so she has grown up knowing what fame can bring, and this is reflected in the Leo first house. She has to live life to her own drumbeat, though: the cardinal and very self-determined sign of Aries is on her MC, with Jupiter, the Moon and Mars (the ruler of Aries) nearby. Her eleventh house Sun in Gemini makes her quick, clever and rather unusual, and my guess is that she reads a great deal and that she has a mind full of interesting facts and snippets of information. Although Angelina's Cancer ascendant and Venus in Cancer, conjunct the Asc, make her the most feminine of women, she has a muscular intellect. Her Sun in Gemini and Moon, Mars, Jupiter, Chiron and MC in Aries, make her an interesting combination and a complex personality.

Angelina's Moon and stellium in the ninth house make her appeal to all kinds of people, all over the world. Her fabulously aspected Neptune in the fifth house makes her creative and attractive, and being in Sagittarius, it helps her to be agile, strong and sporty.

Some sadness lingers in her twelfth house Saturn, possibly due to a lack of any real education. She may have felt pressure during childhood due to parents who didn't really get on with each other, as shown by her Saturn being square to her Moon.

Susan Boyle

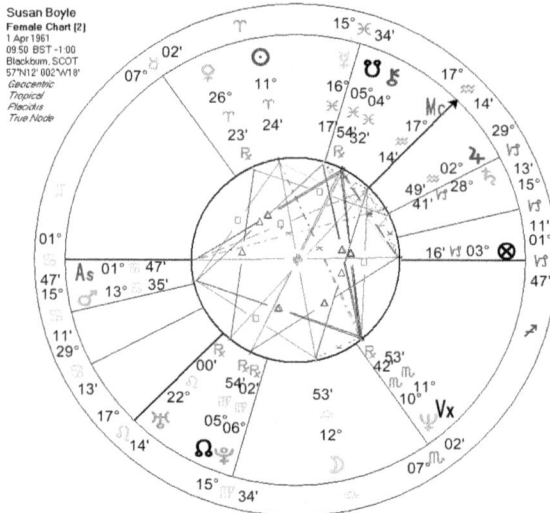

Susan Boyle
Female Chart [2]
1 Apr 1961
09:50 BST -1:00
Blackburn, SCOT
57°N12' 002°W18'
Geocentric
Tropical
Placidus
True Node

On the evening of the 11th of April 2009, in front of millions of people, a phenomenon occurred in the shape of Susan Boyle when she first appeared on the "Britain's Got Talent" TV programme. So let's start with Susan's natal chart - both for the ascendant's sake as far as this book is concerned, and as a whole, because it's really unusual and fascinating.

Mars rules the brain, and the first house rules the early stages of life, the head, the brain and the body as a whole. In Susan's case, Mars rules her Aries Sun sign. There it sits, in the first house, at the fulcrum of a T-square involving the most personal planets of all - the Sun and the Moon. Susan was born with Asperger's Syndrome, making her a slow-learner at school and the victim of bullies. However, this powerful, angular Mars also sits at the leading edge of a grand trine to Mercury and the Neptune/Vertex conjunction, all in sensitive water signs. Susan expresses herself through music, as shown by the link between Mercury (communication) and Neptune (music) for the benefit of others (Vertex). Like a number of Arians and those with Mars rising, she lacks a bit of common sense. She is no beauty, but she has immense beauty in her voice and she was a popular favourite to win the contest. Losing the top spot by a narrow margin was only due to the incredibly strong competition.

Cancer rising suggests a strong bond with the parents, and that is certainly the case for Susan, as she stayed at home and cared for her parents until their death. By her own admission, she is still a virgin who has never been kissed, as shown by the dead weight of Capricorn on the seventh, eighth, and ninth house cusps, and Saturn itself sitting in the eighth house. After her parents died, a lack of opportunities for work and sheer loneliness led her into doing voluntary work for her beloved church. Neptune is well aspected and Jupiter is in her ninth house, both of which indicate benefits from religion. The heavy Saturn and Capricorn situation, especially in the eighth house, shows a huge amount of karma in Susan's life, both in the sense of repaying some massive karmic debt and then gaining massive karmic rewards later in life. For Saturn, life truly does begin at fifty!

So, is there anything in Susan's chart to suggest fame and fortune? Susan's Cancer Asc makes her appear to outsiders as being "mumsy" rather than looking anything remotely like a modern pop star, but Cancer is a cardinal sign, so it can make things happen when it wants to. Her Aries Sun and Libra Moon are also in cardinal signs, as are her Mars in Cancer (Mars is her Sun's ruler) and the Moon in Libra (the Moon is her chart ruler). This denotes that once she gets herself into gear, very little will stop her. When one of the nodes (preferably the north node) is conjunct Pluto, the person will achieve fame and fortune. In Susan's case, the north node is within a few seconds of an exact conjunction with Pluto.

Progressions

So, what happened on the fateful day? The progressions weren't that amazing, but Susan has been singing for years, so she didn't do anything that she hadn't before, albeit to a larger and more important audience. My guess is that the progressions would have been more interesting when her parents died and when she started her church work, but an Asc progressing into Leo has plenty to say about wanting to be a star.

Progressed Asc into Leo.
Progressed MC trine progressed Asc
Progressed MC sextile natal Jupiter.
Progressed Dsc conjunct natal Jupiter.

Transits

If some one came to me with a chart that looked like Susan's did at the time of the competition, all I could have said for certain was that the astonishing number of transiting connections showed that something extraordinary was about to occur. When there is this much activity, it is hard to pin it down to any one thing.

Here is a full list of all the aspects involved; it will be most interesting to follow Susan's progress over the next few years, to see just how her life takes shape from now on. It's most unlikely that her past loneliness and lack of opportunities will continue.

Susan Boyle - transit chart aspects on 11th April, 2009
Transiting Sun trine natal Uranus
Transiting Moon trine natal Mercury
Transiting Mercury trine natal Pluto
Transiting Mercury trine natal north node
Transiting Mercury sextile natal south node
Transiting Mercury sextile natal part of fortune
Transiting Mercury square natal Jupiter
Transiting Venus sextile natal Saturn
Transiting Mars inconjunct natal Uranus
Transiting Jupiter opposite natal Uranus
Transiting Saturn opposite natal Mercury
Transiting Saturn sextile natal Mars
Transiting Uranus sextile natal Venus
Transiting Uranus inconjunct natal Uranus
Transiting Neptune opposite natal Uranus
Transiting Neptune semi-sextile natal Saturn
Transiting Chiron semi-sextile natal Saturn
Transiting Chiron opposite natal Uranus
Transiting Pluto conjunct natal part of fortune (exact)
Transiting north node inconjunct natal north node
Transiting south node inconjunct natal south node
Transiting MC opposite natal Saturn
Transiting MC square natal Venus
Transiting IC conjunct natal Saturn
Transiting Asc opposite natal Venus

Phew! What a day for Susan Boyle! Now at last, she can enjoy the progression of her Asc from Cancer to Leo.
Apparently, according to the internet,Susan is now dating her first boyfriend, who is about her own age. She has continued with a fantastic singing career, winning awards and performing overseas as well. Good luck, Susan!

The BIG
Astrology Guide

Volume One

THE PLANETS

Discover the Power of the Planets!

Introduction to the Planets

I wrote the original version of this book in 1993, and while that feels as though it were only yesterday, it's amazing to think how many years have actually passed since then. In the intervening years, manned and unmanned space travel have added much to our knowledge of the solar system, but how can we incorporate these new discoveries into our existing astrological framework? Astrologers look at everything, and sometimes perhaps at too many things, but eventually the situation shakes down to what actually works, and that's what I have focused on in this book.

I only cover natal charting in this book, but when you are ready to move on to predictive techniques, you'll find a Sasha book for that as well. Is this shameless self-promotion? Maybe so - but my motive is what it has always been, which is to help those who want to understand this fascinating subject.

Let's spend a moment considering that old chestnut of, what does or doesn't make astrology work... Scientists and wannabe scientists are quick to point out that a small rock at the end of the solar system can't possibly exert any magnetic or electrical effect on mankind, and they're quite right. The only explanation I've heard that makes any sense at all comes from my late friend, the wonderful Jon Dee. He used to say that everything in the universe, including us, seems to resonate to some kind of celestial timing device, but whether this is by accident or whether it's something that God created and arranged, is beyond any of us. For my part, after working with the planets for over four decades, I accept that the system works, and that's enough for me.

Basic Information

- I give capitals to "named" objects, such as Mercury, Venus etc. but also to items that are an essential part of this book, such as the Sun, the Moon and the Earth.

- The word "horoscope" means, "map of the hour", and a natal chart is like a snapshot of the sky at the moment that something comes into existence.
- The time of a person's birth is taken from the "first cry", which is the moment the baby draws its first breath and starts to cry. It makes no difference if the birth is premature, late, induced or caesarean; it's the first cry that sets the chart in place.
- Most people don't have an accurate time of birth, even when it is recorded somewhere, so you usually need to jiggle a chart around a bit (rectify it) to find the exact position for the ascendant.

Tools of the Trade

When I wrote my first book, it was already getting hard to suggest what a new astrologer should buy in the way of astrological equipment, but now it's impossible! The items below are the best I can suggest under the circumstances.

You will need two ephemerides (I can't bring myself to say ephemerises...) - one for the 20th century and another for the first half of the 21st century. If your eyesight isn't great, I suggest that you buy "*The Astrolabe World Ephemeris 2001-2050 at Midnight*" because the typeface is clear. That particular ephemeris gives the position of Chiron and the asteroids on a daily basis as well as all the usual planetary data.

Whatever ephemeris you buy, ensure that it's for midnight rather than noon, because that will show you the picture for the whole twenty-four hours that you wish to examine. If you ever take the trouble to learn how to calculate a chart by hand, you will definitely want a midnight ephemeris, because a noon one adds layers of difficulty to the process.

I use the annual "*Raphael's Ephemeris*" for day-to-day work, because it's invaluable for checking planetary and lunar positions, ingresses, eclipses and so much more. It saves me from having to consult a massive tome when I only want a quick glance at something. Study it well, because it really does offer an amazing amount of information in addition to the usual daily planetary data

Software varies from very basic to extremely complex, and with the advent of smart phones and tablets, more programs come onto the market all the time. I suggest you roam the Net or find apps and buy whatever takes your fancy. You'll probably end up buying one or two different products until you find one that suits you. You can set up and run off a few free charts from *Astro.com* (this is a very useful website all round), and there may be other sites that will allow you to do this. A great site for celebrity charts is *www.astrotheme.com*. It's a French site, but it's written in English and it's free to use. It contains the data for hundreds of British and American celebrities, in addition to the European ones, and it frequently updates itself with new faces. This site also contains a number of articles that are worth reading.

The most popular professional quality astrology software in the UK is Solar Fire, but some astrologers use Winstar or one of the other programs. There must be hundreds of programs available in the USA and elsewhere, but some are wildly inaccurate. The best thing I can suggest is to ask other astrologers in your locality what they recommend. I've bought and used most programs that have been available in the UK over the years, but I always come back to my favourite, which is Solar Fire, and I update it from time to time.

Depending upon what kind of astrology takes your fancy, you might want to check out celebrity charts or you might take an interest in historical events or people of the past. The birth of countries, cities and nations might fascinate you, as might politics or finance. You might be into the astrology of climate, or it may be sporting events or rock music that catches your fancy. You may wish to delve into the deeper aspects of psychology, or you may want to choose the right day to start something that's important to you. Each one of us uses our astrology to suit our own needs, and those needs can be different from one day to the next.

Astronomical Data

The Plane of the Ecliptic

Before telescopes were invented and astronomers understood the solar system, it was thought that the Sun travels round the Earth, making one complete circuit each year. The trajectory of this apparent circuit is called the "plane of the ecliptic", or more commonly the "ecliptic", and everything in astrology happens along this line.

The Zodiac

The ecliptic is divided into twelve equal segments of 30 deg. each. About two and a half thousand years ago, astrologers fitted these segments to those constellations that sat along the ecliptic. The constellation of Aries fitted the part of the zodiac that marked the spring equinox, but in the intervening years, the tilt and wobble of the Earth has made the constellations slip back by about 25 degrees. This phenomenon is called "the precession of the equinoxes". Nevertheless, astrologers stick to the standard zodiac signs, simply because the system works.

Western astrologers still use the ancient "tropical zodiac" because it works well for us, so for us, Aries still starts on the 20th of March at the time of the spring equinox. Hindu astrologers use "sidereal" astrology, which takes account of precession, but their astrology isn't the same as ours.

The Planets

For the sake of convenience, we call most of the celestial objects that we deal with "planets", regardless of whether we're talking about the Sun, the Moon, a planet or a dwarf planet.

The Solar System

The Solar system in astrology looks like this:

The Sun
The Moon
Mercury
Venus
Mars
Jupiter
Saturn
Uranus
Neptune
Pluto
Chiron

Apart from the Moon, the above list shows the planets in order of distance from the Sun. Earth is excluded, and isn't part of basic astrological chart calculations.

Also Consider...

The Earth
Vesta
Ceres
The Nodes of the Moon

Several other planets have now been discovered far out in the Solar system, but they take so long to orbit the Sun that they aren't much use in readings. For instance, Eris is a dwarf planet that is larger than Pluto, but it's so far out that it takes about 500 years to orbit the Sun. I guess Eris might be useful to those who like history. The following story is typical of the kind of coincidence that so often occurs to those who are into astrology or spiritual matters.

At the time of writing this book, Eris is at 21 deg. Aries. As it happens, I've just spent the last few months working on two novels that are partly set in modern times and partly in Tudor times. The Tudor era started when the Wars of the Roses came to an end and Henry the Seventh became the first Tudor king. Interestingly, Eris was at 21 deg. Aries then, too!

The Sun

The Sun's mean distance is 149.6 million kilometres from the Earth. It takes 26.9 Earth days to rotate on its axis, and its mean surface temperature is 5,700 degrees Celsius, rising to about 15 million degrees Celsius at the core. It emits electromagnetic radiation of various wavelengths, some of which are harmful, but the radiation of heat and light from the Sun makes life possible on Earth.

The Moon

The Moon's mean distance from the Earth, surface to surface, is 384,400 kilometres. It takes 27.32 days for the Moon to travel round the Earth, and also 27.32 days for it to rotate on its axis; therefore it always has the same face pointing towards the Earth. Its diameter is 3,475.6km and its temperature varies between plus 120 degrees and minus 153 degrees Celsius. The interior of the Moon is still hot enough to be made of molten rock, and there are about 3,000 moonquakes per year. The surface of the Moon is fatter on the side that faces the Earth, and it is also warmer on the Earth side. Water, methane, ammonia, hydrogen, sodium, silver and Mercury have now been discovered on the surface of the Moon.

The Moon and the Earth were both formed when the Solar system came into being. The Moon became attracted to the Earth's gravitational field and formed a double or binary planet system. The Moon is about a quarter the size of the Earth, and its surface area is about the size of Asia. Nevertheless, its mountains reach up to 8,000 metres, which is around the height of Mount Everest. There is no atmosphere on the Moon. The Moon is moving slowly away from the Earth.

The Planets

Mercury, Venus, Earth and Mars are "terrestrial" planets with solid centres. Mercury is the closest to the Sun, albeit still about 35 million miles (58 million kilometres) from the Sun, so its surface temperature on the side that faces the Sun is very high. Its surface is similar to that of the Moon. Being small, it has little gravity and therefore, little atmosphere. What does exist is mainly hydrogen and helium. Dense clouds of carbon dioxide and sulphuric acid cover Venus. The surface of the Earth is mainly covered by water and partially covered by cloud. Surprisingly, the Earth sometimes has up to five Moons, but only one large one. The others are called *Minimoons*, and tend to be captured asteroids whose complicated orbits keep them here for a while – up to a year or so – and then they wander away to be asteroids again. Earth's atmosphere comprises oxygen, carbon dioxide, nitrogen and water vapour. Mars is mainly rocky desert with polar ice caps that were once liquid. A very thin atmosphere consists of carbon dioxide, oxygen and water vapour. Mars has two Moons - Phobos and Deimos.

Jupiter is a huge ball of gas, containing liquid hydrogen and helium with some methane and ethane. Uranus and Neptune are composed of dust, swirling rocks and gas. Saturn, Uranus and Neptune all have ring systems, with many Moons and rocks orbiting around them. Uranus spins in the opposite direction to all the other planets, and its poles are on the east and west alignment, rather than north and south. Uranus alternates between presenting its poles and its equator to the Sun, so that each has a summer of forty-two years, followed by a forty-two-year winter.

Pluto has a very elongated orbit, which, at times, reaches far inside the orbit of Neptune. It is too small to have any atmosphere, although frozen methane has been discovered on its surface. Pluto has a very large Moon called Charon (pronounced like Sharon) that is about one-third its size, plus several tiny ones. Pluto and Charon form a binary planetary system, because they swing around a point that is somewhere between them. Pluto may be small and distant, but its astrological effect is massive.

Chiron is a dwarf planet that moves in an eccentric orbit between Uranus and Neptune.

Astrological Data

Personal, Transpersonal and Impersonal Planets

In astrology, we consider the Sun, Moon, Mercury, Venus and Mars as *personal* planets. These are the closest planets to the Earth and they are concerned with personality and behaviour. Beyond the asteroid belt, you can find Jupiter and Saturn, which are called *transpersonal* planets.

These show how the subject copes with the opposing forces of expansion and limitation, and they are somewhat more concerned with external influences than personal behaviour. The outer planets of Uranus, Neptune and Pluto are called *impersonal* planets, as they have a generational influence rather than a strictly personal one on a natal chart, but no planet is ever really impersonal, because everything in a birthchart makes itself felt.

Retrograde Planets

It's easy to become familiar with the position of planets in the sky overhead, because they tend to show themselves very clearly just after sunset. When you get used to their position, you will notice they move a little from day to day, week to week or month to month, but there are times when the planets appear to move *backwards* for a while before resuming their usual forward motion. This apparent backward motion is caused by the fact that the Earth is also travelling around the Sun, and that all the planets are travelling at different speeds, so it can be something like being on one train that passes another one, moving in the same direction but more slowly, which makes the slower train look as though it's moving backwards.

When a planet is retrograde at birth, it can cause setbacks in the person's life, and when it turns forward by transit or progression, those things should improve. Some of the people born when Mercury was retrograde find their lives are easier at those times when Mercury is retrograde by transit.

The Ancient Divisions

Planets are said to be comfortable in their own sign; for instance, Venus in Libra or Mars in Aries, but they are also comfortable when situated in their own houses, such as Mercury in the third or Jupiter in the ninth. However, there are a series of ancient placements that confer positive or negative energies. The ancient system only uses the planets that can be seen with the naked eye.

PLANET	RULERSHIP	HOUSES	EXALTATION	FALL	DETRIMENT
Sun	Leo	Fifth	Aries	Libra	Aquarius
Moon	Cancer	Fourth	Taurus	Scorpio	Capricorn
Mercury	Gemini/ Virgo	Third/ Sixth	Virgo	Pisces	Sagittarius/ Pisces
Venus	Taurus/ Libra	Second/ Seventh	Pisces	Virgo	Aries/ Scorpio
Mars	Aries/ Scorpio	First/ Eighth	Capricorn	Cancer	Taurus/ Libra
Jupiter	Sagittarius/ Pisces	Ninth/ Twelfth	Cancer	Capricorn	Gemini/ Virgo
Saturn	Capricorn/ Aquarius	Tenth/ Eleventh	Libra	Aries	Cancer/ Leo

One ancient astrologer worked out that certain degrees are actually more important than the signs as a whole as far as exaltations are concerned. I guess the fall of each planet would be at their worst when opposing these points; so for example, Venus would be at its worst point of fall at 27 deg. Virgo.

Degrees of Exaltation
Sun   19 Aries
Moon   03 Taurus
Mercury   15 Virgo
Venus   27 Pisces
Mars   28 Capricorn
Jupiter   15 Cancer
Saturn   21 Libra

The Ruling Planet

The ruling planet is the one that rules the sign that is on the ascendant. For instance, if the chart has Cancer rising, the ruling planet is the Moon. On a chart with Scorpio rising, both Mars and Pluto should be taken into consideration. The sign and house that the ruling planet occupies are important, both natally and when affected by progressions and transits.

The Rising Planet

Some astrologers consider the rising planet to be the first after the ascendant in the first house. Others consider the rising planet to be the one that has risen over the horizon and is in the twelfth house. Most astrologers would be happy to call any planet that is near the ascendant a rising planet.

The rising planet has a bearing on the subject's early life and it can be a strong influence throughout life. For example, Saturn rising will encourage the subject to choose a profession or a lifestyle where self-discipline, a thorough knowledge of a subject, the ability to concentrate on details and to work alone is needed. According to the French statistician, Michel Gauquelin, surgeons tend to have this placement, while I have discovered that many writers also have Saturn close to the ascendant. There are many cases where there is no rising planet, because all the planets are grouped together far from the ascendant.

Mutual Reception

Two planets are in mutual reception when they are in each other's signs, such as the Moon in Taurus and Venus in Cancer. There is a strong connection between these planets and they work well together.

Unaspected Planets

In theory, unaspected planets should "disappear" from a birthchart and have a very weak impact on the subject's life, but it seems that the subject strives to develop the area that's unaspected, so it might actually become quite strong.

The Leading Planet

Some planets have a "stellium" or a bunch of planets in one area of the chart, and the first of this group is said to be the leading planet. When transits occur along the stellium, a train of events is touched off.

Midpoints

These are the halfway points between two planets, between a planet and an angle or between any two important points on a chart. These are hard to work out by hand but software does it in an instant.

Heliocentric Charts

These charts assume that we're standing on the surface of the Sun rather than the Earth. If you have decent software, you can experiment with these charts. There is a great deal missing from these charts, which makes what is left really powerful. For example, there are no houses, every chart starts at zero degrees of Aries and the Earth is placed exactly opposite to where the Sun would be on a geocentric chart, and there are no Moon and no Nodes.

Check out planets in Libra or Scorpio for relationships, Cancer and Capricorn for parents, Leo for children, Taurus for possessions and personal values and so on. Check to see whether your Earth sign represents a past life, the next life or the life you wish to have. The Earth sign may represent the Sun sign you would like to have been born with. Do the planets represent people in your life? Having tried out this method on a number of charts, I am convinced that Mars denotes the querent's father, and Mercury, the mother in a Helios chart. I have discovered that those who had diabolical childhoods and truly dreadful mothers had Mercury in Scorpio! Incidentally, all of these subjects also have enquiring minds and are hard to influence.

The Personal Planets

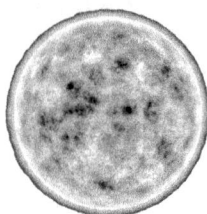

The Sun

The Sun rules the sign of Leo and the fifth house. In Roman mythology, it is associated with the god, Apollo.

The sign the Sun occupies is vitally important, because it represents all that we create and that we are. This is central to our own natures, but the creative aspect of this planet might be linked to the creation of a family, an enterprise or a lifestyle. The desire to create a happy home is a Sun matter. A decision to do something, to take action or to take an active part in anything is a Sun sign matter. The Sun is associated with success and achievement, the fun side of life, holidays, and games and gambling for fun, leisure and pleasure.

Solar Links
- The personality and general outlook on life.
- Winning, succeeding, achieving.
- Creativity in all senses of the word.
- Children.
- Fathers or father figures.
- Business, especially if it is successful or glamorous.
- Show business, glamorous professions and lifestyles.
- Entertainments, holidays, amusements, games and, to some extent, gambling and games of chance.
- Music.

- Love affairs, which are amusing diversions or deeply felt affections but they should be fun.
- Jewellery and the trade in gems and crystals.
- Gold.

Details

The Sun is the largest and most obvious object in the sky, so it's no surprise that it exerts a very strong influence on our birthcharts. Not everyone is typical of their Sun sign, as there are many other features on a chart that have an effect. Nevertheless, the Sun is always a powerful influence.

Traditional astrology tells us that the Sun signifies the self and that it describes behaviour and character. The Sun sign determines the strength of an individual's personality and the way he chooses to live his life, his leadership qualities and his ability to exert power and authority. It can be connected with business matters.

Some older forms of astrology link the Sun to the father or father figure, and that does seem to make some sense. It is also linked with children, so either way; it is a planet that is closely related to the family as well as the self. A badly aspected natal Sun can indicate poor health, but it can also represent repression during childhood, especially by a father or father figure.

Through the association with Leo, the Sun shows how we spend our leisure time, the kind of holidays we enjoy and the things that give us pleasure. Love affairs, sporting activities, gambling, games of chance and amusements of all kinds are attributed to the Sun. Playfulness, childlike behaviour and the pursuit of fun for its own sake are also solar interests.

The Sun presides over all forms of music, entertainment and show business. Even the showbiz side of sports would come under this category. The Sun seeks success, status and pleasure from these ventures. The Sun rules anything that glistens, therefore gold and jewellery, glamorous clothes, glamorous people and fascinating, star-studded events belong to the realm of the Sun.

The Sun can be associated with successful business ventures and the creative aspect of such enterprises. A business is the manifestation of somebody's personal vision, so if the Sun shines on a business venture, it is sure to be a success.

The Moon

The Moon rules the sign of Cancer and the fourth house.

The Moon symbolises the way we feel, and this encompasses far more than just our emotional life or our personal relationships. For instance, a subject may have a job that looks good on the surface, but he may *feel* unhappy about it. The Sun acts, but the Moon reacts, and one's intuitive, reactive response is often the right one. The Moon rules our habits and our behaviour when ill, drunk or otherwise uninhibited. It represents our experience of being nurtured and our capacity to nurture others, and it is associated with the home and any property or premises that we utilise.

Lunar Links
- Inner feelings, emotions and emotional reactions, habitual behaviour and the way we are when ill, drunk or otherwise being our real selves.
- Real inner needs such as ambition, love, revenge or any other personal motivation and driving force, however well-disguised it may be.
- Mothers or mother figures, the experience of being nurtured.
- The home, premises or property and the domestic scene.
- Small shops or businesses that are run on a personal basis, often from home.
- Women, female matters.
- The public.
- Some health matters, especially chronic ones and those brought on by unhappiness.
- Travel and restlessness.
- Moods and changeability.
- Sailors and sewing (sailors were skilled at sewing sails, nets, sacks, clothing and so on).
- Dairymaids, cows.
- The cooking and storage of food, thus the larder, fridge, cooker, implements and, of course, the cook.
- Attachment to the past, patriotism, an interest in history and collecting things that have a history to them, such as antiques.
- Silver and pearls.

Details

The Moon is traditionally associated with the emotions, inner feelings, underlying urges and habitual behaviour. Ancient astrologers considered the Moon restless owing to her rapid movement through the sky, so they changeability, emotional feelings and moods to her. The Moon shows how an individual reacts to situations and how the native behaves when his passions are aroused. Some of this instinctive behaviour refers back to childhood, and it may also have some karmic significance. The underlying lunar personality will show itself when the subject is tired, ill or overwrought. It shows how a person adapts to new situations but it can also rule obsessions and deepest needs.

.   Traditional astrology associates the Moon with mother figures and one's first experience of being nurtured, whether, by one's own mother or by someone else. Some contemporary astrologers consider the Moon to be the childish part of a person's personality. The Moon is associated with the home, both in the sense of domestic harmony and also more practical matters, such as buying, leasing or renting property or premises. These premises may not be for living in but rather for work, renting out or keeping as a holiday home. A well-placed Moon should assure a secure and happy childhood, but the rest of the chart would need to confirm this. Even if the rest of the chart shows areas of difficulty, a comfortable Moon will be a great help to the subject.

The Moon shows the subject's attitude to the feminine, and it suggests whether or not women's issues are an important factor in a subject's life. I find it hard to reconcile the Moon's association with the idea of the public, because it seems to be so firmly tied to the private side of life, but it can show whether a person has connection with the public, serves them in any way, works with them and so on.

The Moon is not specifically associated with health but it can show up a weak area in a subject's body, along with a person's state of mind and emotional condition. Chronic ailments such as rheumatism, migraine and bronchitis can be linked to the Moon, as can cancer and feminine problems.

Earlier astrology books link the Moon with the sea and with travel, and those who have the Moon in signs and houses associated with travel do seem to move around quite a lot. Early astrology books also suggested that someone with the Moon in the ninth house will marry a foreigner and that also seems to fit. I have noticed that people who have the Moon in air signs or the third, seventh or eleventh houses also travel a lot, often in connection with their work.

Some people live overseas for a while, sometimes due to a partner or parent in the military, or working on an overseas project.

Mercury

Mercury rules Gemini and Virgo, the third and sixth houses of the chart. The Roman god, Mercury, was the messenger of the gods. Mercury was associated with medicine, magic and thieves!

Mercury rules thought, words, communications and knowledge. It is associated with local matters, travel, transport and movement of goods and ideas. It also concerns negotiations, paperwork and education, brothers, sisters and neighbours. A fair amount of the things we all do as part of normal daily life are associated with Mercury.

Mercury Links
- Communications.
- Travel and transport.
- Local matters, the neighbourhood.
- Knowledge.
- Primary and secondary education.
- The mind, the mental processes, the way one thinks.
- Brothers and sisters, cousins and similar relationships.
- Youthfulness.
- Health and healing.
- Magic.
- Sales and marketing.
- Thieves and theft.
- Rail and bus termini.
- Boundary markers.
- Cinnabar, mercury.

Details
Mercury rules all forms of communication, such as speech, thought, writing and messages, including those that travel though the body's nervous system. In modern life, Mercury is associated with communication gadgets of all kinds.

Mercury traditionally rules local travel and transport, but the world is so small now that it can be linked to more distant travel. Post, emails and much else related to communications comes under the rule of Mercury. Mercury rules sales, marketing, and many activities associated with business.

Anything that requires skill is typically Mercurial; therefore, craftwork, light engineering, dressmaking and the use of office machinery come into this category. Mercury signifies knowledge, teaching and learning.

Traditional astrology suggests that Mercury rules primary, secondary and further education while Jupiter rules higher education. Languages are particularly Mercurial, as is computer programming. Mercury rules the mind, the ability to think on one's feet and to cope with everyday life. Dyslexia tends to show up when Mercury is retrograde and close to the ascendant.

Mercury rules the locality, neighbours, local shops, schools and anything else that is nearby or places that the subject visits on a frequent basis. Well-placed Mercury suggests living in a friendly area with good local facilities and a happy environment, while badly-aspected Mercury could bring difficult neighbours and an unpleasant neighbourhood.

This planet is associated with brothers, sisters and cousins or other relatives of one's own age, along with close relationships, especially if the friends live nearby. It's also linked to young people and all the things they love to do. Mercurial types stay young at heart even when they get old.

Mercury is concerned with health and healing, especially when the hands are used to diagnose or to heal. The Roman symbol for this god was the caduceus or herald's wand, and this is still used as a healing symbol today. This may be why Mercury is also linked to magic, shamanism and so forth, as there can be positive aspects to healing but it can also be open to charlatanism.

Mercury also rules trickery and sharp practice, along with an element both of concealment and revelation because this planet is the link between this world and the next. He seems to know more than he is prepared to reveal to us and therefore is both wiser and trickier than we realise.

Venus

Venus rules Taurus and Libra, and the second and seventh houses. Venus was the Roman goddess of love.

Venus is associated with the things we hold dear to us, which includes material possessions, land and our values and priorities. Venus is concerned with anything that appeals to the senses, which includes music and art, dancing, food, sex, fresh air and anything else that feels good and does us good. We can be very attached to the things that we own or enjoy, so Venus shows what we will fight to keep. It also rules our image. Venus rules relationships that are open to scrutiny, which may mean a husband or a close associate but it can just as easily concern an open and acknowledged enemy.

- Venus Links
- Values and priorities.
- Valuable goods and personal possessions.
- Personal finances.
- Love, romance and sexuality.
- Leisure and pleasure.
- Music and art.
- Ostentation and luxury.
- Females.
- Emotions connected to love and possessions.
- Open friendships and relationships such as marriage.
- Open enemies and the reason for fighting.
- Mirrors, decorative glass, Venetian blinds.
- Cosmetics, powder compacts (with and without mirrors).
- Sea shells, flowers, oysters.
- Aphrodisiacs and venereal diseases (although AIDS comes under the rulership of Pluto).
- Copper, malachite and emeralds.
- Justice and fair play.
- Legal arguments.
- Balance, harmony.

Details

Venus is associated with the things one values, especially our own personal goods and personal finances, but it also relates to things we value, such as time to oneself, time to do something other than work and of valuing something other than material goods. An important aspect of this is self-value and self-esteem.

Venus was the Roman goddess of love. We tend to see this nowadays as romantic love, but the Romans saw Venus as a sexual being and the temple maidens who were dedicated to her were very far from being Vestal Virgins! Venusian love puts the loved one on a pedestal, but it can also signify greed, possessiveness and jealousy. Don't forget the idea of ownership that is associated with this planet. In some cases, a partner can be seen as a meal ticket or a status symbol. Pets can be loved to distraction but they are also a form of possession.

Venus is associated with leisure and pleasure, also with singing, playing an instrument and with music. Sometimes Venus can go over the top and sink into hedonism, drunkenness, self-indulgence and a love of luxury. All sorts of surprisingly deep emotions are wrapped up with this planet, such as a need for comfort and safety but also envy, jealousy and possessiveness and sentimentality. Venus signifies relationships that are open and above board, so it rules love partnerships, business partnerships and close associations of all kinds, but it is also concerned with open enemies.

The position of Venus can give some clue as to whether or not the subject will ever have children. When activated by progression or transit, it can indicate birth, with female children being more likely than male ones. Be careful when dealing with this because you may give someone who can't have children false hopes.

Venus rules anything that appeals to the senses, so this applies to nice food, perfume, a beautiful garden or a lovely house, music, dancing, singing, art, culture, colour, shape, fashion or anything else which we enjoy.

Venus denotes the feminine principle and is associated with all that is soft and feminine within every one of us but paradoxically Venus is too materialistic to make sacrifices for others. This planet represents the beauty and sexual attractiveness of women. Venus in a man's chart can suggest the kind of woman who would interest him.

Venus is also concerned with justice, balance and harmony, and she will go openly into battle against an injustice if necessary. Venus rules arbitration, adjudication, marriage counselling, family counselling and brokering of any kind, which brings an attachment to the law, especially where it specialises in settling financial or family arguments.

Mars

Mars rules Aries and before the discovery of Pluto, it was also assigned to the sign of Scorpio. It rules the first house and was once also the ruler of the eighth house. Mars was, of course, the Roman god of war.

Mars rules energy and drive. On one hand, Mars adds assertiveness, courage and sexuality but it can add aggression, violence and danger. Too much Mars is much like too much adrenalin or testosterone, while the right amount gives a subject the heart to fight when the need is there. This planet is not concerned with actual possessions and material objects but it can show how these are acquired.

Mars Links
- Energy, assertiveness, forcefulness, initiative, etc.
- Passion, the desire for something.
- The drive to obtain the person or the object of one's desire.
- Decision-making and decisive action.
- Arguments and violence.
- Masculine occupations such as engineering steel making and (with Pluto) coal mining.
- Competitive activities, especially sports.
- Iron and steel, surgical instruments.
- Tools, especially knives, blades.
- Warfare, weapons, the tools of destruction.
- Blood.
- Iron.

Details
Mars is associated with energy, force, drive, courage and the masculine side within all of us. This planet represents the macho aspect of the personality, and without Mars somewhere on our charts, nobody would ever get up out of bed to do anything! A subject with a strong Mars is assertive, energetic and courageous, but if the Mars

energy is overdone, the subject will be hot tempered, apt to leap before he looks and possibly even violent or self-destructive.

Mars relates to masculine activities, such as car maintenance and engineering, along with the tools that are used in these activities, especially metal ones. It can have some connection with explosives, especially those used for an engineering purpose. The red planet concerns driving at speed and all kind of sports, especially team games and fast or dangerous sports, along with the armed services, the police, the fire service and paramedics, or any other job that requires courage and the wearing of a special uniform. It rules courage and perseverance in the face of major obstacles.

This planet rules the masculine aspect of sexuality and one's sex drive. It also suggests the kind of man who a woman finds attractive. For instance, I've known women with Mars in Aries or Scorpio who are attracted to men in uniforms and men who do what we would consider particularly masculine jobs.

The Transpersonal Planets

Jupiter

Jupiter was the king of the Roman gods, and he could be very generous and philanthropic, but also angry and destructive. Jupiter rules the sign of Sagittarius and the ninth house. Before the discovery of Neptune, Jupiter was also associated with the sign of Pisces and the twelfth house. Jupiter is a transpersonal planet, so it is less concerned with a subject's actions and feelings than with the person's experiences of life in general. Jupiter signifies expansion, exploration and anything that pushes back boundaries, surmounts barriers and creates opportunities. The general idea is to take a concept, a desire or an opportunity and run with it as far as you can go, although Jupiter can destroy some things to make room for something better

Jupiter Links
- Foreign travel or exploration of new places.
- The law and the legal system.
- Belief, religion and philosophy.
- What you believe in and feel strongly about.
- Education, especially higher education.
- Business and success.
- Opportunities.
- Meeting new and influential people.
- Publishing and broadcasting.
- Large animals.

- Outdoor life and sporting activities.
- Gambling and winning – traditionally, gambling on horses.
- Tin.

Details

Jupiter expands the native's horizons in several different ways, these being higher education, religion and philosophy, the law and travel or overseas exploration. The notion of exploration and expansion in connection with foreign travel is obvious but it is also inherent in the other Jupiterian concepts.

Education expands an individual's knowledge and understanding, and because Jupiter is concerned with higher education, this allows the person to explore an idea or area of knowledge much further than basic schooling can achieve. Jupiter takes the time to think, to dream and to explore widely. Nobody finds religion, philosophy, belief or propaganda interesting unless they think about these things. Depth of knowledge and understanding characterise education and religion, but sadly, certain religious beliefs engender fear, hatred and intolerance, which are the darker side of the old Roman god's nature.

Legal matters require specialist help and advice. In the past, solicitors administered land, inheritances, money matters and to some extent, they still do, but the complications of taxation and modem business mean that accountancy has now become a separate field. However, this too is Jupiterian, as it is the legal aspect of these topics, while business itself is assigned to Saturn. The law may not seem to link to exploration but lawyers test ideas and people and they push against the boundaries. The law can be used to protect the populace or to repress it, a fact that once again illustrates the dark side of Jupiter.

Jupiter is associated with publishing and also with broadcasting, which are ways of getting one's words and one's ideas "out there". It is linked to tolerance and acceptance of ethnic and racial differences and of being interested in new or different ways of thinking. It's also associated with large animals, and thus to horse racing and gambling. It is a planet of glamour; grandeur and a life lived to the full. Other Jupiterian concepts include sports and competitive activities, although in the sense of competition for the fun of it rather than serious dedication. Jupiter is linked to a sense of humour and enjoyment of life. There is a lucky aspect to this planet as it can bring opportunity and change for the better. It also brings meetings with new people, growth and depth to an enterprise. However, Jupiter was known for tossing down thunderbolts from time to time, so it can bring problems in its wake.

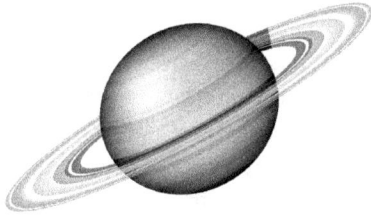

Saturn

Saturn is the second and last transpersonal planet, and it rules Capricorn and the tenth house. Before Uranus was discovered, Saturn also ruled Aquarius and the eleventh house. Saturn was the Roman god of time and of old age.

Saturn helps us reach our goals and see the rewards for our efforts, but he also rules difficult circumstances and times of restriction or limitation. This planet presides over foundations, craftsmanship and attention to detail and ultimate success through hard work and persistence, so it can rule long-winded tasks.

Saturn sets boundaries and it shows where and how we may be limited by circumstances. Saturn should not be considered as an enemy but a means of learning and developing and of giving us the character and backbone that we need in order to get through life.

Saturn Links
- Endurance, persistence, restraint and caution.
- Self-discipline, organisation, knowing the right time to do something.
- Ambition, success that is well deserved.
- Maturity, senior citizenship, old age.
- Some aspects of pain and suffering, especially if the situation is lasting or chronic.
- Banking, big business, large organisations.
- Structure and a firm foundation.
- Authority and status.
- Lead, pipes - especially household plumbing, and of course, plumbers.
- Clocks, watches and timepieces of all kinds.
- Measuring instruments of all kinds, such as rulers, weights, slide rules, computers used for mathematical purposes.
- Calculations and in ancient times, astrology.
- Coffin makers.
- Masonry, building materials, the building trade.
- Taboos.

Details

Saturn rules structure, foundations and work that is carried out in an orderly, structured and disciplined manner. Anything that we do thoroughly is Saturnian, so this planet rules craftsmanship, attention to detail and finishing what one starts. Saturn is connected to responsibilities, obligations and the idea of getting the work done before we can rush off and have a good time. We respect the type of person who works hard, and despise the one who walks away from responsibilities or refuses to put himself out to help others. Too much Saturn can result in a person being under the control of others, but the subject may cope with this situation by enduring it, because endurance is another Saturnian concept.

A well-placed Saturn, along with other pleasant factors on a chart suggests that the person had a childhood of encouragement and reasonable discipline along with love, security and proper care.

Saturn rules team games, joint efforts and the family pulling together in order to achieve something worthwhile.

As far as material concepts are concerned, Saturn rules banking, big business, large structures and organisations, trees, wood and probably the earth itself, along with lead and radiation shields. It also rules heaviness in all its forms ranging from a heavy object to a heavy heart! Saturn is considered to be the ruler of old age and things that are worth working for or waiting for, such as well-deserved feeling of success, increased status, wealth, an organised kitchen, a royalty payment or a myriad other well-earned blessings. It rules serious people who have real knowledge and are therefore, worthy of our respect.

There are some really unpleasant concepts that come under the realm of Saturn, such as crippling shyness, self-doubt, low self-esteem, self-hatred, severe embarrassment, a blow to the ego, and also suffering and loss. Also, chronic illness and disability, but before you slide back into the habit of blaming Saturn for every ill, please remember that all the planets have a downside.

The Impersonal Planets

Uranus

Uranus rules Aquarius and the eleventh house.

According to mythology, Uranus was the god of the stormy heavens, and he was the son of the earth goddess, Gaia. Saturn castrated him and threw his genitals into the sea, upon which the foaming stormy mess of blood and semen bubbled and boiled and eventually gave birth to Venus.

Uranus is the first of the outer planets, which are known in astrology as the impersonal planets. These planets take several years to move through each sign, so they represent a particular era. Uranus is considered to be the planet of change, revolution, rebellion and refusal to conform. It's concerned with ideas rather than feelings, and it's especially associated with group and political activities, so it relates to original thinking, new inventions and fresh ideas.

Uranian people like to consider themselves "different", and they may have a point, because their planet certainly is different from all the others: it revolves in the opposite direction to all the other planets. It's also the coldest of all the planets.

Uranus Links
- Groups and political activities, especially green or humanitarian ones.
- Idealism, humanitarianism, any other "ism" that supposedly benefits the group as a whole.
- Individualism, independence, self-motivation.

- Ideas, concepts.
- Technical innovation and inventions that may change the world.
- Originality.
- Shocks and surprises - some nice, some nasty, but all enlightening.
- Obstinacy and eccentricity.
- Uranium.

Details

In the 1960s and early 1970s when I was learning astrology, much was made of the totalitarian nature of Uranus which was due to usher in the age of Big Brother and the thought police, because Uranian ideas were considered to be utilitarian, devoted to equality and the submergence of individual feelings, desires and needs. Nowadays, Uranus is associated with quirky individualism, a desire for freedom and independence and with all people being equal. Uranus rules group activities and organisations, which may range from racist or militant religions, to "green" organisations, trades unions, new political parties and issues, along with gentler kinds of clubs, societies and community centres geared to the needs of particular groups of people.

Uranus rules friendship and acquaintanceship rather than close personal relationships. It relates to the need to learn for oneself and to find out the hard way. Uranus is associated with education in all its forms it wants to see ideas and knowledge being spread as far and wide as possible. It's particularly linked to educational organisations and groups.

Uranus can signify obstinacy and the determination to get things done. It is unconventional and original in it's thinking, and it links to flashes of intuition, genius, clairvoyance, sudden shocks and life-changing events. It denotes science fact and science fiction and the kind of imagination that produces both of these, and almost anything else which is weird and different. Uranian people are so individual that they aren't even like other Uranian people. They march to their own drumbeat and don't follow the herd. Many Uranian people have strong feelings about some cause or other, such as the needs of animals, education, religion or politics. It's a waste of time trying to argue with a Uranian type. They consider themselves hugely logical and open minded, but they are devoted to their own opinions and can't be influenced – not even when common sense stares them in the face.

Neptune

Neptune rules Pisces and the twelfth house.

In mythology, Neptune was the god of the sea, and the cause of earthquakes. This planet is something of a misnomer in astrology, because its attributes have more to do with the god Morpheus than with Neptune, except for the odd fact that two of Neptune's moons are Oberon and Titania, who were the god and goddess of dreams, in addition to being the King and Queen of the fairies.

Neptune rules the highest that we can aspire to and the lowest levels of degradation. It brings confusion, but also revelation, self-delusion but also compassion and pure love. This planet presides over the creation of illusion for entertainment in films, television and music, also illusions brought on by strange moods, alcohol and drugs.

Neptune Links
- Illusions, both good and bad kinds.
- Appreciation of things other than the basic needs of food, clothing and shelter.
- Love of God and religious or mystical revelations.
- Romantic love, especially when one endows the lover with virtues that he or she doesn't actually have.
- Creativity, especially if the creation depends upon illusion, as in film.
- Shifting sands, nothing being what it seems.
- Lies, deception and self-deception.
- The sea and fishing.
- Travel to or over water.
- Holidays on or by water or snow.
- Gas, smells, perfume, anaesthetics.
- Alcohol and drugs.
- Glass, especially when used in a functional rather than in a decorative manner, such as for windows or spectacles, microscopes, telescopes and so on.
- Photography and film.

- Self-sacrifice, social work, doing things for others.
- Places of seclusion such as hospitals, prisons and mental institutions.
- The workers and the work that is associated with these places.
- Voluntary workers.

Details

Neptune rules concepts that are hard to describe, such as inspiration, imagination, illusion and delusion. The planet rules the appreciation of those things that are beyond the basic needs of food, clothing and shelter, so it presides over artistry, music, film and television programmes.

Neptune brings truth, light and wisdom but it also causes muddles and confusion, and it causes us to lose our way. This planet is associated with kindness, pity, charity and love but these concepts can all too easily be twisted and misused. Many ordinary people give freely to the starving people in Somalia, Ethiopia and the Sudan only to discover that the goods they have bought have been hi-jacked and used to feed warlords and their armies or to pay for their armaments. Mysticism, religious inspiration and a life dedicated to doing God's work, but also to fanaticism and religious intolerance. This planet is associated with the sea, fish and fishing, which give it a powerful link to Christianity.

Neptune denotes escape from the world and sometimes to confinement. This can be due to a spell in hospital, prison or simply staying at home. It rules orphanages, asylums, hospitals, prisons and hospices or any other place where people are confined either for their own good or for the good of society. This planet is also connected to religious retreats, enclosed orders and any other means of escape or of retreat from the world. It is linked to charity and self-less giving.

Neptune is especially associated with escape from normal life by means of alcohol and drugs. This planet can lead to deceptions, lies and swindles, along with muddles, mistakes and things that go missing. When someone falls in love, he is confused, unable to think straight and he may be unable to eat, sleep and function normally for a while. Unrequited love is particularly Neptunian, as is the kind of love that blinds an individual to the truth.

Neptune is associated with hypnotherapy and altered states of consciousness, with joy and ecstasy and with gloom and depression. It can lead one to see others through rose coloured glasses or to see them as the enemy when they are not.

Pluto

Pluto rules Scorpio and the eighth house.

In Roman mythology, Pluto was the hugely wealthy god of the underworld. Astronomers have recently demoted Pluto to a dwarf planet, and it certainly is a small object compared to others, but it has a profound effect in astrology.

Pluto is associated with transformation and commitment but also with deeply held resentment and hatred. It rules partnerships, joint financial arrangements and important financial matters, particularly where other people are involved. It presides over things that are hidden from the eye and the means of uncovering or extracting these. Most of all it symbolises transformation and the collective unconscious.

Pluto rules the deeper and more difficult aspects of our lives and with transforming events, up to and including birth and death. It changes people and circumstances on a deep and profound level, but on a lighter note, it rules recycling, having a clear out and transforming our lives for the better. It is linked with shared resources and with financial dealings, especially those that crop up at times of great change, such as the joining of one's resources when forming a partnership or dealing with banks, legacies, business finances and other people's money or goods.

Pluto Links
- Birth and death.
- The passage to the "other side".
- Transformation, recycling, changing from one state to another.
- Sex, procreation and committed relationships.
- Wills, legacies, taxes, accountancy on behalf of others.
- Business matters related to money, stocks and shares, insurance.
- Business commitments.
- Mining, excavation, archaeology.
- Butchery, surgery, cutting with knives.
- Psychiatry, unlocking the unconscious.
- Investigation, espionage, counter espionage.

- Engineering, military matters, macho images.
- Power broking, power behind the scenes, manipulation.
- Jealousy, resentment, bitterness.
- Surgery, surgeons, healing.

Details

Pluto is associated with wills, legacies and corporate matters. It may not rule business as such but the act of becoming involved in a business or changes that occur within that business are linked to Pluto. This planet rules taxes and bills, bank accounts, the stock market and shares, pensions and insurance, especially life insurance and the administration of other people's finances.

Pluto rules procreation, both in the sense of bringing a new life into the world as well as the birth of an enterprise or an idea. Pluto also rules sex, sexual scandals and sexual indiscretions, but on the other hand, Pluto is also concerned with committed relationships and married love.

Pluto rules mining and the act of digging out things that are buried, such as gold, diamonds, oil and coal. It also rules bank vaults and archaeology. This planet relates to all that is covert, such as spies and spying, but also the police, investigation, intelligence, military matters and atomic weapons.

Pluto signifies power games and manipulative behaviour and those who act as the power behind the throne. It also rules psychiatry and the ability to get to the bottom of things, such as hidden motives and corrosive resentments. Some health problems are Plutonic, especially those that affect the lower spine, reproductive organs or things that can't easily be seen or got at. Surgery is linked to Pluto because it cuts through to what is inside. Pluto is concerned with butchery and engineering. Pluto is far from being bad, because everything has to be recycled one way or another, including life itself.

Chiron

In mythology, Chiron was the king of the centaurs and the teacher of heroes, including Hercules, Jason and Perseus. He was accidentally shot in the heel by one of Hercules' poisoned arrows and the wound festered. Chiron couldn't be cured, but being immortal, he couldn't die either, so he suffered terribly until he exchanged his immortality with Prometheus, who had lost his. It interesting to note that, before his accident, Chiron was known as the greatest of the healers. His daughter, Manta, was said to have invented astrology and the other mantic arts.

Chiron is a dwarf planet that is associated with sickness that comes on suddenly, accidents that lead to pain and suffering, along with physical, mental and emotional pain and chronic ailments. It's also associated with healing of all kinds. There is a slight link with teaching and with martial arts. There is no definite rule, but I have always associated Chiron with the sign of Virgo and the sixth house.

Chiron links:
- Illness, accidents and pain.
- Emotional and psychological damage.
- Healing of all kinds.
- Slight attachment to learning combat techniques.
- Slight attachment to learning music.
- Changes in relationships and family structure.

Details
A strong Chiron in a birthchart denotes a subject who wishes to work in medicine, teaching or counselling, possibly due to a desire to alleviate suffering or to encourage others to make something of themselves. It is said to represent the area of hurt in our charts, and this may be a practical health problem or a psychological one.

It seems to have the greatest influence when it is close to the angles or in angular houses, such as the fourth and tenth houses for difficult relationships with parents, or close to the ascendant or descendant for personal problems or difficulties in love relationships.

Other Features on a Chart

The Asteroid - Vesta

Vesta rules the comfort and cosiness of a nice home and a good family. It also seems to show the kind of home life we come from or that we choose to have. The Romans believed that bad behaviour would bring Vesta down on one's head in the form of karmic retribution.

The Asteroid - Ceres

Ceres rules the harvest and cereals, and thus symbolically comfort and abundance.

The Nodes of the Moon

When the Moon crosses the ecliptic in an upward direction, the crossing point is called the North Node of that planet and the southward crossing point becomes the South Node.

The North Node of the Moon

- Your present and future karma.
- How you fit into current social and political thinking.
- Some astrologers see this as a lucky point, others as the opposite.
- Good luck with matters related to the family, property and premises.

The South Node of the Moon

- Your past karma and your past life.
- How your desires differ from "political correctness" or from the society in which you live.
- Difficulty in getting things off the ground.
- Some astrologers see this as a lucky point, others as the opposite.

Details

There are three ways of looking at the Nodes of the Moon, starting with an idea taken from Hindu astrology, which says that the Nodes are connected to karma and reincarnation. Indian astrologers refer to the North Node as the dragon's head (Rahu) and the South Node as the dragon's tail (Kethu), and they consider the dragon itself to be a pretty evil influence.

The idea is that the South Node represents our previous lives and those things that we have already learned or overcome, but we struggle to come to terms with the lessons of our current life, as represented by the North Node. The Moon itself has a connection with the past, so previous experiences and past-life experiences do seem to have relevance when looking at the Nodes.

Western astrologers see the North Node as an area on our charts where we are attuned to the current outlook that prevails in society, while the South Node might put us against the general trend and make us seem rebellious and out of tune with the views of others. A common effect is something related to property or premises. Minor transits to the Nodes indicate trivial events such as going on holiday, having visitors or decorating and renovating the home.

If you look at the transits of the Nodes in the ephemeris, in addition to looking at progressions and transits of other planets to your own Nodes, you will be surprised at how important they can be.

The Angles

The Ascendant is on the left of the chart, and it marks the start of the first house. It's usually abbreviated as Asc. It rules the following concepts:

- Childhood programming.
- Outer manner, and thus the way others see you.
- Some aspects of the body and health.

The Descendant is opposite the Ascendant on the chart, and it marks the start of the seventh house. It's usually expressed as Dsc. It is linked with the following items:

- The kind of people we attract.
- What we enjoy in others.
- Some aspects of partners and friends.

At the top is the Midheaven or Medium Coeli, which is usually expressed as the MC, and it marks the start of the tenth house in most house systems. It is associated with the following:

- Reputation.
- Aims and aspirations.
- Career or where you would like to be in life.
- What you would like to achieve.
- Some aspects of partners and friends.
- The future.
- Father figures or paternal role models.
- Authority figures.

The bottom is the Nadir or Imum Coeli, and it marks the start of the fourth house in most house systems. It is known as the IC and it links to the following ideas:

- The family background and collective unconscious.
- What the family wanted the subject to be.
- Mother figures and maternal role models.
- Nurturing figures.
- Where the person is coming from, so to speak.
- The past.

Sensitive Points

There are many of these, but here are two that you might like to experiment with:

- The Vertex rules important events that occur via other people, and the most obvious ones are falling in love or bereavement, but there are many other less dramatic ones.

- The Part of Fortune comes from an Arabic system of astrology and it shows how you get ahead in life and even how you might make your fortune.

The Sun in Aries

Aries is a masculine, cardinal, fire sign, ruled by Mars.

Arians are energetic, enterprising, outgoing and competitive and they can be impulsive, so a typical Arian won't let the grass grow under his feet but he is impatient with details, easily bored and needs to be busy both at work and socially. Arians like to be part of a large organisation with a set structure and a ladder to climb, but if they work for themselves, they will find a way of joining up with others or of leading a team.

Somewhat impulsive and always optimistic, Arians look forward with faith in the future and they don't usually bear grudges. These subjects are kind hearted and very good to their friends and family, they are generous, helpful and very good hosts or hostesses. Arians are competitive and they like to be the best of the bunch, but can lack the persistence. Aries women need a career outside the home, and both men and women often have hobbies in addition to demanding careers. These subjects cannot sit about for long and they are not great television viewers because they become restless and easily bored.

They make loving parents and while they may push their children a bit too much, they will do anything they can to help them. Arians surprisingly home loving and most are not actually keen on too much travel. Most appreciate art, beauty, poetry and music and they have an excellent sense of humour. Arians have a surprisingly spiritual side to them that attracts them to religion or a spiritual way of thinking. A surprising number of them are drawn to psychic matters, and their intuition and keen interest in spiritual life can make them excellent clairvoyants and psychic mediums.

The Sun in Taurus
Taurus is a feminine, fixed, earth sign, ruled by Venus.

Taureans are practical, patient, thorough, tenacious and reliable. The Sun in Taurus acts in a slow and patient manner and it has a common sense attitude. The creativity of the Sun is expressed in something solid, such as a building project, landscape gardening, dancing, cookery or singing. The chief fault of this sign is stubbornness or to drop whatever hobbyhorse they climb on.

Taureans need to feel secure and to have a well-filled bank account behind them. These subjects are close to their families and loyal to their friends but if they take a dislike to someone, they make implacable enemies. They may irritate their partners or their children by wanting to know exactly where they are going and what time they are coming home. These dexterous people often find work in artistic or creative fields and many of them make inspired builders, decorators, hairdressers and make-up artists. Taurean people are extremely sociable, so they love to meet new people and to be out and about at all kinds of function. They love holidays with their family and friends, but if they go alone or with a partner, they soon make new friends. They just love strolling around in the sunshine. These people are usually pleasant, ordinary, reliable and shrewd. They can sometimes be taken for fools, but they can use that to their advantage on occasion.

Some choose to wear weird and wonderful clothing, either to amuse people when at a function or because they simply enjoy dressing differently. Some like to shock people, and some can be quite offensive. Most are reliable workers but they don't like to be rushed, so they keep going at their own pace.

The Sun in Gemini
Gemini is a masculine, mutable, air sign,
ruled by Mercury.

Gemini is flexible in its approach, changeable and sometimes intellectual. The Sun here expresses itself by taking in information and then releasing it again. Gemini people can live and work alone, but draw people towards them, so their phone is rarely at rest. Gemini subjects are astute but they may hop from one subject to another without studying anything too deeply. However, if their interest is aroused, they can get into something to a greater depth.

These subjects are loyal to their families and they care deeply for their children, and while they don't like too many changes in their relationships, like all air signs, they can drift in and out of friendships as the mood takes them. These excellent communicators often work in jobs that keep them in touch with others, which is why so many of them work in the media. Many Geminis are attracted to figure-work so they find jobs in banking and accountancy.

Geminis enjoy travel and sports but they are not particularly strong, so they need to conserve their easily depleted physical energies. These subjects are more sensible and hard-working than they are given credit for, and they can be determined when they set their sights on something. Geminis are good homemakers but they need the stimulus of a decent job or a strong outside interest. They also appreciate having money to spend and they are happy to earn it. Geminis need personal freedom and they hate being questioned about their comings and goings. Their main downside is a tendency to become depressed.

The Sun in Cancer
Cancer is a feminine, cardinal, water sign,
ruled by the Moon.

Cardinal signs like to make their own decisions, while the water element brings emotion, intuition and sensitivity. Their combination of shrewdness, common sense and intuition makes them excellent sales people who have a sure touch with the public.

Cancerians do well in any job that deals with the public, because they have an instinctive feel for what people need, and they provide this with charm and efficiency. They can calm those who are angry or hysterical without becoming infected with anger themselves, assuming this situation occurs in a business or working environment and not inside their own homes and families. They tend to fall apart when the going gets rough at home. They do best when they ally themselves either to a calm and resilient partner or to an adventurous one. Cancerians enjoy family life and they often work with family members. Cancerians are sensitive and easily hurt but they learn to hide their sensitivity under a hard shell and, in some cases over a period of time, the soft heart atrophies, making them unfeeling to the point of cruelty.

Cancer is careful with money, so they usually save and avoid getting into debt. Many Cancerians love to travel and while they need the security of a home base, they love getting away from it to explore new places. These people make good teachers and caring friends.

The Sun in Leo
Leo is a masculine, fixed, fire sign, ruled by the Sun.

Leos are playful in nature so they like their lives to have an element in fun in them. These people are successful, glamorous and popular but they can be stubborn, determined and arrogant. Leo people are proud and their standards are high. These people are not materialistic in the sense of needing a large pile of savings in the bank or of wanting to have more than the Joneses, but they want everything life can offer. They want to succeed and they want their families to be happy and successful.

Leos are usually kind and generous, good natured and sociable but they can become mean and cranky if life doesn't go their way. These subjects can be restless, impatient and critical but they are often harder on themselves than they are on others. Leos have old-fashioned values, being basically honest, hard-working family people.

These subjects need an adventurous life and a prestigious or glamorous line of work, but they will stick to a poor job if necessary. Leos often choose jobs that allow them to travel or to get out and about and talk to people. Leos are not usually intellectual or academic, so their thinking is slow and rather inflexible and their ideas and interests quite mundane. One of their greatest assets is their organisational talents and their sheer ability to get things done. Leos are not as dramatic or as outgoing as most astrologers seem to think, because they are easily embarrassed and they don't like to make a spectacle of themselves. Their kindness and sympathy can make them a soft touch for less scrupulous people.

The Sun in Virgo
Virgo is a feminine, mutable, earth sign,
ruled by Mercury; also, arguably, by Chiron.

Virgos are concerned with detail and they make good database managers, record keepers and bookkeepers, but they don't catch on to new ideas too quickly. They are modest and sometimes fussy. The earth element signifies that they do things thoroughly and they don't like to be rushed. They make good editors and journalists, and many are into cooking or needlework, farming or draughtsmanship.

Their standards are very high and they blame themselves when things go wrong. They are sensitive and easily hurt, but also critical of others. They have a reputation for tidiness but they are no more tidy or untidy than any other sign, but they get annoyed if others tidy up their stuff for them. Virgos are careful and discriminating, and they have a talent for analysis. They may have some special area of knowledge, but they also have a good range of general knowledge.

Some Virgoans have strangely split personalities, being extremely modest and retiring in some situations, and outgoing in others. Some are defensive and difficult, while other Virgos are the salt of the earth, being kind, gentle and witty, with delightful senses of humour and hearts of gold. The nicest Virgoans are drawn to work in fields where they can help others. Their worst fault is a tendency to shoot themselves in the foot and ruin things for themselves. Virgos are very good to their parents and other relatives and they don't usually let others down.

The Sun in Libra
Libra is a masculine, cardinal, air sign, ruled by Venus.

Libra is concerned with balance, harmony and fair play but it is also quite a tough and adventurous sign. The Sun in Libra expresses itself in a co-operative manner, and any enterprise is carried out in as pleasant and charming a way as possible. Librans have a deceptive appearance, because they are good looking and they can look soft and gentle, but they have a tough core that allows them to cope with difficult situations.

Librans can be very persuasive, so they make wonderful agents, excellent diplomats, lawyers and negotiators. Librans can't take too much stress, so they need a reliable career and good relationships, but they are more ambitious than they appear. There are some strange polarities with this sign, as some are extremely clean and tidy, while others are the opposite. Similarly, some are extremely well organised and hard working, while others are the exact opposite. As you can see, this sign can run to extremes. Some Librans have a problem with decision-making, while others just need time to come to their conclusions. The reason for this shilly-shallying is their finely balanced legal minds, which tend to look at all sides of a question and examine the rightness of their choices, along with a preference for stopping and thinking before committing themselves.

These subjects are very flirtatious, and some of them have a real problem with fidelity. Some prefer to keep their options open and to explore a variety of relationships. Librans are cheerful, optimistic, humorous, good-natured and loving, but they can be sharp tongued and cruel when the mood hits them. Boredom is their worst enemy. Librans are wonderful company and great talkers and they have the knack of understanding other people. Many Librans tend to live in cloud cuckoo land sometimes, rather than facing reality.

The Sun in Scorpio
Scorpio is a feminine, fixed, water sign,
ruled by Pluto and, in older traditions, Mars.

There is a resilience and determination about this sign that makes them able to live through difficult times and to cope with hardship in ways that would poleaxe others. These people are the workers of the zodiac who like to turn up on time, do a good job and to finish what they start. Their motto is "if you are going do to something, do it properly!" They tackle things with great energy and enthusiasm, and once they start something, they stick with it until the end. Scorpios are reliable, resourceful, hard working and intensely loyal. They are well organised and they have good memories. They are excellent salespeople because they have the tenacity and determination to see things through. They expect others to be as thorough and as capable as they are, and they can show contempt for those who aren't. Scorpios prefer to be the second in command than to lead an organisation. They make good marriage partners but they are moody and they don't always tell their partners what is on their minds. If Scorpios have problems at work or in a social setting, they may release their tensions by behaving badly to their loved ones.

Most are charming and likeable, and they genuinely love to help others. Their tough appearance and manner often hides a kind and generous heart, although some Scorpios actually relate better to animals than to people. They make wonderful friends and they can be the most loyal and dependable partners. Their feelings are very deep and they don't forgive those who hurt them. Some have a fear of abandonment, while others tend to worry over small things. These inexplicable feelings may be carried forward from childhood experiences or even a previous life. Being an all or nothing sign, some are very generous while others are very tight fisted, while some drink too much and others barely drink at all. Some are tidy, while others live in a mess. They can be romantic and very loving.

The Sun in Sagittarius
Sagittarius is a masculine, mutable, fire sign,
ruled by Jupiter.

People born under Sagittarius usually fall on their feet. These people are pleasant, cheerful and optimistic, but their intense honesty can make them tactless and outspoken. Astrology books tell us that Sagittarians live very exciting lives, travelling, exploring and making new friends wherever they go, but many prefer to plod along with a secure home life and nothing to rock the boat.

They are artistic and creative and many are very capable, especially when it comes to building work or do-in-yourself. These subjects enjoy working for large organisations where they can meet a variety of people, and they are good at dealing with the public or with people who have problems. They make excellent teachers and are often happiest in that line of work. There is a common belief that all Sagittarians love horses but the reality is that they are like the rest of us, in that they may enjoy having a dog or a cat as a pet, but that's about all.

Some of these individuals are rather rebellious in childhood while others reject parental affection, but many have poor childhoods with fathers who abandon the family and mothers who find it hard to cope. Both sexes are generous with their time and some are generous with money and goods, so they can lay themselves open to being used or taken advantage of. If they are hurt or let down, they don't forgive or forget. They aren't prejudiced on the grounds of race or religion - indeed, they fight against such prejudice. Sagittarians can be great fighters for justice and fair play, and their strong social conscience can lead them to work in the law or the Church. They are often into spirituality, religion, New Age thinking or psychism. They question the religion they were brought up with and find their own way later in life.

The Sun in Capricorn
Capricorn is a feminine, cardinal, earth sign,
ruled by Saturn.

The Sun expresses itself in a steady and thorough manner in Capricorn. Capricorn folks are patient, realistic, respectable, responsible and hard working. They don't walk away from unpalatable situations lightly and they stick to marriages and partnerships as long as possible. However, this is a cardinal sign, not a fixed one, which means that they won't put up with something unnecessarily. Capricorns are refined and gentle, so they dislike rough or crude people. Most of all, they hate to be embarrassed.

These subjects are ambitious, but they have the patience to wait for things to work out. They love things that give them status but they avoid the flashier symbols of success. Capricorns are interested in business and money and they often do well. Such subjects may be shy when young but they gain confidence and become more sociable as they get older. They can be too easily offended when no offence is intended.

Capricorns make good marriage partners because they truly prefer to be settled in a happy family than flitting from one partner to another. They make good parents because they care about their children and rarely let them down. They particularly adore their parents and they love having them around. These subjects are not as dull as they sound because they can be gently humorous and they can be quite flirtatious. They are often nice looking and they keep their looks when they get old. Capricorns can be insecure and they do best in life if they have an encouraging partner. Most prefer an outgoing partner, and they will do all they can to help that person to get on. Most have a difficult family member somewhere in their lives, but they do what they can for them.

The Sun in Aquarius
Aquarius is a masculine, fixed, air sign that is ruled by Uranus, and in old types of astrology, also by Saturn.

NB: Many people mistake Aquarius for a water sign, because its symbol is the Water Carrier.

Aquarians are clever, friendly, kind, independent and humane. They take a reasonable, unsentimental and impersonal attitude to most things, but they can get very worked up when things go wrong in their own lives. Friendship is often easier for these people than family life, and some of them prefer animals to people. Some Aquarians seem to live in a dream world, finding it hard to get anything done or tackling too many things at one time. These people are so individual that they are unlike anybody else, including other Aquarians! They march to their own drumbeat and live in their own chosen manner. Some of them seem to live entirely inside their own heads, while others throw themselves into causes of one kind or another. Aquarians make excellent teachers and they have a great deal of patience with anyone who is willing to learn. They can express themselves clearly and put points across to others in an imaginative manner. These apparently cool, calm people are actually quite tense inside and sometimes bad tempered. Most can argue the hind leg of a donkey, which is possibly why so many of them love politics. The age of gadgets and technology is made for them, as they seem to have a real affinity for these things.

Aquarian minds are logical and broad-minded, and most of them are clever. Many Aquarians work in the caring professions and they can be excellent counsellors and arbitrators. These subjects make the most loyal and wonderful friends.

The Sun in Pisces

Pisces is a feminine, mutable, water sign, ruled by Neptune, and in old types of astrology, also by Jupiter.

The Sun's energies often turn to such things as teaching, caring for others or developing the spiritual side of life when in Pisces. The creative energies of the Sun are used in a gentle way and everything is done in a slow and gentle manner. Pisceans are kind-hearted.

Pisceans are very hard to quantify because they can present themselves in so many guises. Most of them are gentle and quiet, while some can be surprisingly fiery. Pisceans will rush to give practical help when it is needed. Many of these subjects work in the psychic field because they're drawn to the hidden and mystical sides of life and most are pretty psychic. Despite their gentle, artistic, mystical nature, they are ambitious and often achieve success one way or another. They never seem to earn big money but they always have enough for their needs, and sometimes more than one would suppose. Their biggest fault is a tendency to expect others to run around after them, and some can be surprisingly bossy to their children.

These subjects are often very good with their hands and many of them are gifted artists or musicians. They can create a home out of nothing. Many Pisceans lack confidence and they are very vulnerable when young, but they gain strength in their decision-making abilities later. They do well if matched to a practical and supportive partner and they blossom in a happy family. Some seem to miss the boat where emotional happiness is concerned.

Pisceans can be happy living in a rambling house filled with relatives, children and animals but they also need their own space and time for themselves. Many of these subjects travel to escape, while others bury themselves in a hobby or escape into drink or drugs. Some have a strong hold on life while others seem to have a very tenuous one. Few Pisceans fear death, because they know there is an afterlife.

The Moon through the Signs

The Moon in Aries

These subjects are quick thinkers and talkers who are clever large-scale planners but they need help with details. They are starters rather than runners, and they may be happier in an executive position than as one of the workers. Moon in Aries people can be successful in executive positions, but their confidence evaporates quickly and they need the support and admiration of others. Women with this placement need a career. Enthusiastic, headstrong and freedom loving, they cannot take restriction or unnecessary discipline. Such people may have stormy love lives, either because they are changeable and easily bored or because they are unwilling to compromise, but they are usually honest and they don't try to manipulate others.

Moon Aries subjects can be deft and dexterous and their excellent co-ordination can make them successful at sports. The Moon is a water planet and when it is in a fire sign, emotions are expressed quickly and easily. These individuals have hot tempers but they usually cool down fairly quickly and they rarely sulk for long. They feel entitled to their emotions and are not shy about exhibiting them. In a way, I guess, what you see is what you get! Some are brought up in a military atmosphere or in a family that values sports. Many teach or work in large organisations that benefit the public in some way.

While the childhood is often reasonable, there may be arguments between the individual and the father and this seems to affect father/daughter relationships especially badly. Many grow up to become caring but pushy parents who want the best for their own children.

The Moon in Taurus

This Moon sign is very stable and sensible when the lives of the natives are in perfect working order but when emotional problems come along, these people fall apart. Moon Taurus subjects are pleasant and sociable, respectable, reliable and decent. These subjects need a settled and happy family life, a comfortable home and a good job. They make good parents and successful family members as long as they have the love and support they need. These subjects can be confrontational and uncompromising though, and some are too fond of alcohol. They are tough but fair in business and rarely stupid with money. Moon in Taurus people love music, gardening, cooking, the outdoors and travelling. Lunar Taureans seem to love their fathers but they may feel let down by them. The father may be week, ailing or unable to stand up to their mothers. Some experience a childhood that is materially comfortable but lacking in wholehearted love.

The Moon in Gemini

These subjects have active minds that may be academic, imaginative, creative or logical, depending upon other features on the birthchart. They are dexterous and versatile and they can cope with most tasks at work or in the home. Some need freedom and may avoid getting into permanent relationships while others need a practical partner. Some love films and television, while others are into sports. Many work in jobs where they communicate with the public or provide services for the public, such as travel advice, journalism or teaching. Moon in Gemini types stay young, even when they get older.

   This Moon placement can indicate a difficult childhood and there may have been problems at school where they suffered from bullying or unfair treatment. They are bright though, and they often love to read when they are young so they tend to educate themselves. They have shrewd minds and excellent business ability, so they do well later in life. They are excellent parents and they keep a close relationship with their children throughout life.

The Moon in Cancer

The Moon rules Cancer, so it is comfortable in this sign. The subjects are sensitive and sometimes moody, imaginative, creative and possibly artistic. They use their intuition in daily life and they may be into religion or psychic subjects. They can be emotionally demanding and moody.

   These subjects make good family members and excellent parents, and both sexes are domesticated and many are excellent do-it-yourselves. Lunar Cancerians are shrewd in business matters and sometimes very successful. They don't like taking chances and they need financial and emotional security. They are wonderful teachers and may seek work in that arena. They plan for their old age and they often remain quite youthful in spirit even when old. They love the sea and enjoy travelling with their families. Moon in Cancer subjects normally have quite reasonable parents and they are good to their children.

The Moon in Leo

These people are friendly and welcoming, and while some are genuinely confident, many are quite shy. They are loyal, loving and idealistic and they only leave a partner if it becomes absolutely necessary. They are happiest when they are loved and appreciated. They can put a partner on a pedestal or expect too much from them. These individuals are good organisers who enjoy an orderly life, shouldering responsibility well and having good leadership qualities.

The Lunar Leo childhood is usually good although there may be an emphasis on religion, tradition or educational attainment. The mother is normally warm-hearted and energetic and the childhood home is comfortable and well organised. This is not normally a difficult Moon placement, but pride and arrogance can become a problem. The subject's father figure isn't great.

The Moon in Virgo

These subjects are keenly intellectual, discriminating and capable of dealing with details. They are emotionally contained, reserved and slow to push themselves forward. They can keep their emotions on a tight leash, being easily embarrassed by displays of emotion. Strong emotions such as anger, jealousy, desire, love and hate may all be buried, denied or deflected into other activities, such as money-making, cleaning the home and so on. This may eventually turn inwards to make them ill.

Moon Virgo folk are keen on matters related to health, hygiene, fitness and alternative therapies. They may be fussy eaters and they are often sensitive to certain types of foods, although many are excellent cooks. Some Lunar Virgoans are timid and full of worries, nerves and negativity, but most are actually rather stubborn and determined. Some can be critical and tactless. These subjects are conscientious providers and excellent at the practical sides of family life, but they may find it hard to show loving feelings to their partners or their children. They make sacrifices for their families. Lunar Virgo subjects are clever with money and they often make shrewd investments and purchases. They work in areas where they can use their communications skills while also helping humanity.

Moon in Virgo subjects have difficult childhoods, and this is probably behind their self-protective attitude. Fortunately, these subjects are not fools and if they take the trouble to look into the reasons behind their unhappiness, they develop the kind of understanding which allows them to change and to grow.

The Moon in Libra

These subjects are charming, optimistic and sociable. They are skilled and tactful diplomats who are popular in all kinds of social settings and some are good looking. Lunar Librans can appear soft, but they are hard workers who can display considerable determination when they have a particular goal in sight. They like having things their way. These subjects don't enjoy being alone, so they seek partnerships in business and personal life and they have many friends. In days gone by, these subjects married young, but nowadays they may live with someone to start with and move on again later but they are faithful when in a stable relationship.

Moon Libra subjects need pleasant living and working surroundings, and they are fussy about decor and colour schemes. They make excellent architects, interior designers and even software designers. Their diplomatic skills can take them into agency work, marketing or union negotiating, and while good company much of the time, they can be arrogant, outspoken and hurtful.

A Moon-Libra childhood is usually a pleasant one with kindly, clever parents who do all they can to stimulate the child's intellect. In some cases, the father is a distant figure, possibly due to business commitments or not being fully committed to family life. There is little strict discipline and everything is reasonable, including the child himself most of the time. These children come under pressure at school, because they can be lazy.

The Moon in Scorpio

Whenever the Moon is in a water sign, the emotions are intense and in Scorpio, the feelings can be quite close to the surface. If these folk are let down in love, they can go on about the situation too much, but if they keep their troubles to themselves, they can fester inside and become ill as a result. Lunar Scorpios never forget those who hurt them but they also remember those who are good to them. These subjects hate to owe money and they hate people who borrow without paying them back. These individuals do best when allied to a cheerful, capable and emotionally stable partner, but their own vulnerability can lead them to choose vulnerable, sensitive or chaotic mates. Although stubborn and inclined to stick to their choices, they can be driven to leave a relationship, but they then learn from their mistakes and go on to make better choices in future.

Lunar Scorpios struggle to achieve financial security but if they suffer financial setbacks, they pick themselves up and to start again. They may experience great gains and losses, and can suffer extremes of tragedy or joy in their lives. They love challenges and they can put a lot into their careers, partnerships and children. They find it easy attract friends, lovers or even money when they put their minds to it. Tough, masculine jobs appeal to some of them while the world of health and healing appeals to others, and they are especially gifted at subjects like psychology and hypnotherapy.

Something seems to have been wrong in the childhood. A parent or sibling may have died; there may have been intense poverty sickness or abandonment. The subject may have become resentful because a brother or sister was more successful and more popular with the parents and grandparents than the Lunar Scorpio was.

The Moon in Sagittarius

There are many Lunar Sagittarians in the worlds of astrology and the psychic sciences and many are excellent dowsers, palmists and anything else of the kind. It seems that these people are driven to explore the inner world of mind, body and spirit and to seek enlightenment at a deep and inner level. Superficially, Lunar Sagittarians are optimistic, outgoing and friendly. Many of them travel a great deal or have strong connections to people from lands, cultures or backgrounds. They seek to learn from these people.

Most Lunar Sagittarians feel the need to contact as many people as they can during their lifetime, which leads them to choose jobs in teaching or dealing with the public. These subjects need personal freedom, so they don't settle with one partner for life, but they keep friendships going for years. Some Lunar Sagittarians relate better with animals than people. These individuals may have distant relationships with their parents. They need an interesting lifestyle that offers them plenty of variety. Many are deep thinkers who read, study and expand their knowledge base throughout their lives. These subjects are surprisingly ambitious and they can be quite competitive, which may lead some of them into a sporting lifestyle.

These subjects may have strange childhood experiences in which they are made to feel different from those who are around them. They rarely receive enough nurturing and they miss out on cuddles and affection. They may not stick to one partner for life but they have the ability to draw others to them so they are rarely lonely for long. Lunar Sagittarians can do well at school but they do most of their studying and learning later.

The Moon in Capricorn

These subjects learn early in life that security is hard to find, as they may come from circumstances that are difficult in some way. If the subject himself does not experience severe difficulties in childhood, it is likely that his mother would have suffered, so there is a kind of collective unconsciousness that drives the person to seek financial security. These people work hard and provide for themselves and their families, but they can be too materialistic, too inclined to worry about money and tight-fisted. Some use other people and take advantage of them.

It can take a long time before they gain courage and confidence in themselves to open up to others. They may find an outlet in a career or a happy family life later and they overcome most of their problems by patient stoicism. Lunar Capricorns rarely abandon their families or friends. They have a good sense of humour and they are able to laugh at themselves, but they can be touchy and they don't care to have others laugh at them. They have love lives, and they make up in old age for the unhappiness or insecurity of their childhood.

Moon in Aquarius

Lunar Aquarians need independence, and they cannot live under someone else's thumb or be dictated to by others. If any of these subjects have to face a particularly difficult situation, they prefer to do it on their own and without an audience. These subjects are very imaginative and they can be extremely creative. Under stress, these subjects can become aloof, sarcastic or unpredictable. These people are broadminded, always up-to-date and they are keen to live their lives to the full. They can be obstinate, argumentative and keen to have their own way. They need a partner whom they can respect.

These people are very friendly and they keep their friends for a very long time. They are humorous, good company and kind hearted but they can attract too many lame ducks. Many have a strangely distant relationship with their parents, while others are forced to take on the job of parenting their own parents at some point in time. They would have grown up in a household that is full of books and with ample opportunity to obtain a good education, but they tend to prefer having a good time with their friends to putting themselves to a lot of trouble at school.

The Moon in Pisces

This Lunar placement can lead the subject into an unusual lifestyle. Many are deeply into mind, body and spirit subjects, and they can be drawn to religion or spiritualism. This Moon placement leads to a great deal of vulnerability and shyness. There is often something wrong in childhood and these natives may feel extremely lonely during childhood and even throughout life. These subjects may choose to be alone for much of the time because the continual presence of other people can upset the delicate balance of their aura. These natives are psychic sponges, who pick up the moods and vibrations of all with whom they come into contact. In some cases, low self-esteem leads to apathy and an inability to get anything done, but when these indecisive worriers have the support of a strong, steadfast and reliable partner they blossom.

These people love deeply and can become obsessed with their lovers. They may not know how to turn down a request, and thus they can allow others to take advantage of their good natures. Sympathetic, romantic and sweet natured, they have an inner strength that comes to the fore in times of crisis, and they have a truly magical gift for helping those who are troubled. Retiring and often in poor health, these strange people achieve more, show more courage and cope with far more than all the other Moon signs of the zodiac put together. Their considerable creative and artistic talents, allied to their instinct for finding gaps in the market means that they find ways of supplying the public with the goods and services that they need. Lunar Pisceans end up surprising others by unexpectedly gaining fame and fortune, and that makes them targets for jealousy.

The Personal Planets through the Signs

Mercury in Aries

The mind is impulsive, quick-witted and the tongue can be sharp and sarcastic. There is often a good memory, particularly for poetry, literary quotations or quiz trivia. The nature is self-assertive and there is a fighting spirit. These subjects can be nervous, impulsive and hyperactive. They may act first and then think later. They concentrate on things that interest them, but skip lightly over other things without studying them deeply.

Mercury in Taurus

The mind is retentive and the thought processes slow but logical. Learning may be easier through pictures than words. This subject is dexterous and practical and may be better with his hands than with academic subjects. Sensible and cheerful, but possibly a bit slow and stodgy, this person can be stubborn, inflexible and incapable of lateral thinking. If nearby planets are in Gemini, this placement acts as a settling or grounding factor.

Mercury in Gemini

These subjects are clever, versatile and inventive, with quick minds. They can think on their feet but they may find it hard to concentrate on one thing at a time. They are excellent communicators who are quick to learn and they can be dexterous or good with computers. They prefer jobs with plenty of variety or opportunities to move from place to place. Highly-strung and nervous, they may talk too much when under stress.

Mercury in Cancer

These people may live in the past or they may take an interest in history or in objects that have historical connections, such as antiques. Their memory is excellent but they are opinionated. They can harbour grudges. Kind and loyal, they dislike major change but they do enjoy novelty and a change of scene from time to time. They may be hypochondriacs.

Mercury in Leo

Optimistic and creative, these subjects can be arrogant, sharp tongued and unfeeling at times. Good public speakers or teachers, they are strong minded and tough in business. They are excellent organisers but they are inclined to get involved in over-optimistic schemes, or carried away with glamorous but unrealistic projects. On the whole, however, these subjects are fairly sensible and they are also generous.

Mercury in Virgo

These subjects are analytical, shrewd and practical, being good at specialisation and problem solving. These individuals may be excellent writers or journalists but they may also be long-winded talkers because they see every detail so clearly and expect others to be as interested in details as they are. These natives are critical of others but even more critical of themselves. Their standards are very high. They have an affinity to the suffering of others and may be interested in healthy living, possibly to the point of hypochondria.

Mercury in Libra

These people are gentle and tactful, and they make excellent ambassadors. They have excellent taste in decor with a strong sense of colour, and they love their creature comforts. They have good business sense but they may lose opportunities through idleness. Sociable and humorous, they can be great fun.

Mercury in Scorpio

The mind is sharp and critical and there may be tendencies towards manipulation, suspicion, jealousy or possessiveness. These subjects may be interested in medical matters, the police or military subjects, and they can be excellent historians or specialists. They can be clever in business but they can lose interest or forget to tie up loose ends. Some are into art or music.

Mercury in Sagittarius

Some of these subjects do well at college, while others fall aside when young but educate themselves later. Broad-minded and lacking in prejudice, these people are interested in everything and everyone. They find it hard to concentrate and they may be involved in so many things that they never really grasp or finish any of them. Frank, versatile and restless, they love travel, foreigners and anything unusual. Some of these subjects are sportsmen and women, while others are drawn to religious or philosophical lifestyles due to their attraction to mystical or spiritual matters.

Mercury in Capricorn

Rational, practical, careful and patient, these subjects take life seriously. Their minds are scientific, mathematical, or attuned to business. Some are keen linguists while others make excellent teachers while others do well in banking or economics. These subjects are traditional in outlook, reliable in business, kind hearted and loyal friends. They do their duty!

Mercury in Aquarius

Intuitive, inventive, modern and interested in science and social progress, these subjects are excellent communicators who may choose to work for the public. A detached attitude makes them appear to be good judges of human behaviour, but they may be too distanced to really understand others. They can have an unrealistic outlook.

Mercury in Pisces

Intuitive, imaginative, flexible and kind, these people have broad minds and they are drawn to mysticism, spirituality and the meaning of life and the after life. Many are clairvoyant and spiritual, while others are very creative and imaginative. They can be chaotic and prone to escapism through drink, drugs or sex. Over emotional, secretive and manipulative, these subjects lack confidence, but they find ways of succeeding anyway. These people can be drawn to spiritual healing or novel writing.

Venus in Aries

Affectionate and sexy, these people are fond of giving unusual presents. They enjoy social life and outings. They are creative, popular and flirtatious. They can be headstrong and reckless with money or fluctuate between generosity and meanness. They aren't bothered about possessions, although they will value their sports equipment, motorcar and they may collect unusual items.

Venus in Taurus

These people are affectionate and passionate. Some are into cooking, eating, art, music or crafts. They can be self-indulgent but they are shrewd with money, being careful and possibly somewhat tight fisted. They need a nice home and a great garden.

Venus in Gemini

Flirtatious, light-hearted, restless and possibly fickle, some of these subjects feel trapped by close personal relationships. They are fond of their relatives. Some love travel, music, art and drama. Although adaptable, some find themselves the odd one out in their family. They love to collect books or equipment although they are actually more interested in ideas than in goods.

Venus in Cancer

Affectionate and sympathetic, these people may smother their loved ones or lean on them. Emotional, clinging and imaginative, these subjects react badly to loss or rejection. They are home loving, good cooks and good hosts. They love history and antiques and need a nice home and garden. They may spend their lives seeking security. They need a settled relationship and money in the bank. They may be subject to weight gain.

Venus in Leo

These subjects need love but they may dominate their partners. They are generous and loving, and they love their children deeply. They love good clothes and a nice home. They can be creative and they love to produce goods that others admire. They are flirtatious and fun. They usually obtain property and goods during their lives.

Venus in Virgo

These people can be critical of others but they are even more self-critical, which leads to low self-esteem. They hate dirt and mess. They can be sexy, but while they seek close and loving relationships, they are choosy, and may not find them until later in life. Although reserved and quietly charming, they may be fault finding or fussy. They have good practical business sense and can be shrewd but while they like money, they aren't hoarders and they can spend freely.

Venus in Libra

Kind hearted, lovable and sociable, these people are nice looking with really lovely eyes. They find it hard to maintain one strong relationship if it requires effort, and they may drift away from lovers and friends. They are very artistic and probably also musical. Despite their gentle, dreamy nature, they are good in business and not as soft as they look.

Venus in Scorpio

Sensual, passionate and possessive, these subjects hang onto what is theirs, and they don't forgive a hurt. They can be extremely generous or amazingly stingy. They often have executive ability but their pig-headed attitude can spoil their efforts. Some of them are jealous of the ability of others. They are not especially acquisitive, being more interested in a good lifestyle than in accumulating things. These subjects make good and loyal friends but they can take advantage of those who they perceive as being weak. This placement also indicates strong intuition, with possible clairvoyant powers and a need to be close to the spiritual side of life.

Venus in Sagittarius

These subjects must feel free. They choose jobs where they can come and go as they please and they love to travel. Some are very adventurous and unsettled, so they may delay marriage until late in life. Some are spiritual and psychic. Most are humanitarian and idealistic but they can be tactless and thoughtless. They only need money for the freedom it allows them, as they aren't particularly into possessions. They make good friends and very good teachers.

Venus in Capricorn

Conventional and stable in matters of affection, these people can be undemonstrative, but they can actually be quite sexy. They may be calculating and fussy at work and also status conscious. They are reliable workers who will get on with things if left in peace. If challenged, they dig their heels in and fight back hard. They are shrewd and business like. They are deeply into their family and very caring towards older family members. They value education, art and literature, but also money making.

Venus in Aquarius

These subjects don't like conventional jobs or home life, and they need to feel that they can come and go as they please. They can cope with a lot because they don't become too attached to anyone or anything. They are friendly and helpful to others but they don't like people who cling to them. Possessions aren't as important to them as being with people who share their ideas and their needs.

Venus in Pisces

These subjects are creative, artistic or musical and they may be very good looking. They are emotional and sentimental. They need a creative outlet or one that allows them to express themselves. They may sacrifice too much for loved ones or their families. Some are sensible with money while others aren't, while some are generous and others tight fisted. They are often misunderstood.

***

Mars in Aries

Argumentative, outspoken, impulsive and obstinate, such subjects can be a real handful. They may appear self-assured on the surface but they may actually be quite unsure of themselves underneath. There is a small child hidden not too far under the surface and it is this that makes them so attractive. Other attractive features are their openness and friendliness, in addition to their intelligence and their witty sense of humour. They may be practical and have mechanical talent, and they may love gadgets. They may be prone to fevers, high blood pressure, eye troubles and accidents to the head.

Mars in Taurus

These people are hard practical workers who have the strength of character and obstinacy to finish what they start. Some of these subjects are good singers or dancers, and many are clever cooks, gardeners or craft workers.

These people have a smouldering and somewhat grudging temperament, and they don't like to be opposed or deflected from their chosen path. Passionate about life and love, they have strong feelings that are not always apparent to others, while they can be secretive and quite difficult to live with. These subjects have excellent organising talents and shrewd business abilities. They like money and they can be sexy.These subjects may have bad throats and have accidents.

Mars in Gemini

Clever, talented and dexterous, these subjects may not have the staying power to finish what they start. Talkative, restless and nervous, they need a life that does not give them too many problems. These subjects are clever inventors and problem-solvers but they are easily bored by too much routine or detail. They are adaptable and interested in travel and communications. There may be a tendency to accidents to the hands, shoulders and arms.

Mars in Cancer

Ambitious and clinging, emotional, sensitive and sensuous, these subjects need security and they need to be loved and cared for. Both sexes are domesticated and may be good at cooking, do-it-yourself jobs and creative gardening. These people make excellent but rather possessive parents and marriage partners and they may also be inclined to lean on their spouses. Very intuitive and probably psychic, these subjects may be attracted to the psychic sciences. They may have weak stomachs.

Mars in Leo

These folk like excitement and change and cannot put up with a dull or routine job. They enjoy travel, meeting new people and tackling a variety of problems. They appear confident but this may be something of a pose. They are attractive and popular and they have friendly personalities. There may be problems with the spine or the heart.

Mars in Virgo

These subjects should be hard workers but sometimes they spend more time talking and fiddling about than actually doing anything, but when their interest is aroused, they can get on extremely well and at great speed. These people need a job that holds their attention and which provides them with plenty of variety because boredom is their worst enemy. They are shrewd operators and they are capable of attending to details. They are drawn to work in the communications or medical industries. These people can be too critical, nervous, fussy and demanding, and they may talk too much. Worry makes them ill and their weak spots are the bowels and skin.

Mars in Libra

These subjects are clever and perceptive about people. They are interested in communicating with others and they may be good business people. These people are friendly and sociable but they can be very laid back and rather lazy. They have a strong survival instinct and they will fight hard for what is theirs. Mars in Libra people are flirtatious and very fond of the opposite sex. Their marriage-type relationships should have a strongly sexual content. Their weak spots are the kidneys, pancreas and bladder.

Mars in Scorpio

These subjects have very strong characters and they can bully weaker types. They aim high and work hard for their chosen goals. They can be secretive, relentless and even cruel at times. They are very perceptive, intuitive and even quite psychic. They may be interested in the occult or anything that is hidden. Some choose to work as detectives while others are drawn to the military life. They need self-discipline and an organised lifestyle. As far as health is concerned, they are very strong and resilient, but they can drink too much and they may suffer spinal or reproductive problems.

Mars in Sagittarius

Boisterous and energetic, these people may take life by storm. They are independent thinkers who may choose unusual or unconventional lifestyles. Some are sceptical and questioning, while others are drawn to mysticism and astrology. They love travel, sports and adventure. Some are outspoken, tactless and argumentative, while others use their intellect to fight injustice wherever they see it. Some never really settle down but drift from one partner to another throughout their lives. Some are very sexually experimental. Their weak spots are the hips, thighs and arteries.

Mars in Capricorn

These people are strong characters and they may be power hungry and obstinate. They have excellent organisational ability and they can be practical, self-reliant and capable. They can also be cold, distant and irritable, but they get things done. They hate waste. Their health areas are the ears, teeth, bones, knees and skin.

Mars in Aquarius

These individuals are impulsive and idealistic, so they are often found working for good causes. They may be intellectual but also unpredictable, while they can also be determined and obstinate. They may find it hard to express their feelings. They need freedom and they don't like to be smothered or for anyone to get in their way. Their health problem areas are their circulation, ankles and legs.

Mars in Pisces

Some of these people are self-sacrificial, emotional and lacking in drive and concentration, while others are artistic and dreamy. Some make exceptional designers and engineers who do very well when allowed to work on their own projects. They can be unrealistic and disloyal. They love music, dance and the arts. They can be penny wise and pound-foolish. Some are psychic and spiritual. The weak spots are the feet, lungs and circulation.

The Transpersonal Planets
through the Signs

Jupiter takes about a year to traverse a sign, while Saturn takes about two and a half years to do so.

Jupiter in Aries

Self-sufficient, freedom loving, honest and extravagant, these subjects can be overly optimistic, reckless or thoughtless. They may bully others. They need to learn to budget their time, money and energy. They can be clever workers who do well in large organisations. They value freedom to express their opinions but they also value the organisations to which they belong.

Jupiter in Taurus

These people love comfort, rich living and good food, and they may overindulge in all of these things. They have sound judgement and their feet are on the ground. They are, for the most part, good-hearted, reliable friends and steady workers. They can be possessive or materialistic. They enjoy practical work, especially if it is on a large scale, such as construction work or landscape gardening. These people value what they can see, hear, feel, taste and touch.

Jupiter in Gemini

These people are clever but possibly somewhat superficial. They make good teachers and journalists and they can be affable but unreliable as friends. Mentally alert, versatile and good conversationalists, they need constant stimulation because they are easily bored. They enjoy word games and literature and they are dexterous and inventive, valuing ideas and intellectual freedom. They love to travel and explore. They can be crafty.

Jupiter in Cancer

These individuals are kind, good-humoured and sympathetic. They are more ambitious than one realises and they can be restless. They are emotional by nature and they can become emotionally attached to job, a house, an area or an idea. They are sociable, patriotic and fairly old-fashioned in their values. Such people are loyal to their families but their possessiveness and touchiness can make them hard to live with. They may draw invisible lines which one crosses at one's peril. These subjects have good business sense but they can incline towards nepotism especially where their parents are concerned. They can make money from antiques.

Jupiter in Leo

The natives are big-hearted, generous and creative. They can be popular and they have the ability to draw people and for the public to like them. They are intelligent, honest and vital, and they like to live in a glamorous or exciting world. They can be overbearing, pompous and arrogant. They enjoy prestige and money and like to do everything on a grand scale. Their work brings them fame but not always fortune. They love to teach or train others. These humorous people enjoy music and dancing and they feel that life is for living.

Jupiter in Virgo

These people are kind, conscientious, moral and ethical. They have an analytical approach to their work. They should try not to bottle up their emotions or divert too many of their feelings into their work. They enjoy research, analysis and intellectual pursuits and they may have success in the medical or scientific fields. They can be critical, pernickety or absent-minded. These people value material goods, money, education and ideas.

Jupiter in Libra

These subjects are sympathetic, kind, harmonious and charitable. They work best in a partnership or as part of a team, although they can be lazy and self-indulgent. They are interested in legal matters and may work in that field. They enjoy music, art, literature and culture. They need to be admired or praised and they value marriage and companionship.

Jupiter in Scorpio

These folk are often sexy, and they live life to the full. They can be dramatic and self-centred. These subjects are shrewd, ambitious and strong-willed. They can overwork or overdo almost anything to which they set their minds. These individuals may be proud and conceited but they can also relate to the underdog or to the animal world. They love a challenge and they enjoy seeking out things that are hidden, solving mysteries and solving problems. Some subjects are very drawn to the occult. They value personal achievement and strength of character.

Jupiter in Sagittarius

These subjects are optimistic, forward thinking and philanthropic. They may choose to work the law, the church or the travel trade. They are supposed to like large animals but they seem to actually prefer small ones. These people are sympathetic and kind, but they may be erratic and tactless. They are broad-minded and they enjoy travelling or being in the company of foreigners. Most of them enjoy visiting wide-open spaces. They may be a bit lazy and inclined to let things drift or they may jump from one idea to the next without getting anything done. Many of these subjects are intuitive and interested in astrology or the psychic and mystical world. They value personal freedom, independence and intelligence.

Jupiter in Capricorn

These subjects are resourceful, responsible and thoughtful. They can be stingy, penny-wise and pound-foolish, austere and cold. On the other hand, they can be productive and thorough. They work hard and may put their jobs before personal relationships. Some of these subjects can be egotistical, unsociable and unpopular, but they are deep thinkers, and they value structure and old-fashioned ideas. They may value the Earth and all that is in it, and they may seek to save it in practical ways. These people may be religious.

Jupiter in Aquarius

Humanitarian, impartial and imaginative, these subjects can be tactless, unpredictable, restless or obstinate and wilful. They are high-minded, idealistic and attached to causes, but they may be unrealistic. These subjects need a definite goal to focus upon. They can be extremely intuitive and very attracted to astrology or the occult. They work hard on group projects, and they value freedom, intellect and working for the betterment of the world.

Jupiter in Pisces.

This is a good placement for work in the medical or the caring professions. These subjects are intuitive, imaginative and artistic. They are kind, humane, romantic and idealistic, but they can become detached from reality. These people need clear goals, and they can be psychic, spiritual and attracted to the occult.

***

Saturn in Aries

This results in a seesaw personality that can be nice or nasty depending upon mood. These people are ambitious, determined and self-reliant, or jealous, defiant and impatient. They may have a good eye for mechanical matters or they may be into computing. They could be interested in military matters. They may have had a destructive parent or possibly a rough time at school, and they may have difficulty in expressing themselves or in being themselves. They can achieve high esteem, especially in the field of politics..

Saturn in Taurus

Patient, cautious, methodical and economical, these subjects can be frugal and obstinate but they know how to persevere and they may produce things of beauty. They work well under pressure but hate to be rushed. There may be a background of poverty and of life in uncongenial places, or over-materialistic parents.

Saturn in Gemini

Logical, conscientious and serious, these subjects can be deeply intellectual, very dexterous and they have the patience to complete long and complex tasks. They may be good at maths, astrology and science and they make thorough and well-prepared teachers. Their early education is poor and they may suffer from bullying at school, but they make up for it later. The father may have left home, disappeared or died. The person would have been lonely as a child, living in the world of books and imagination.

Saturn in Cancer

Shrewd, ambitious, tenacious and hard working, these subjects are very attached to their families and they may try to control them. These people are emotionally controlled and they can become melancholy or self-absorbed. One of the parents or parent figures could have made the childhood home unhappy.

Saturn in Leo

This subject could be self-assured or very self-effacing, depending upon how Saturn affects them. There is excellent organising ability and a natural attitude of authority. They may have a good deal of knowledge about something glamorous, such as jewellery or fashion. Some find it hard to relax and enjoy life. Some have bad-tempered or disciplinarian parents or ungrateful children.

Saturn in Virgo

These subjects are methodical, prudent and tidy but they can critical, faultfinding and mistrustful. They have high personal standards and they are good at keeping confidences. They are good at detailed or analytical work and may be drawn to editing or the medical world. They tend to mistrust the motives of others. They may have had cold or demanding parents.

Saturn in Libra

On one hand, these individuals may be lonely due to failed partnerships, even though they are kind, pleasant and honourable. They can work hard for a chosen goal or in order to right an injustice and they can be successful due to Saturn being exalted in Libra. Their parents are reasonable people, but there is a possibility that one of the parents was weak or deserted the family.

Saturn in Scorpio

These people are resilient and capable. They have executive ability and a shrewd idea of what will or won't work and can be very successful in business. They can hold a grudge and punish others, be ruthless, jealous, possessive and inflexible. They can also be impractical. However, they love deeply and can be very good to their loved ones.

Saturn in Sagittarius

This softens Saturn's tendency to dourness, so it's a good placement, but it can make the person hurtful and tactless or dedicated to strange causes. These subjects are forward-looking and keen on higher education for themselves and others. They can be religious, philosophical and intellectual but they can also be fanatical.

Saturn in Capricorn

Methodical, hard working, disciplined and ambitious, these subjects advance slowly in life and overcome obstacles. They can be selfish, pessimistic and they may worry unnecessarily over money but they are generally sensible and often successful in business or politics. They can have a dry sense of humour. They are attached to their parents and other family members. These people choose partners who are much older or much younger than they are.

Saturn in Aquarius

These folk are serious, intellectual and good thinkers. They may have scientific or mathematical abilities. If they decide to work for causes, they do so in a thorough manner and they finish what they start. These people are reserved but quite sociable, especially towards their families and their trusted friends. They also have a dry and witty sense of humour. They are forgiving, but also judgemental and opinionated. They can lead lonely lives.

Saturn in Pisces

This is an excellent placement for those who work in the medical profession, teaching or the church. These subjects are humanitarian, idealistic and romantic, and they implement their beliefs in a realistic manner. They can be indecisive, moody and manipulative, and their strong emotional nature can bring them problems. They need a steady partner and a secure home life.

The Impersonal Planets through the Signs

Uranus in Aries
These people are freedom loving, unconventional, positive and independent. They could be inventive engineers or craft workers. There may be unexpected events in life and the grandparents could be a strong influence.

Uranus in Taurus
These subjects have fixed opinions, and are headstrong, resourceful, disruptive and intense. They attack problems forcefully. They have sudden financial ups and downs and also strange values. They may inherit money from grandparents.

Uranus in Gemini
Versatile, imaginative and nervy, these people may have telepathic ability. They have unusual brothers and sisters or an unusual family situation, as well as an unusual education and possibly an unusual career. Grandparents could have a hand in the subject's education or upbringing.

Uranus in Cancer
These subjects may be emotionally unstable, touchy and eccentric. An original or unusual domestic life may be chosen. They may have had a disrupted childhood, possibly brought up by grandparents.

Uranus in Leo
Hard working, adventurous, bold, defiant and powerful, these subjects may have interesting children or be interested in child development. They may be domineering and eccentric. Such subjects may have strange grandparents who were a strong influence in childhood or a powerful father.

Uranus in Virgo

There may be an interest in diet and health, cleanliness and alternative therapies. These subjects have good critical faculties and could be inventive teachers. They may be funny about food and they may have strange but rather distant grandparents.

Uranus in Libra

This signifies a dual personality that is both charming and disruptive. There is definite evidence of an unusual marriage or partnerships. They have literary ability and a fondness for television and the media. They are scientific, artistic, and possibly psychic. They may have loving grandparents.

Uranus in Scorpio

These people could be somewhat odd, swinging between being very helpful to others and then being dictatorial or distant. These subjects can be independent, determined and emotional but they can also be vindictive and explosive. Weird grandparents may have brought them up.

Uranus in Sagittarius

These people may be reckless and independent with some really original ideas about life, love, religion and the world in general. They reach out for higher knowledge or spiritual understanding. They may have grown up with grandparents who emigrated from one country to another, bringing knowledge of a different culture with them.

Uranus in Capricorn

These people may be interested in politics and they may live through a time of change. With penetrating minds and an authoritative manner, they may be rebellious and domineering or thoughtful and thorough. They come from family backgrounds that encourage their ambition.

Uranus in Aquarius

Resourceful and clever, intuitive and imaginative, these subjects may be into astrology or the psychic sciences. They have original ideas for reform and an interest in science. They are modern thinkers who are humanitarian and idealistic but they may be cool and mechanical. They seem to come from clever families.

Uranus in Pisces

This person will look into religion and mysticism. Highly intuitive, secretive and emotional with changeable moods, they may have mediumistic dreams. They are great ups and downs in life, with scandals and losses, balanced by sudden gains in status and wealth.

***

Neptune in Aries

These subjects have unusual personalities. They are emotional, romantic and artistic, and they love to travel. They may be interested in psychic research or some strange form of politics. This links people to the enterprising eras of discovery and development.

Neptune in Taurus

Musical, artistic and creative, they may work in the arts. They experience fluctuating finances. This links to the early stages of modern banking and business practices, also to a better way of life for most people.

Neptune in Gemini

These people are mystical, imaginative and prophetic with many new ideas on religion. They may be peevish and gossipy. This links to the spread of education for ordinary people.

Neptune in Cancer

These individuals are emotional and imaginative. They choose artistic home surroundings and they love the sea. This links to the start of ordinary people having decent housing and enjoying the cinema and theatre.

Neptune in Leo

There is an interest in glamour and escapist entertainment, so they love dance, film and the theatre. They are dramatic, artistic, magnetic and often kind hearted. This links people to the glamour of Hollywood during the Second World War.

Neptune in Virgo

Critical of orthodox religion, these subjects may be intellectual, intuitive and sensitive. They may suffer from allergies to food and drugs, although they are interested in nutrition and health. This links people to the Welfare State, National Insurance and the National Health Service.

Neptune in Libra

These subjects are gentle, artistic, romantic and keen on love. They also love music and the poetry inherent in much popular music. They dislike war and materialism. This connects people to the hippy and New Age era, a lack of interest in marriage and the end of illegitimate children.

Neptune in Scorpio

These people are sensitive, emotional and mediumistic. They may be secretive with a strong sense of justice. They overturn their parents' religious or social beliefs. This links people to improvements in medicine but also new health scares.

Neptune in Sagittarius

These individuals love travel and new ideas. They may look for new religious ideas. There is an interest in research, language and literature. This is when religion begins to grow again, including the revival of Wicca and paganism.

Neptune in Capricorn

This links practical ability with business insight and inspiration. Changes in religious outlook start to connect with ideas, such as power, domination, control and money in some cases and a love the earth and a dislike of materialism in others.

Neptune in Aquarius

Natives with this sign will look for new ideas, philosophies and ways of life. They may be idealistic but unrealistic and they may have new ideas about religion, love, marriage, romance and the social order. This links people with different ideas about marriage, gay marriage and the rise of different religious ideas.

Neptune in Pisces

Mysterious religions are signified here, and this generation might reach the heights or sink into the depths of depravity, possibly making their religion an excuse for their bad behaviour. Allergies and strange ailments will abound, including Corona Virus.

The Dwarf Planets through the Signs

Pluto in Gemini – 1900 to 1914

- A time of scientific discoveries and new means of transport.
- The rise of socialism and trades unions.
- Universal education in Europe and America.
- Beginning of film, which educates and entertains.

Pluto in Cancer – 1914 to 1939

- The horror of the First World War and families broken up by the war.
- Fight for better rights for ordinary people.
- Depression and financial desperation.
- House prices tumble but much good council house building.
- Government impinges more on the lives of ordinary people.

Pluto in Leo – 1939 to 1958

- Wars of ideology, bringing death on a mega scale.
- Famines and disease in other countries.
- Rationing and austerity in the West
- Rise of Welfare State, National Health Service, child welfare.
- The Marshall Plan and post war reconstruction.
- Rise of democracy but also communism.

Pluto in Virgo – 1958 to 1971

- Changes in social and sexual rules.
- Improvements in health, living and working conditions.
- Analytical attitude to world problems.
- Rise of TV news broadcasting and TV age.
- The Vietnam War, civil rights, women's liberation.
- Beginning of space exploration.

Pluto in Libra – 1971 to 1983

- Changes in methods of business.

- New attitudes to marriage and family life.
- Women's lib and racial equality.
- Striving to end war and nuclear threat.
- Real interest in ecology.
- First real power struggles over oil and fuel.

Pluto in Scorpio - 1983 to 1995
- Soviet Union and communism ends.
- Reduction in nuclear arms, but changes in power bases.
- AIDS, but also openness about sexual behaviour.
- Changes in family structure.
- Changes in oil and fuel industry.
- Rise of terrorism.

Pluto in Sagittarius - 1995 to 2008
- Rise of Islam.
- Rise of terrorism.
- Major wars in the Middle East.
- Welfare state at its height, but beginning to tail off.
- New technology changes communications.
- Ordinary people relatively well off.
- Hidden problems in banking and governments.
- Space exploration grows.

Pluto in Capricorn - 2008 to 2024
- Bad banking practices exposed.
- Fiddles and scandals in high places exposed.
- Recession and possibly depression.
- Trying to extract the West from Middle East wars, but with limited success.
- Space exploration still growing.
- Health improves in some ways but bad lifestyles take their toll.

***

Chiron in Aries - 2019 to 2027
- Accidents to the head, eyes and upper jaw.
- Desire to be independent but this is hard to achieve.
- Difficult relationship with the father.

Chiron in Taurus - 1977 to 1984

- Health issues in the throat, lower jaw or neck.
- Health issues affecting the bladder or lower spine.
- Issues in the family regarding money, goods and inheritance.

Chiron in Gemini - 1984 to 1988

- Health issues relating to the hands, arms, shoulders and lungs.
- Family problems with siblings.
- Living in a difficult neighbourhood or with difficult neighbours.
- Educational problems.

Chiron in Cancer - 1988 to 1991

- Problems with lungs, chest area or breasts.
- Difficulties with mother or mother figures.
- Hard to get or keep a nice home.

Chiron in Leo - 1991 to 1993

- Accidents and problems with the spine and heart.
- Desire for success but this is hard to achieve.
- Difficulties with father figures.

Chiron in Virgo - 1993 to 1995

- Digestive and bowel problems.
- Problems with hands, arms or shoulders.
- Problems with siblings and other relatives.

Chiron in Libra - 1995 to 1997

- Problems with kidneys or bladder.
- Problems with lower spine and mobility.
- Too much or too little discipline.
- Marriage, divorce, or partnerships very good or very bad.

Chiron in Scorpio - 1997 to 1999

- Problems with reproductive organs or bowels.
- Head injuries or problems with head and eyes.
- Financial problems, due to banking, legal or inheritance matters.
- Marriage, divorce or partnerships very good or very bad.

Chiron in Sagittarius - 1999 to 2002

- Problems with hips and thighs.

- Problems with siblings.
- Delayed or poor education.
- Problems with travel, religion or the law.

Chiron in Capricorn - 2002 to 2005
- Health issues with knees, bones and ears.
- Problems with skin, lungs and arteries.
- Financial problems not of one's making.
- Responsibilities and problems related to father figures.

Chiron in Aquarius - 2005 to 2010
- Health issues with legs and ankles, also skin.
- Problems with arteries.
- Great ideas but others may not take the person seriously.
- Revolutions and changes disrupt normal life.

Chiron in Pisces - 2010 to 2019
- Health issues affecting the feet, lungs and mental state.
- Religious or political changes may disrupt life.
- Mysteries, swindles, scandals and weird events.

Chiron Transits

There still isn't much practical information around on the Chiron effect, so it's worth mentioning it here. Chiron takes around 51 years to orbit the Sun, but it has an eccentric orbit in the area between Saturn and Uranus. As an early watcher of the Chiron effect, I discovered that most people go through some kind of upheaval when Chiron reaches its "return" at around the age of fifty-one. Any transit of Chiron, from sextile, square, trine, opposition or return, will bring a dose of reality or a change of direction. It often connects with health problems, especially accidents and operations, menopause, the start of a long illness, the break-up of a partnership, falling deeply in love, the start of a new relationship, a change of career, a move of house or a change of country.

Asteroids

I sometimes use Ceres and Vesta in readings because they have pleasant effects on a chart, which helps to balance the preponderance of harsh influences. Ceres brings financial benefits in both the natal and transiting chart, while Vesta improves home life.

Angles, Hemispheres, Elements and Qualities

The Ascendant (Asc)

The ascendant is the degree of the sign of the zodiac that was coming up over the horizon when a new baby made his first cry, or at the start of a new enterprise. You can see the Asc in action by running an Astro-Cartography chart, being sure to include the ecliptic, then run a line from the person's place of birth to the Sun's rise line, and finally, to drop a line downwards from that point to the ecliptic. If none of that makes any sense to you, don't worry about it, just make up your chart in your usual way and use the Asc that your software gives you.

The ascendant relates to the kind of programming the person received in childhood from his family, school, friends and society. Thus, it has a bearing on a subject's outer manner, his appearance and the way he lives. It may determine the kind of career he takes up. The ascendant is linked to the first house and thus to a person's physical health and appearance and personal manner. Nothing is cut and dried in astrology, but the ascendant is a strong modifying factor on a chart and it is often more obvious than the Sun sign. Any planet that is close to the ascendant will have a powerful effect on the subject's personality and lifestyle.

The Descendant (Dsc)

This is the cusp of the seventh house and it is always found opposite the ascendant. We tend to choose people as partners, lovers and colleagues who have the kind of character and values which can be found in the sign on the descendant. Planets close to the descendant can show the influence that others have on us or perhaps the way we think about relationships.

The Midheaven,
Also Known as the Medium Coeli or MC

The MC denotes the direction a person tries to take in life and it can indicate career choices, what someone tries to achieve and the subject's reputation. Planets around the Midheaven suggest a need for public recognition, and they can denote a search for something that the father failed to provide. The MC can also show the choice of marriage partner.

The Nadir,
Also Known as the Imum Coeli or IC

This relates to a person's past, family background or where they came from. It also speaks about his or her home and domestic circumstances. It concerns the circumstances that prevailed at the beginning of a subject's life and those that might apply at the end of life. It may throw some light on relationships with the parents, especially the mother. Planets in this area show a need for financial or emotional security.

Hemispheres

Bear in mind that any astrological chart points to the south! So if you want to make sense of how it works, sit or stand facing the south and look at the position of the sun in the sky.

The upper hemisphere contains the 7th, 8th, 9th, 10th, 11th and 12th houses. A subject with most of his planets in this part of his chart will not be too deeply affected by the actions of other people and he may be able to distance himself from those around him. He keeps his eye on the main chance or on his own needs and feelings, but also on the needs of humanity in general. He needs a career or lifestyle that fulfils him. If the planets are grouped in the 8th, 9th or 12th houses, the subject will have strong spiritual needs and will see life in terms of related spiritual values. If in the 10th, he will be ambitious and politically astute, while if they are in the 11th, he will be interested in humanity in general and education in particular.

The lower hemisphere contains the 1st, 2nd, 3rd, 4th, 5th and 6th houses, and someone who has most of his planets in this part of the chart will be sensitive to the moods and feelings of those around him and he may suffer a good deal as a result. His family may bully him or wear him down, or he may live through his family rather than for himself. He may be too subjective or he may choose to do most of his thinking and working at home.

The eastern hemisphere contains the 10th, 11th, 12th, 1st, 2nd and 3rd houses. A subject who has most of his planets in this area of the chart is a self-starter who chooses his own path through life and sets his own boundaries. He is not happy living off other people or being kept by someone else, and other people don't do much for him. When the planets are in the first three houses, the subject is self-absorbed and convinced that his own opinions are the only ones that matter.

The western hemisphere contains the 4th, 5th, 6th, 7th, 8th and 9th houses. A subject who has most of his planets in this area of the chart will use diplomacy to keep others on his side. Others may look after him or he may spend his life supporting and motivating others. When the majority of planets are in the 6th, 7th and 8th houses, he will use his energy to fulfil the needs of others. This subject may bring up several children.

The Elements

The element of fire:
The key ideas here are of enthusiasm, initiative, intuition, optimism and faith in the future. Fiery people never quite relinquish their childhood, so they are in tune with young people and young ideas. These entertaining people display considerable egotism but also spontaneous generosity. They get things started, create action and pace but they may leave the details to others. Fire sign people are quick to grasp an idea and they approach life with a degree of sportsmanship as if it were a kind of game. These people find it difficult to save money but they can usually earn their way out of disaster. Fire subjects have very hot tempers but once they have shouted and raved a little, the steam goes out of them and they settle back into their usual good-humoured nature, although Leos can hold grudges.

The element of earth:
This element is concerned with security, structure, slow growth, conventional behaviour and concrete results. Earth people are sensible, possibly rather plodding and practical in outlook. They do things thoroughly and carefully and they are unlikely to be extravagant. They are very caring towards family and friends. They hold on to their possessions and may be a little too money-minded at times. They try to finish any job that they start. There is a sense of maturity with these people but perhaps a lack of spontaneity. Their virtue is their reliability and their vice, fussiness. They are slow to rouse to anger but they can be very angry indeed if hurt.

The element of air:
This element is concerned with networks of all kinds, along with education, theoretical ideas, finding answers to questions and all-round enlightenment. These subjects may be serious-minded or they can be chirpy, streetwise people. They can be found expounding on a pet idea or arguing a point over anything from a literary reference to a sporting event. They make good journalists and shopkeepers, teachers and travellers because they are always up to date. Although kind-hearted, they tend to forget their friends when out of sight. They are not especially hot-tempered but they can become extremely angry over an injustice.

The element of water:
Water people respond slowly when asked a question and they may appear slow when grasping a new concept. However, they are not slow or stupid, it's just that they need time for everything to filter through their highly intuitive aura before it hits the brain. Water people are slow to change, preferring to stay on a tried and tested path. Their chief need is financial security, and this is sometimes hard for them to obtain. Faithful, loyal and rather tense, water people have an intuitive feeling for what is right for themselves and their families. They are usually sensible and reliable but if their feelings are stirred up, they can react strangely. They can become depressed and ill if they are not loved enough. Water people are very sympathetic to the needs of others and they appreciate artistic or creative matters. These people don't lose their temper easily but they can be very destructive to themselves or others when they do, but their biggest problem is that they make decisions based on their feelings rather than on logic.

The Qualities

The cardinal signs:
Cardinal sign people are ambitious for themselves, their families and if appropriate, their organisation. There is a dynastic feel to all these signs and, once they have found the right avenue for their talents, they go as far as they can. They don't listen to others very much as they only really value their own opinions and they like having their own way.

The fixed signs:
Fixed people don't like change. They stick to their jobs, homes and families through thick and thin and they have the strength and

determination to see things through. They may stick in a bad job or a bad relationship too long. These subjects are stubborn and determined, and they work hard to obtain financial security and to keep it.

The mutable signs:

Mutable people have the courage to go their own way and do things differently, so many choose an alternative lifestyle, change countries or just life in a way that is different from the rest of their family and friends. They are adaptable and they will fit in with most situations and most types of people. They try to reach a point of contact or understanding between themselves and even the oddest people. Their thinking is wider and more lateral than the other two types and their friendliness and good humour make them good fun to be with. They have jobs or lifestyles that lead many people or things to pass through their hands. They don't usually have happy childhoods, and they can suffer from loneliness at times.

The Houses

There are twelve houses on a birthchart, starting from the ascendant and working their way round the chart in an anti-clockwise direction. There are many house systems to choose from, and each country seems to have its favourites, as do many astrologers. We tend to use those that feel right, and our choices are entirely subjective. I use Placidus for character reading, but I will also check out equal house, especially when it comes to predictive work.

Each house is linked to a sign:

HOUSE	SIGN
First	Aries
Second	Taurus
Third	Gemini
Fourth	Cancer
Fifth	Leo
Sixth	Virgo
Seventh	Libra
Eighth	Scorpio
Ninth	Sagittarius
Tenth	Capricorn
Eleventh	Aquarius
Twelfth	Pisces

Each house is linked to one or more planets:

HOUSE	PLANET
First	Mars
Second	Venus
Third	Mercury
Fourth	Moon
Fifth	Sun
Sixth	Mercury, Chiron
Seventh	Venus
Eighth	Pluto, Mars
Ninth	Jupiter
Tenth	Saturn
Eleventh	Uranus, Saturn
Twelfth	Neptune, Jupiter

If the ascendant falls near the beginning of a sign, the sign will occupy most of the first house, but if it falls towards the end of the sign, there will be a small part of the sign in the first house, but the next sign along will take up most of the first house. I am a good example of this, as I have Gemini rising, but my ascendant is 25 deg. Gemini, so only four degrees fall in Gemini and most of my first house is Cancer. The shape and layout of the houses can be further complicated by the house system that you decide to use. (The thirty degrees in each sign run from 0 deg. to 29 deg.)

The First House
Similar to Aries and Mars, and
it is an Angular house.

Many people resemble their rising sign, and it often represents the person's outward appearance and mode of behaviour, but sometimes the Sun sign or some other factor is stronger. Unfortunately, there are no hard and fast rules and one has to approach each chart with an open mind.

The first house should rule the subject's looks, outer manner and some aspects of health. It may throw light on the way he was treated or taught as a child. His behaviour and manner may be the result of his background and upbringing. It can show how he approaches life, the career he chooses or where he directs his energies. Planets are found in this house are likely to have a strong influence.

The Second House
Similar to Taurus and Venus, and
it is a Succedent house.

This is concerned with personal possessions and personal finances, along with basic needs such as food, clothing and shelter. It is concerned with values, priorities and self-esteem, some aspects of the feelings and of relationships, and the five senses. Along with the first house, it can refer to a person's image.

The Third House
This is similar to Gemini and Mercury, and
it is a Cadent house.

This house rules brothers and sisters, cousins and other relatives of one's own generation, along with neighbours and local matters. Traditionally, it concerns local travel and short journeys but this could now be extended into any kind of travel that is normal for the subject. It rules communications and information of all kinds, plus paperwork, negotiations, and basic education. This house shows the capacity to think and such things as a talent for figure work or dexterity, or the lack of these things.

The Fourth House
Similar to Cancer and the Moon, and
it is an angular house.

In all but the equal house system, this house starts at the IC. This rules the parents, especially the mother figure or the person who nurtured the subject. It concerns the childhood home and domestic circumstances throughout life, as well as land or property matters. Traditionally, it represents the beginning and the end of life.

The Fifth House
Similar to Leo and the Sun,
this is a Succedent house.

This house rules anything that the subject creates, which may relate to artistry, music and creativity. It also rules the creation of a family and especially children. It rules pleasures, holidays and hobbies which are fun or amusing; love affairs and any spontaneous affection, such as that for pets, small children and so on. It also rules time off from the struggle of daily life, love affairs and fun.

The Sixth House
Similar to Virgo and Mercury (also possibly, Chiron),
this is a cadent house.

Traditionally, this is the house of employers and employees, so it has much to do with work and duty. This house also rules health and prevention of illness, food and the harvest, and duties to others. It's associated with pets, especially small animals.

The Seventh House
Similar to Libra and Venus,
this is an angular house.

This house is linked to open relationships and all that happens in connection with them, so it rules marriage and partnerships but also open enemies. This house rules business partnerships and agreements, and many kinds of legal agreements between two parties, such as contracts and so on.

The Eighth House
Similar to Scorpio, Pluto and Mars,
this is a Succedent house.

This house is connected with those heavy-duty turning points in life, such as birth, death, marriage, divorce and commitments of all kinds. It links to shared resources and other people's money, which in turn concerns such things as banking, legacies, taxes, corporate matters and everything linked to the care of other people's goods or those that are shared. It can rule dealings with the police, crime and forensics, as well as surgery. Resentment and hatred are hidden in his house, as are sexual secrets and even hidden abuse of many kinds. This house can show karmic difficulties.

The Ninth House
Similar to Sagittarius and Jupiter,
this is a cadent house.

This house is concerned with escape, freedom and expanding one's horizons, so it denotes foreign travel and dealings with foreign people and goods. It can relate to business that crosses frontiers. It tests limits, which means that it's concerned with the law and the rules of religion and belief. It links to further education and an interest in spiritual and philosophic matters. This house is said to connect to a dealings with large animals, gambling and sports.

The Tenth House
Similar to Capricorn and Saturn,
this is an Angular house.
In all but the equal house system, this house starts at the MC. It rules the subject's aims and ambitions, what he or she would like to achieve in life and the status that the person strives to reach. It is linked to parents, especially father figures, and to people in authority who can be helpful or obstructive. It can rule the subject's immediate circle along with his or her achievements, responsibilities and public image (along with the first and second houses). This house represents limiting circumstances and limits to opportunity.

The Eleventh House
Similar to Aquarius, Uranus and Saturn,
this is a Succedent house.
This house rules friends and acquaintances, and detached or more distant relationships. It's also associated with education and the acquisition of knowledge. It concerns activities that affect groups of people, such as clubs, societies, unions, workshops, political groups and so on. It can be associated with intellectual pleasures such as crosswords, but also astrology. It shows the person's hopes and wishes.

The Twelfth House
Similar to Pisces, Neptune and Jupiter,
this is a Cadent house.
This house rules service to others, self-sacrifice and care for the weak. It also concerns self-undoing, escapism, the mystical side of life and the occult. It talks of the unconscious and therefore of deeply hidden urges or needs, also the need to escape through alcohol or drugs. It is associated with sensitivity, creativity and artistry, sports and music. Also secrets and hidden liaisons.

Planets in Houses

The planets don't work in quite the same way in the houses as they do in the signs. The sign modifies the character of the planet, but the house shows how the planet is used. For example, Mercury in Virgo is analytical in character, but when in the second house, it would be used to gain wealth or to conserve one's money or possessions, and in the ninth house, it would be used to stretch the mind and gain a good education or to travel for study or business.

The Sun

First House
These subjects are concerned with themselves and the projection of their personalities. They can be sunny, cheerful and fun. They achieve some kind of celebrity. They enjoy the company of children and young people.

Second House
Centred on money and possessions, these subjects should be wealthy. They are materialistic or they may simply want a comfortable life. They have a high earning capacity and can be possessive over goods or people. They are cautious over decisions and they usually seek harmonious relationships with others.

Third House
Fluent talkers who need to communicate. They may work in journalism, the media, teaching or writing, or they may deal with neighbourhood matters. These people can be closely attached to sisters, brothers and cousins. They can lack patience and consistency.

Fourth House

These subjects are interested in home and family and they will help family members. They are conscious of background and family history and may take up genealogy or history as a hobby. They may be collectors. Many choose to work from home. They have a caring personality but they can be shy or withdrawn. Some of them lose out on parental love in childhood. Excellent listeners.

Fifth House

These subjects can be over-generous. They need to enjoy life to the full but may want more than is possible. They are very fond of children. They may be musical, creative or sporty. Some have many love affairs while others are unusually faithful to one partner. Stubborn. They are drawn to showbiz and glamorous professions.

Sixth House

Hardworking with good organising ability and a head for details but forgetful about things that don't interest them. These people are health conscious and they can be hypochondriacs. They can be difficult and exacting, and they are better talkers than listeners.

Seventh House

These subjects want to be liked. They enjoy marriage and working partnerships. They want to express themselves but they may do what others dictate. These subjects may be lazy or prefer to lean on others who make decisions for them. Good looking, musical, creative, popular.

Eighth House

Interested in the afterlife, possibly involved in deeds, wills and official matters related to life and death. These subjects can be interested in medicine, forensic investigation, detective work or the occult. These people have powerful but difficult personalities. They may be involved with other people's finances.

Ninth House

Many of these subjects choose to live in different countries from those in which they grew up. They are tolerant of different cultures and they may have a flair for languages. Broadminded outlook. They may be attracted to religion, education or the law. Some choose to work with animals, while others become involved in publishing or broadcasting.

Tenth House

Interested in career, status, advancement, politics and public image. They may have a vocation that causes them to neglect family and friends, because they are hardworking, dedicated and somewhat austere.

Eleventh House

May officiate in clubs and societies or work for the betterment of humanity. Friendly and open-minded, they try to make others happy. They can be detached in personal relationships and not particularly fond of family life.

Twelfth House

These subjects may work alone and they may also choose to live alone. They are very sensitive and introverted. They may be interested in art, music and creative pursuits and they may want to escape from reality from time to time. These people are interested in the occult and they may be quite clairvoyant. They may have hidden sides to their personality that only comes out after one lives or works with them for a while. They are natural strategists.

The Moon

First House

These subjects are strongly affected by their mothers and the relationship is either very good or pretty awful, but always unforgettable. The emotions are strong and the subject is sensitive, but the feelings and emotions can be suppressed, especially in males. These people can take their anguish out on a partner, or try to heal the world or put the environment to rights. Childhood experiences can lead to difficult behaviour patterns in adult life. This may be eased if the Moon is in a feminine sign or if it is well aspected. It can indicate a talent for art or music, an interest in the food trades, or a desire to save the planet. The sign which is rising is strongly emphasised and the effects of the Moon will be coloured by whatever sign is involved.

Second House

These subjects need security, so they may save or collect articles of value. They may simply surround themselves with clutter in order to feel safe and secure. These people have good business instincts but their income and their luck can ebb and flow. Their feelings towards their loved ones are very strong and they can be possessive.

Third House

Attached to their siblings or to a neighbourhood that they know well. They may take responsibility for other family members. Their early education is unsettled and they may never really find it easy to concentrate deeply or to stick to one idea.

Fourth House

Maternal and home loving, these subjects may demand more love and affection than anyone can reasonably give them. They may cling to old lovers, children, friends and their past. They are loyal to their family and friends. These people may be interested in history or objects with a provenance. Some choose to work from home, or to work with children in a family atmosphere.

Fifth House

Outgoing and rather dramatic or over-emotional, they may be attracted to a glamorous lifestyle, possibly in the world of the arts, the stage or sports.

Alternatively, they might fill their homes and their lives with children. They may marry someone who has children or they may teach.

Sixth House
These subjects may have been ailing in childhood, or they may be obsessed by health, hygiene or food. They may work from home or move to be close to their work. They may grow up with a demanding mother or they may in their turn be difficult to live with. They are hard workers and good with details.

Seventh House
May be emotionally vulnerable and dependent, needing a strong, maternal partner or they may try to smother or control others. They are very interested in business matters and they make successful working partnerships.

Eighth House
Interested in psychic or intuitive subjects with strong powers of ESP. They may be preoccupied with life, death and the spiritual side of things. Sex is another strong interest for these subjects. These people may become involved in public finances or they may be strongly influenced by a partner's financial position. They have a talent for business and can be extremely successful in business partnerships.

Ninth House
They have many interests, particularly ecology, animals, legal matters and spirituality. May pursue an interest in a variety of esoteric interests and they may be keen on languages. They usually travel a good deal and they may choose to live or work in a different country from the one in which they grew up. Some marry foreigners. They may write or broadcast. These subjects often carry around resentment from their childhood, perhaps due to difficult sibling relationships.

Tenth House
These subjects work very hard, either because they want to or because they have to in order to keep their families and homes in tact. Life can be hard. Their careers may take precedence over their private lives. They may be drawn to politics or public service and they may achieve wealth or fame, although this can be at the cost of their family life. Their families may be drawn into the public world (such as a politician's husband or wife).

Eleventh House

These subjects are keen on friends, clubs and group activities, so they are very sociable but not always so keen on family life. Some are happier at work than at home. Their objectives are changeable and their interests varied. They have many friends and acquaintances.

Twelfth House

These subjects need time (sometimes years) in order to cope with their childhoods and their feelings towards parents, previous spouses or other members of their families. They may learn hard lessons through relatives. They appear tough but they are very soft inside and they are easily hurt. In some cases, the proximity of the Moon to the ascendant makes these subjects similar to those who have the Moon in the first house. There may be a hidden and unresolved problem that has been left over from the subject's childhood.

Mercury

First House

These subjects are clever and literate but if Mercury is afflicted, they can find thinking, talking or writing difficult. Similarly, they can be computer and accounts wizards or unable to cope with numbers. They try to make an intellectual impact on the world. They can speak without thinking and hurt others with their words. They can push their friends and relatives away by this behaviour. Some overrule feelings with logic, while others are too self-centred.

Second House

Businesslike and business-minded. Possibly large scale wheeler-dealers. Practical and dexterous. Good craftsmen or musicians. Interested in food and cookery. Good with words and music.

Third House

Keen on education, good teachers. They may be closely involved with brothers and sisters, neighbours or neighbourhood matters. Local travel and vehicles could figure strongly in their lives. They may release pent up tension by writing poetry or music.

Fourth House

These subjects are fond of their home surroundings and they may choose to work from home. Maternal and domesticated, they make a point of talking and listening to their children and they are also keen on educating them. These people may be interested in history or collecting things that have a past. They can work from home, possibly writing historical novels.

Fifth House

May teach or be intellectually involved with children. Good at intellectual games but easily bored by work that requires attention to detail or a rigid routine. They want love and sex; they see sex as an essential part of communication, but they also need conversation.

Sixth House

These subjects have very analytical minds and they make excellent secretaries. They can be academic, musical or good at craft and design. They may be nervous, fussy or health-conscious. They find it hard to plan or to look forward with optimism, and they may suffer from a low sense of self-esteem. Some talk incessantly about nothing.

Seventh House

These subjects seek an intellectual rapport with others. They are good friends and also excellent diplomats or liaison officers. They have a good attitude to marriage and working partnerships. They may be better talkers than listeners. Some are excellent designers or craftsmen. If Mercury is afflicted, these subjects may be prone to illness.

Eighth House

Successful businessmen and women who have clever ideas. They are deep thinkers. They may be interested in the occult, religion and the afterlife. They may be keen on reading or writing thrillers or working in the undertaking industry. Their emotions are deep but they may be expressed in an intellectual manner. They have good concentration but afflicted Mercury can cause blockages in the thinking processes.

Ninth House

Good students and teachers with a flair for English or foreign languages. They may have too many ideas to bring any of them to fruition and they need to apply themselves conscientiously.

Tenth House

Can be drawn to a career in communications or a business that has a communicative basis. They need a mental outlet or they can become unhappy or frustrated.

Eleventh House

These subjects enjoy being involved with clubs and societies and they have many friends. They are approachable and friendly, although they can be sarcastic and tactless at times. They have wide-ranging ideas about politics.

Twelfth House

Inward looking and secretive, their inner feelings are very important to them. They are sensitive, thoughtful and kind. Some are attracted to mysticism and they may write or compose music on these themes. These people may have problems in connection with their work or their health and they need a happy and stable marriage in order to function successfully.

Venus

First House
Good looking. This is a good placement for models, starlets or work in the fashion or glamour industry. Interested in art, music, fashion, hair and makeup, and things of beauty. They enjoy flattery. They can become wealthy. Charming.

Second House
Could collect or create attractive and valuable artefacts. Could be interested in the arts or the business side of art or beauty. Clever business people who are materialistic. May be interested in craftwork, fashion, makeup, cookery and gardening. Sensual and charming.

Third House
Sociable and friendly. They get on well with siblings, relatives and neighbours. Could attract wealthy or influential friends or colleagues. Can study successfully, especially if the chosen subject has an artistic, musical, cultural or beauty bias. Could be extravagant, especially where the family is concerned. Could collect valuable items of an intellectual nature, such as books. They make good agents or liaison officers.

Fourth House
These subjects make beautiful homes with lovely decor, flower arrangements, etc. May be extravagant, especially where the family is concerned. Could be successful antique collectors or dealers, or may succeed in the fields of insurance, property or small businesses. Could have wealthy parents, especially the mother.

Fifth House
Children are liked, may work with them in some way. These subjects' children should become rich or successful in some glamorous industry. Love of glamour and the fun side of life. Could enjoy flirtation, love affairs, travel, games, sports, gambling and all kinds of amusements and treats. May be very creative and artistic, also fond of music. Could have very creative children.

Sixth House
These subjects need to work in pleasant surroundings with good working conditions. May choose a glamorous career. They dislike hard physical or

dirty work. May be health-conscious, but basically strong, unless Venus is afflicted. Will gain money and influence through work.

Seventh House
These people could marry for money but even if they marry for love, they could still find themselves in easy circumstances as a result. Good placement for a happy marriage or for marriage to a successful partner. Affectionate and loving, but needing validation and encouragement from others.

Eighth House
Very intense and rather jealous feelings. May inherit or marry money. Could make career out of the police, medical, or some other kind of diagnostic or investigative work.

Ninth House
These subjects will well at school or university and they will certainly enjoy their time there. They may partner people from other countries. May make money from the travel trade or will travel for fun. May inherit money or obtain it through a second marriage or through in-laws. Could become happily involved in spiritual or religious matters, possibly through marriage. May make a career in the law, arbitration or liaison work.

Tenth House
These subjects should have happy and successful careers, especially in something that makes money and also brings fame. Could work in a feminine or glamour career. Good manner with people, especially in business. Could make money by being associated with influential people.

Eleventh House
Diplomatic, discreet and good with people. Could be happy working for clubs, societies or with specialised groups of people. Clever politicians. Could have rich or influential friends. Powerful inner fantasy life.

Twelfth House
Attracted to the occult or to mysticism. May have secret love affairs or a need for seclusion and time alone. Creative, imaginative, artistic and musical. Not terribly practical.

Mars

First House
These subjects have assertive personalities and they may be pushy, domineering and difficult. Alternatively, the Mars energy can be channelled into sport, adventure, the military life, pioneering or exploration. They may be impulsive, passionate, reckless and full of daring. These subjects can have red hair and a hot temper to go with it. Alternatively, they may have a mole, wart, strawberry or other mark on the head or face. They can suffer from headaches, head injuries or high blood pressure.

Second House
Aggressive money-makers who are competitive in business or in any sphere where land, possessions and money are concerned. They may have wonderful singing voices or simply loud voices that they use to dominate a conversation. These subjects can be high earners but they can also be extravagant. The throat is sensitive.

Third House
These subjects could be keen students both at school and later in life. They have quick and active minds. These people are protective towards their families and, either especially close to, or antagonistic towards their siblings. They can be argumentative or verbally aggressive. Alternatively, they may use words as part of a job, for instance as a writer, broadcaster or salesperson. These subjects are unlikely to be attracted to a slow or stupid partner. The arms, shoulders, wrists and hands are weak points, as are the lungs.

Fourth House
These subjects work hard in the home and are very attached to their homes and families. This placement can be a considerably softening factor in a hard and aggressive chart but it can be the worst thing in the world in a soft chart. These subjects may enjoy carpentry, car maintenance and so on. They may move house fairly frequently and they may make money out of property. They can be quarrelsome in the home or they may simply shout rather ineffectually at their spouses and children. They may whine about supposed problems or about their health. They need to connect with the loved one on the deepest level. The breasts, lungs and stomachs are sensitive.

Fifth House

These subjects are usually strong and robust. They are keen on sports and games and may be very competitive. They make excellent salesmen and women. They can be pushy parents who want their children to compete and win. They are good with children and young people and they may work or spend their spare time with them. Passion may be channelled into work or creativity rather than lovemaking. The spine and heart are weak spots.

Sixth House

These subjects can work very hard when their interest is aroused but they can switch off and simply serve time if their jobs don't hold their interest. Some are hard on subordinates, using their considerable communications skills to cutting effect, while others with this placement are kind and thoughtful to other people. These people make good critics and they can use their critical skills to hurt or to amuse. Some of them talk incessantly, others are fussy, but they bring more pain to themselves than they do to others. The skin, bowels and intestines may be sensitive.

Seventh House

An energetic attitude to marriage and partnerships. Can be quarrelsome and the cause of their own disappointments in relationships. Some people with this placement wait for others to validate them because they have no clear idea of their own worth. Passionate. The kidneys, bladder and other internal organs can be weak.

Eighth House

Attracted to the medical profession, especially surgery. Butchery is another possible career as are mining, engineering, the armed forces or weaponry. Can be keen on detection and investigation, forensic or insurance matters. There may be a deep interest in death or the afterlife. These subjects can be passionate, jealous and possibly conscience-ridden. They may have health problems relating to the reproductive organs or the lower back. The throat can be sensitive too.

Ninth House

These subjects are more active than intellectual. They make good sportspeople or adventurers, being interested in travel, often to unknown regions. They love to hunt, and may chase the opposite sex. These people have a well-developed sense of fair play and they may be keen lawyers. They may choose to work in the travel trade or the legal, educational, literary or religious professions. Their hips and legs may be weak spots.

Tenth House

Can be hard, energetic workers who reach the top alone. These subjects can be ruthlessly ambitious. They may be attracted to politics, engineering or the armed forces. Very big business enterprises attract them, as does banking. Depending upon other factors on the chart, these people have good family relationships. Others can concentrate their energies on their ambitions. Their weak spots are the skin, ears, teeth, bones, knees and shins.

Eleventh House

Clubs and societies are liked and group work or group activities of all kinds appeal. These subjects make wonderfully enthusiastic friends but they can fall out with others just as quickly as they fall in with them. They are attracted to causes and may be interested in politics. The ankles and circulation are the weak spots.

Twelfth House

These subjects live a rich inner life and they will spend some part of their lives on an inward or spiritual journey. They don't have an aggressive bone in their bodies and they may be unassertive and self-sacrificial. Their weak spots are their feet and legs, their circulation and in some cases, their lungs or body fluids.

Jupiter

First House
Broad-minded and cheerful. These subjects are lucky in life, either making money easily or attaching themselves to partners who become rich. Attracted to travel, education, publishing and broadcasting, religion or the law. They learn a great deal about whatever is represented by the sign that this planet occupies.

Second House
These subjects are lucky with money and possessions, but while they can make money easily but they may be too generous or open-handed to keep it. They can earn money dealing with foreigners or foreign goods. Landowning, farming, animal husbandry or some other form of outdoor life can feature in their lives.

Third House
These subjects get on well with siblings and neighbours. They are quite studious and successful academically at school or later in life. They have a deep interest in communications and they may drive, write or travel as part of their working lives.

Fourth House
Good relationships with parents and a good home life characterise this placement. May move house often or may make money out of property matters. Some inherit property while others win a share in property through the courts. They can lack perspective or be too closely focused on home or family matters. Some work from home.

Fifth House
All forms of speculation are lucky for these subjects and they are good at sports and the creative arts. They may make money from sports, art or some kind of glamour business. They may enjoy working with children. They are religious or spiritual and they may teach in a Sunday school. These subjects may have a dramatic, larger-than-life manner and they may be reckless and easily bored. Their children do well and can have lucky lives in their turn.

Sixth House
These subjects are happy at work and they enjoy what they do. They make money from working and they could inherit a business. They may work in travel, the law, education and religion. Travel interests them and they are

fond of animals. Hips and thighs may be weak or may suffer from accidents if other factors on the chart point to this.

Seventh House
This is an excellent placement for partnerships both of the working and the personal kind. Marriage may be either very good or very bad. These subjects are friendly and flirtatious and they are especially attracted to foreigners or anyone who is different in some way. Pleasant and patient personalities. Very interested in the law and all legal matters.

Eighth House
There is a strong chance that these subjects could inherit money. There may be a particularly easy or casual attitude towards death and the afterlife. These subjects may do very well from marriage and they could be attracted to partners from other countries or who are unusual.

Ninth House
These subjects may travel a lot or be interested in religious or spiritual matters. They may teach or work in the law, publishing or the media. These people are happy, lucky and sometimes reckless. They can be outspoken, eccentric or tactless. Their hips and thighs may be weak.

Tenth House
These subjects do well in their chosen career and may achieve public acclaim. They can be successful without making a great deal of effort. These people may have a rather dramatic personality. They may need a good deal of variety in their working lives. They want to leave the world a better or a happier place than when they found it.

Eleventh House
These subjects have many friends and acquaintances, some of them being rich and influential. They may have a strangely casual or a pompously high-minded attitude to others. They may embrace causes and they may use their wealth philanthropically.

Twelfth House
These people prefer to work alone and they may achieve success in something like poetry, art or dancing. They like the sea and are keen on travel. These subjects are also interested in medicine. They are talented and musical, but shy and possibly psychic.

Saturn

First House
These subjects' parents may have had difficulty in conceiving them or giving birth. They may be conscious of having lived before. These people are serious, hard working and ambitious. They take life seriously and they take a responsible attitude to all that they do. This placement can lead to fame and fortune!

Second House
These subjects work hard to make money and they succeed in due course. Success is hard-won but almost inevitable. They can be possessive and too thrifty.

Third House
A hard early life with problems at school, but success and self-education come later through their own efforts. They help their brothers and sisters and have good relations with neighbours.

Fourth House
An unhappy and deprived early life. Could have restrictive parents who may have been mean or cruel. These subjects work hard to obtain a good family and home of their own and they value these things when they have them. Their early problems may not have been due to bad parenting but to poverty or tribulation in the family.

Fifth House
These subjects may have a domineering parent (usually the father). They may lack joy, or they may work too hard and forget how to play. Alternatively, they may take a serious attitude to creative endeavours and make a great success out of these. Children may be seen as a burden but they are loved and can become successful in their turn. Some people with this placement choose not to have children or they may have difficulty in producing children.

Sixth House
There may be difficulty in connection with childbirth or with a sick child. I have found that Saturn placed here can bring difficulties in either having children or bringing them up. These subjects may suffer with bad backs or arthritis. They work hard and can be successful in the long term.

Seventh House

These people may marry late or marry someone who is much older or much younger than them. There may be restriction or frustration in marriage or as a result of marriage or business partnerships. They are faithful partners with a serious attitude to the partnership or quite frankly, they may be uninterested in their partner.

Eighth House

A careful, responsible attitude to money, especially when dealing with other people's resources, but they can be morbid and miserable. On the other hand, all these areas of life may work out well once the subject gets into middle age.

Ninth House

Deep thinkers who are dedicated to causes that benefit mankind. These subjects are happier when they get older. Long-distance travel and foreigners may bring them trouble but also status or money. These subjects may spend a lifetime searching for spiritual experiences or some kind of meaning to their lives.

Tenth House

Could be ambitious to the exclusion of social and family life. Obligations can weigh heavily. These subjects may be efficient and conscientious at work despite not enjoying their work. They may switch career in mid-life and achieve a great deal of success later on. They may achieve fame and fortune or suffer public disgrace.

Eleventh House

These subjects may take committees and group activities very seriously. They may have influential friends. Alternatively, they may be too busy with their jobs to have any friends. Elderly relatives and friends may help them to get on in life.

Twelfth House

This placement can lead to sadness and also to mental problems or an inability to express thoughts. These people may find themselves married to a partner who doesn't talk or listen to them. They may feel lonely even when surrounded by family. They may be their own worst enemy. Some turn early suffering, an ailing childhood or their own super-sensitivity to suffering to advantage by becoming nurses, counsellors, astrologers or carers. These subjects learn to discipline their inner selves and may learn to cope by using meditative techniques.

Uranus

First House
Intelligent, unpredictable, individualistic. Should have a modern, scientific mind but may have unusual ideas or an unusual lifestyle. May have nerve or circulation problems. Friends could be extremely important to these subjects.

Second House
Unpredictable income. These subjects may have gains and losses on a grand scale or they may have two or more different sources of income. Sudden loss or gains of job or an unusual way of gaining possessions, resources. Non-materialist attitude to life. Friends may help these subjects find something they value in life, but their values would be unusual in any case.

Third House
Frequent changes of school or an unusual education. Lively, intelligent mind with unusual ideas. Odd experiences regarding brothers and sisters. May become close to friends and treat them like brothers and sisters. Friends may educate these subjects.

Fourth House
Unstable situation early in life, with many upheavals or changes of home. May have behaved badly as a child. May choose to live in an unusual home, or under strange circumstances later in life. May choose to make a home with a friend.

Fifth House
May have love affairs or affairs with friends who become lovers and then slip back to being friends once again. Friends offer inspiration. Lively, intelligent mind, possibly an inventor; certainly creative in an unusual way. Could have unusual pastimes or hobbies. Will have clever children.

Sixth House
Can be unpredictable at work. May have two jobs, or one very unusual one. May have sudden illnesses, such as circulation problems or paralysis. May have many friends at or through work.

Seventh House

An unusual and very free marriage is needed. Must have mental rapport with the partner. Could choose unusual partners. Working partnerships could be very odd. Could choose to live with a friend and have sexual relationships away from the home.

Eighth House

Unusual, ideas in the realm of work, money and sex. Could gain and lose money from business partnerships or marriage circumstances. May inherit. May be attached to a strange partner. May have an unusual attitude to friends.

Ninth House

Could spend a lot of time travelling and have great gains and losses as a result. Could be a very lucky gambler. Accident-prone and also prone to mental stress. Could be an excellent clairvoyant or medium. May be keen on helping groups of people to understand religion and spirituality. Could make friends through hobbies, interests or while travelling.

Tenth House

Possible sudden changes in career, because these subjects dislike routine. Far-sighted with leadership qualities. May have two jobs that are equally important to each other, but very different from one another. May make good friends at work or choose to work with groups of friends. May work with or for groups of people. Keen on education in order to get on in life. May work as astrologers.

Eleventh House

Fond of clubs, societies and group activities. They have many friends but they gain and lose them quickly. These people might be eccentric or different in some way. May be keen astrologers. Far-sighted, broad-minded, these people never stop educating themselves.

Twelfth House

These subjects may have terrific clairvoyant abilities and they may be keen on astrology. Secretive, they may harbour odd ideas and feelings. Could be very spiritual and mystical or eccentric. These people may hide their emotions or they may be confused by them or be upset by feelings of inner turmoil.

Neptune

First House

These subjects are dreamy, sensitive and artistic. They may be impractical, disorganised, chaotic and forgetful. Some are eccentric, whereas others are drawn to mystical or artistic pursuits. They are often talented, musical or artistic and some make excellent photographers. May like the sea and fishing.

Second House

May not be able to keep money for long. Usually non-materialistic in outlook. These subjects value kindness and caring for others. They may make money from mystical or other unusual interests. They may work successfully in something to do with liquids such as the oil industry, sailing, fishing, shipping, plumbing, etc. They like aesthetic or artistic objects.

Third House

These subjects are intuitive and imaginative. They may lack concentration or they may have a wonderful gift of communication through visual effects (video, photography) or through descriptive writing. Could work as a therapist. Good actor, but may be something of a drifter.

Fourth House

These subjects may love their homes but they may not keep them very tidy. Alternatively, the home may be a thing of great beauty. There should be a good relationship with the parents with an intuitive, telepathic link. May be disorganised in practical matters, but with a strong imagination or inner life.

Fifth House

Very creative and imaginative. Could have a career on the stage or something similar. These subjects tend to be escapist at times, they may prefer television and books to real life or they may simply have a strong inner life. Fond of dancing and of the sea. May love wild countryside, and trees in particular. Should have excellent rapport with small children and a good relationship with their own children.

Sixth House

Can be very creative and may work hard on their chosen projects, but otherwise, they can be lazy and uninterested in work. Interested in humanitarian causes or working in an artistic or mystical sphere. May work as a nurse, with the mentally-handicapped, or a similar kind of occupation. May have allergies. May be drawn to work near water or with liquids (cooking, hairdressing).

Seventh House
These subjects either have wonderfully happy marriages or confused and difficult ones. They may be very independent or they may lean heavily on their partners. They may have vague attitudes to life or they may be quite sensible but with a tendency to draw drunken or chaotic people to them. They may have an idealised vision of relationships. They would be taken for a ride in any kind of business or working partnership.

Eighth House
Could be very psychic and drawn to the world of mysticism, the occult or to spiritualism. Very intuitive and mediumistic, more in touch with the other side than here for much of the time. Could squander inheritance or a partner's money or alternatively a partner may take them for a fool. They may choose an artistic partner and/or enjoy an absolutely ideal relationship where sex is elevated to a spiritual fuel. They may have strange love affairs with peculiar people.

Ninth House
Could work in the fields of philosophy or religion. May be inspired. May do well in trades connected to the sea or to liquids, such as the oil industry, hairdressing, etc. Could travel a great deal and could fall in love while travelling. May be involved in strange legal cases that go on for years. These subjects help people who are in trouble or who cannot help themselves.

Tenth House
These subjects may choose a career for idealistic reasons. They may work in feminine or creative fields such as photography, art, dancing, poetry or something similar. Alternatively, they could choose nursing, working with prisoners, the mentally-handicapped, or in some other form of caring occupation. They aspire to something greater than simply earning money and they want to heal the world. Some work with liquids such as oil, the sea or the alcohol industry. They may go through many changes in life and they could be greatly helped or let

down by others in career matters. May start off well and then let everything come to naught.

Eleventh House

Idealistic, artistic and creative, these subjects may find it hard to get anything done at all. Their aims are intellectual and artistic and they are keen on groups who have the same kind of goal. Could be greatly helped or badly let down by friends. May be mystical, intuitive and interested in astrology.

Twelfth House

Likely to be interested in poetry, ballet, culture, art and music. Could be a great animal lover or a lover of people, especially those who need help. Mystical, spiritual and other-worldly. May have great sadness in life or simply be drawn inwards to a contemplative existence.

Pluto

First House
These subjects have attractive, magnetic personalities and dynamic natures. They are attracted to big business or to positions of power and authority. Their lives go in distinct phases with gains and losses every few years. Can brood and have a terrible temper. They tend to control or rule others if they can. They lose people through death or they may have brushes with death. Resentful and possibly jealous or suffer from the jealousy of others.

Second House
Can make very big money, but may lose it on a grand scale. These subjects have a good grasp of business affairs. They also have a deep need for security, and may see money and possessions as a form of this. They can be covetous or they may be hoarders.

Third House
These subjects have terrific powers of concentration and they finish the projects that they start. They can be moody and depressed at times. They may do much to help their siblings or, alternatively, they can be beastly to them. These people can make money by teaching and writing and they enjoy influencing others via the medium of words.

Fourth House
These people feel very deeply about their homes, their parents and their marriage partners. They may try to control or dominate their families and they may be too fond of their own point of view when in the home situation. They may inherit property.

Fifth House
Children are important to these subjects and they may go to a lot of trouble, either to have children or to bring them up. They may live for pleasure or they may take a serious view of pastimes, sports and so on. These people enjoy the arts and music, and they could be drawn to gambling in order to make money. Some have many affairs while others put their energies into creative schemes.

Sixth House
May be a very hard worker or may simply be too concerned with working life. These people try to reform or change their colleagues' working

practices. They may have weak health or irritable bowels and some of these problems may be due to tension.

Seventh House

Could be very good business partners but a bit overbearing. Could be demanding marriage partners, with too much emphasis on sex. Feelings are intense and jealousy is a problem, but these subjects may be on the receiving end of this kind of treatment rather than dishing it out themselves. May inherit from a partner.

Eighth House

Very intuitive, especially where money and business is concerned. May inherit from a partner. May work for the community or in a mediumistic or spiritual manner. Could be very keen on Plutonic interests such as the afterlife, death, sex, birth, medical or forensic and investigative matters. Could deal with the insides or the underneath of things, e.g. butchery, mining or simply digging out secrets. Very secretive themselves. Analytical, logical, with very searching minds. Resentful.

Ninth House

Very spiritual. These people may be bound up with foreigners or distant places. They may force their religious or spiritual views on others, or they may drag others through the courts. Could be very keen on educating themselves and others. Could be very fond of animals, or keen to travel to strange places.

Tenth House

These subjects can reach great heights of influence or they can attach themselves to influential people. They may work in fields where they can influence others or even take them over in some way. For instance, this is a good placement for hypnotherapists, anaesthetists and dream analysts. There may be powerful urges to rule and these subjects may be obsessed with dreams of grandeur. May be attracted to drugs or may work with them. Dynamic, powerful or nuts.

Eleventh House

These people may be looking for the truth and may choose astrology as a method for doing this. These subjects may have powerful and influential friends or they may try to influence groups of people or make friends of people in order to change or influence them. Mainly well-balanced and sensible, although with one or two funny ideas from time to time.

Twelfth House

These subjects have hidden talents and interests. They may go in for hidden or taboo love affairs. They may have hidden problems of a psychological kind, such as suppressed anger or hatred for something that has been done to them by others. They may strive to find some kind of mystical or astrological truth and to express this to others in the form of poetry or music.

Chiron

First House
Could have health problems in the head, brain, eyes or upper jaw. May have a difficult personality that alienates others, or may have to put up with someone like this in a partnership.

Second House
Health problems related to the lower jaw, throat and neck. May find it difficult to obtain or keep money and goods. May be over-generous.

Third House
May have health problems in connection with the bronchial tubes, shoulders, arms or hands, while the nervous system may be vulnerable. May find school difficult or have difficult brothers or sisters.

Fourth House
May have weak lungs or chest area, or digestive problems. The home life may be difficult. May have an unpleasant mother or mother figures to contend with.

Fifth House
Health problems will concern the spine and heart. May have problems related to children or one or more children may be ill or disabled in some way.

Sixth House
May suffer with bowel problems or abdominal pain. Diabetes possible. The working life will be blocked and difficult at time.

Seventh House
May suffer with inner organs, such as the pancreas, kidneys and bladder. Diabetes possible. Troubled partnerships both of a personal and a work kind.

Eighth House
May suffer with the reproductive organs or lower abdomen and lower spine. Relationships may be extremely difficult at times and that goes for business or financial ones as well as romantic ones. Sex may cause some kind of problem.

Ninth House
May suffer with hip and thigh problems, also liver trouble. May feel trapped and need to escape a bad situation. Grandparents may be difficult or second marriage could be difficult. Lack of higher education or qualifications. May have to deal with religious people who cause pain and difficulty.

Tenth House
Bones, hearing, teeth and skin will cause difficulties, along with possible asthma and eczema. The knees and shins may also be vulnerable. Blockages to career and in achieving aims and ambitions.

Eleventh House
There may be a problem with the ankles, skin, breathing, hearing, teeth and bones. Friends may need help or they may be fine until they turn on the subject and cause him a deep hurt.

Twelfth House
The feet, lungs, brain, nerves and mind may cause problems. Could be assailed by psychic events of some strange kind. Very imaginative, and drawn to healing and helping others. May suffer times of isolation or intense loneliness.

Ceres and Vesta

Both of these asteroids can bring peace in the home, or bounty of some kind, to the area of the chart that they touch.

Nodes of the Moon

There are many views on these, but the majority of astrologers consider the north node to be a point where life is difficult and lessons need to be learned, while the south is an easy area.

Aspects

Hard and Soft Aspects

Hard aspects aren't automatically bad or difficult, because this simply means that a planet is in conjunction, square or opposition to another planet or to the ascendant, descendant, midheaven or the nadir. These are the aspects that we are most likely to become aware of during the course of our lives.

Soft aspects, such as the sextile and trine are pleasant but others such as the inconjunct and semi-square can be awkward, so once again the terms refer to the geometrical type of aspect rather than the way it affects a subject.

The words good, beneficial or easy can be applied to aspects that work well for the subject, while difficult or challenging ones are building blocks that enable us to learn from experience, or they can be a handicap. Often it is by overcoming our limitations that we actually manage to succeed; therefore a bad aspect can turn out to be a blessing in disguise.

Allowable Orbs

It's rare that two planets make an exact aspect, so a few degrees either way are allowable. Astrologers used to disagree somewhat on the orbs but astrological software sets these by default, so we no longer worry much about this. You can change the default settings on your computer if you feel strongly about it.

The Aspects

ASPECT	DISTANCE BETWEEN PLANETS	EFFECT
Conjunction	0 deg.	Mainly good. But depends upon the planets involved
Semi-sextile	30 deg.	Mild effect, usually good
Sextile	60 deg.	Good, especially for intellectual matters
Quintile	70 deg.	Supposed to endow the native with brains
Square	90 deg.	Very difficult
Trine	120 deg.	Good, especially for family or creative matters
Inconjunct	150 deg.	Awkward and irritating
Opposition	180 deg.	Usually difficult, but there may be help from other people

Also Worth Mentioning

A "Yod" aspect takes its name from a Hebrew letter that is a kind of "Y" shape, and it means a double inconjunct, which happens when one planet is 150 degrees away from a planet in one direction and 150 degrees away from another planet in the other direction. This can be extremely irritating, and it may have an effect on the health of the person, or the financial aspects of his relationships with others.

There are several minor aspects, such as the bi-quintile, sesquiquadrate and others, but I suggest you leave these for now. Minor aspects and any aspect to the nodes of the moon should have a tight orb of no more than a couple of degrees.

The Body and Astrology

Signs, Planets and the Body

- Aries and Mars rule the head, eyes, brain and upper jaw.
- Taurus and Venus rule the throat and neck, along with the lower jaw.
- Gemini and Mercury rule the bronchial tubes, shoulders, arms and hands.
- Cancer and the Moon rule the lungs, digestion and breasts.
- Leo and the Sun rule the spine and heart.
- Virgo and Mercury (or possibly Chiron) rule the bowels.
- Libra and Venus rule the bladder and kidneys, along with mobility matters.
- Scorpio and Pluto rule the base of the spine and the reproductive organs.
- Sagittarius and Jupiter rule the hips, thighs and liver.
- Capricorn and Saturn rule the skin, breathing, bones, hearing, knees and shins.
- Aquarius and Uranus rule the ankles and breathing.
- Pisces rules the feet, also the lungs and nerves.

The BIG
Astrology Guide

Volume One

ASPECTS

Introduction

Introduction
I will show each planet's conjunctions, beneficial and challenging aspects here, but only as an overview because this chapter could quickly grow into a large book on its own account if I took it further.

As we go through the planets in this chapter and the subsequent ones, some aspects drop away because they will have already been dealt with earlier in this section.

The Nodes of the Moon
The Nodes of the Moon are interesting as far as household, property, family, and business plans are involved. Either node can register an improvement in these things or a setback, depending upon the aspect. If someone is born with a planet in conjunction with either node, and especially the north node, it leads to a certain amount of fame and fortune, especially if this happens to be the Sun, Moon or even Pluto.

The Angles
Planets that conjunct the ascendant are always mega-important and must be taken into consideration. Saturn is an excellent example of this, as Saturn conjunct the Asc brings success due to very hard work. Neptune conjunct the IC suggests a mystery surrounding the person's background, or drunkenness in the family. A planet on the Dsc symbolises interesting partnerships, while a planet near the MC enhances the person's reputation and may determine the kind of career she chooses. An example might be Uranus conjunct the MC, bringing a career in one job but an equally important interest in humanitarian matters.

Other Features
Planets can aspect the Part of Fortune, the Vertex, the East Point or anything else that interests you, and it is always worth studying these matters.

ASPECT	DISTANCE BETWEEN PLANETS	EFFECT
Conjunction	0 deg.	Mainly good. But depends upon the planets involved
Semi-sextile	30 deg.	Mild effect, usually good
Sextile	60 deg.	Good, especially for intellectual matters
Quintile	70 deg.	Supposed to endow the native with brains
Square	90 deg.	Very difficult
Trine	120 deg.	Good, especially for family or creative matters
Inconjunct	150 deg.	Awkward and irritating
Opposition	180 deg.	Usually difficult, but there may be help from other people

Sun Aspects

Sun Conjunct Moon
If both planets are in the same sign, the person is similar on the inside to the way she is on the outside. If the Moon is behind the Sun, the person will be a little shy, while if it is ahead of the Sun, she will be more outgoing and more emotional.

Sun Conjunct Mercury
This person is determined and somewhat closed-minded, depending upon the signs and houses involved. She is intelligent with plenty of willpower, and she is an excellent communicator who may work as a salesperson or a negotiator.

Sun Conjunct Venus
This conjunction makes for charm and good looks. The subject likes to be fair and to take a balanced view of things. Women will be helpful to this person. She may be somewhat lazy and fond of nice clothes and luxury.

Sun Conjunct Mars
Whatever the sign or house this is in, this person has the kind of personality that makes her hard to ignore. She may be competitive and argumentative, or she may be talented, hardworking, sexy and successful in life.

Sun Conjunct Jupiter
As the saying goes, some people have all the luck, and to some extent, this applies to this person. She may not have a great childhood, but she spreads her wings and succeeds in her life once she grows up. She may travel a lot or get involved in teaching.

Sun Conjunct Saturn
Saturn always has a dampening effect on any planet that it aspects, so this person may lack confidence and self-worth and have to work hard to

overcome a tough start in life. She isn't afraid of hard work and finds a way of getting ahead over time.

Sun Conjunct Uranus

This lady is unconventional, or she gets drawn into an unconventional lifestyle. She is an independent and original thinker and interested in everything unusual and a bit different. She may be highly intuitive and prone to real psychic flashes.

Sun Conjunct Neptune

This aspect is the sign of an artist or musician, or possibly someone who never quite gets her act together. This talented lady is attractive, friendly and good fun. She may be clairvoyant. Some parts of her life are chaotic, while others are well organised.

Sun Conjunct Pluto

This talented person is friendly, generous, broadminded and fun, but she can become downhearted and drink too much to make herself feel better. The sextile makes her a good teacher and the trine an artistic and creative person.

Sun Conjunct Chiron

You will be faced with problems from the past or the present that upset you, make you feel uncomfortable or even ill. You will need to deal with these issues and maybe put them permanently to rest.

Sun Sextile or Trine Mars

This will be a hectic time with lots to do and not much time in which to do it. You may have to stand up for yourself against others, and luckily, you will find the right way to do this; you will have the stomach for the fight.

Sun Sextile or trine Jupiter

This is a lucky phase where windfalls or new opportunities are possible, and if new people come into your life now, they will be helpful and useful. You may travel or soon find yourself dealing with foreigners or foreign trade.

Sun Sextile or Trine Saturn

This individual is a hard worker who keeps going when others give up. A sextile confers a good brain and a desire to study, teach or write, while the trine makes the person a practical artist, such as a wonderful decorator or gardener.

Sun Sextile or Trine Uranus

The sextile makes this person happy to take on new and untested projects and explore new ideas, while the trine makes this person happy to do anything originally and differently. This subject is honest, determined and friendly.

Sun Sextile or Trine Neptune

This is the true artist who may be a writer or illustrator if the aspect is sextile and a musician, singer, dancer or sculptor if it is trine. The person is kind and happy to help those who need a helping hand, especially if they are ill or unhappy.

Sun Sextile or Trine Pluto

There is intensity here and deep feelings. She loves mysteries, so she might work in the police or the forensic world, but she may write plays or stories about crimes, spies or that have powerful psychological content.

Sun Sextile or Trine Chiron

This is an excellent position for someone who wants to study health, nutrition, healing, medicine or anything else of the kind. This person has a sound mind and likes to explore her chosen subject. She may also be musical or at least interested in listening to music.

Sun Square, Opposition, Semi-Square or Inconjunct Moon

This individual learns to keep her feelings hidden, and she may be different on the inside to the outside. She doesn't trust others easily. She may be aware of difficulties in her family background, and she may have a home that is not as happy as it looks from the outside.

Sun Square, Opposition, Semi-Square or Inconjunct Mercury

The only aspect Mercury can make is a semi-sextile, so these aspects can't exist.

Sun Square, Opposition, Semi-Square or Inconjunct Venus

Venus can make a semi-sextile and possibly a widely orbed semi-square, making it hard to find love.

Sun Square, Opposition, Semi-Square or Inconjunct Mars

This makes the subject hard working and competitive. She may prefer to back away from a fight than being confrontational, but that doesn't mean she forgets those who hurt her. She may be sporty or a good dancer.

Sun Square, Opposition, Semi-Square or Inconjunct Jupiter
This person means well, but things tend to go wrong, possibly due to a lack of common sense or a refusal to accept boundaries. Despite the challenging nature of these aspects, the person is quite lucky and has good friends.

Sun Square, Opposition, Semi-Square or Inconjunct Saturn
The ordinarily happy nature of the Sun is dampened by Saturn, which can cause a lack of self-confidence or self-worth. This can also show a severe problem concerning the father because both planets are linked to father figures.

Sun Square, Opposition, Semi-Square or Inconjunct Uranus
This person may not fit in with others, and she may find it hard to stick to anything unless it really grips her. She may be clever and intuitive, but it can all be wasted due to a peculiar attitude towards others.

Sun Square, Opposition, Semi-Square or Inconjunct Neptune
It is all very well being dreamy, but sometimes we have to deal with reality, and this person may find it hard to do so. Artistic and intelligent but lacking common sense, this subject may have an interesting life, albeit chaotic.

Sun Square, Opposition, Semi-Square or Inconjunct Pluto
This is a very intense personality that can understand the nature of people very well, and she could become a wonderful counsellor. Still, she has to overcome her own fears, resentment and inner pain before she can do this.

Sun Square, Opposition, Semi-Square or Inconjunct Chiron
This can lead to long term health issues, such as auto-immune ailments that make life difficult. The person has no choice but to become an expert in dealing with her own ailments, as she will understand them better than most doctors do.

Moon Aspects

Moon Conjunct Mercury
The mental side of this person works in harness with the feeling side of the individual. On a more mundane level, this person should be able to make a success out of a family business, especially if it involved catering or property development.

Moon Conjunct Venus
Charm, beauty and a happy, laid back attitude characterise this person. Home like will be great, and she may work in food, real estate, décor and artistic fields, and she will love to sing and make music. She must take care not to overeat or drink too much.

Moon Conjunct Mars
This confers energy and vitality, so this person may be interested in sports or outdoor activities. She may be happy to run a farm or to work in engineering or the police. This is a sexy lady who enjoys life to the full.

Moon Conjunct Jupiter
The home will be a centre for education, religion or culture, and there may be many people coming through the front door. This subject may travel a lot or even have a second home in another country. Money should come easily to this person.

Moon Conjunct Saturn
The childhood may have been difficult, and the relationship with mother figures depressing, and this may lead to a lack of self-confidence and problems with the love life. This person is a hard worker who will make a success of her career.

Moon Conjunct Uranus

This denotes an original mind and an unconventional way of life. This person may have moved around a lot in childhood, and her home life may never be really settled, but she will find work in a field that suits her, and she will have lots of friends.

Moon Conjunct Neptune

Artistic and creative talent characterise this conjunction, so this person may become a musician, artist, creative cook or designer or possibly a psychic medium or healer. She is kind and well-meaning but perhaps a bit vague and disorganised.

Moon Conjunct Pluto

This is a powerful personality that knows how to give the public what it wants. The person might choose a career as a funeral director, in forensic investigation or possibly in psychology. The individual will have a strong sex drive.

Moon Conjunct Chiron

There may be a mother figure who is ill and who needs help, so the child grows up knowing how to give sick or desperate people what they need. This person is a good teacher, and she may play an instrument, so she is quite talented.

Moon Sextile or Trine Mercury

The conscious and unconscious mind are both active here, so this person is both intelligent and intuitive. She can make a living out of real estate, domestic matters and things that are important to women, and she makes friends easily.

Moon Sextile or Trine Venus

This person is cheerful and happy, and she strives to create domestic harmony in her home. She does well in any career that makes women feel good, such as hairdressing, nail art or illustrating and writing children's books.

Moon Sextile or Trine Mars

This confers energy and vitality, which makes this person a good sportswoman or dancer. She may be hot-tempered or highly sexed due to the amount of emotion that is being stirred up by her assertive Mars.

Moon Sextile or Trine Jupiter
This person could love the sea, and she may choose to work on the sea in a fishing capacity or by finding work on a cruise liner. She is a happy person who is also a deep thinker with a strong religious or spiritual side to her nature.

Moon Sextile or Trine Saturn
This is a hard worker who can cope with details. She is studious and good at mathematics or figure work. She may be a bit too serious, and she needs to lighten up and have fun from time to time. Her health may give her problems at times.

Moon Sextile or Trine Uranus
This person has an original and inventive mind; she may choose to work in an unusual field or have an unusual home. She probably has loads of books and is interested in educating herself and keeping up to date.

Moon Sextile or Trine Neptune
Sensitivity characterises this aspect to the point where the person is almost telepathic in her ability to read the motives of others. The individual may be artistic or musical, and she is undoubtedly kind-hearted, if a bit vague and forgetful at times.

Moon Sextile or Trine Pluto
The subject has a good instinct for business and financial matters, so she is unlikely to be taken for a fool. If family members fall out, this person will be the peacemaker who restores harmony to the group as a whole.

Moon Sextile or Trine Chiron
There is a natural tendency to want to help those in trouble with this sextile, but probably by coming up with ideas on a committee rather than in a hands-on manner. This person may be interested in psychology and also spiritual healing.

Moon Square, Opposition, Semi-Square or Inconjunct Mercury
The emotions are so strong that they may overwhelm the mental faculties, so this person needs to find ways of avoiding becoming neurotic. There may be health problems or a lack of attention to personal hygiene.

Moon Square, Opposition, Semi-Square or Inconjunct Venus
Women may be a source of difficulty in this person's life, starting with her mother and moving on to other females in her life. She may try to smother her own children to compensate for the shortage of love in her life.

Moon Square, Opposition, Semi-Square or Inconjunct Mars
Family problems may beset this person to the point where she cuts off from them and makes her own way in life. She must take care when dealing with sharp objects or fires, such as barbecues, as these could pose a danger to her.

Moon Square, Opposition, Semi-Square or Inconjunct Jupiter
As challenging aspects go, this isn't too bad, but it can make it hard to pay off a mortgage or find security in other ways. It can also lead to weight problems, so this person will have to keep an eye on her diet throughout life.

Moon Square, Opposition, Semi-Square or Inconjunct Saturn
The parents aren't an outstanding influence on this person, and even if they are reasonable, there may be difficult or unpleasant in-laws. This isn't a great aspect for business or complicated financial matters, either.

Moon Square, Opposition, Semi-Square or Inconjunct Uranus
This person is intelligent and an original thinker, which, allied to her powerful intuition, could give her psychic or mediumistic gifts. A woman will cause trouble and drive a wedge between her and a close family member.

Moon Square, Opposition, Semi-Square or Inconjunct Neptune
It is all very well being interested in spirituality and New Age ideas, but this subject could take it much too far, perhaps joining a cult or following a false guru. It is hard for her to think straight, and she spends too much time daydreaming.

Moon Square, Opposition, Semi-Square or Inconjunct Pluto
This could belong to a successful business person, but it may be hard for her to maintain family relationships due to some other family member being the favoured one. There may be some tragedy in the family background.

Moon Square, Opposition, Semi-Square or Inconjunct Chiron
Health could be an issue for this person, or she may make herself ill by worrying about nothing, but it could work in a better way by leading her into a career in nursing or caring for the elderly or the disabled.

Mercury Aspects

Mercury Conjunct Venus

This person has a sure touch where business is concerned, as she can see gaps in the market and make the best of them. Salesmanship and charm characterise this aspect, and the person must have a lovely home and attractive surroundings at work.

Mercury Conjunct Mars

The mind is sharp and there is a good instinct for business and money matters, but the person has to avoid jumping into things without checking them out thoroughly first. She may have a sharp tongue, or she may talk too much.

Mercury Conjunct Jupiter

This is a wonderful aspect for a writer or broadcaster or, for that matter, a publisher of books or music. It is a lucky aspect for someone who wants to work in business, but it also bestows honesty and a fondness for ethical behaviour.

Mercury Conjunct Saturn

This is an ideal placement for an intellectual because the mind is both sharp and deep. At times, the person might be inclined to depression, so she must do things that ease her mind, such as walking in the country or by the sea.

Mercury Conjunct Uranus

Science is one possibility here, as is advanced computer programming, but so is an interest in spiritual or psychic subjects. This person is intelligent but also an original thinker with an inventive mind.

Mercury Conjunct Neptune

As long as this person is involved in the artistic, musical or psychic world, she will do well, but the mind is too woolly for business matters. Her imagination is excellent, to the point where she could write wonderful novels.

Mercury Conjunct Pluto

This person has a deep and penetrating mind, and she may be an excellent psychologist. She would do well with scientific subjects or something like parapsychology, as she needs to know what is behind or inside everything.

Mercury Conjunct Chiron

Health and healing are essential to this person, and she may work in the world of established medicine, dentistry, optics or spiritual healing. She can sense inner pain and emotional wounds and help people to heal.

Mercury Sextile Venus

Mercury can't be far enough from Venus to make a trine aspect, so we only have the sextile here. This is a harmonious aspect that belongs to someone who creates peace and happiness all around her. She would succeed in public relations work.

Mercury Sextile or Trine Mars

Energy is the keyword here, but in the case of the sextile, it is mental energy, which makes it easy for this person to study or learn something complex, such as engineering design. The trine is a more artistic and creative aspect.

Mercury Sextile or Trine Jupiter

A good aspect for someone who wants to be a translator or deal with foreign people, foreign goods or work in the travel trade. This person is broadminded, cheerful and lucky, and she may be interested in mind, body and spirit subjects.

Mercury Sextile or Trine Saturn

This subject has a serious mind that is good at retaining details. This could be a specialist in antiques, where knowledge of hallmarks is essential, or something deep and detailed. She may not be much fun, but she is reliable.

Mercury Sextile or Trine Uranus

Friendships and groups of like-minded people characterise this aspect, so this person would be happy to join committees or get involved in humanitarian or ecological issues. She has a bright and original turn of mind.

Mercury Sextile or Trine Neptune

It wouldn't be surprising to find this subject travelling around her neighbourhood to give psychic readings or to work as a medium. Another avenue would be working in the field of art, design, music and beauty.

Mercury Sextile or Trine Pluto

This individual would be interested in health, both in the sense of nutrition and maybe herbalism and psychological healing. She has an investigative mind and likes to get to the bottom of mystical or spiritual subjects.

Mercury Sextile or Trine Chiron

Healing and helping characterise this aspect, so this person might work in conventional medicine, optics, dentistry or even as a vet. She might be a complementary healer or a psychologist, using sound and music in her work.

Mercury Semi-Square Venus

This is about the only aspect that these two planets can make to each other. This person wants to find love, but she may be too shy to socialise, and she may be over-sensitive, seeing insults and hurt where none exist. She needs to lighten up.

Mercury Square, Opposition, Semi-Square or Inconjunct Mars

There could be difficulties in business or negotiations with this aspect, and the person may be on the wrong end of back-biting, sarcasm and insults from family and colleagues. She needs to get away from this stressful environment.

Mercury Square, Opposition, Semi-Square or Inconjunct Jupiter

This person may find it hard to think straight because, on the one hand, she may be blindly optimistic and unwilling to believe that anything could go wrong. On the other, she may put her sympathies in the wrong place.

Mercury Square, Opposition, Semi-Square or Inconjunct Saturn

There are some people for whom the glass is always completely empty, so they become miseries and pessimists. This person must do all she can to avoid falling into this kind of behaviour, and she should avoid too much alcohol.

Mercury Square, Opposition, Semi-Square or Inconjunct Uranus
It can be a mistake to jump to conclusions without doing any research, and this person is prone to do that. She may be arrogant and convinced that her ideas are correct. She should avoid signing contracts or getting in negotiations.

Mercury Square, Opposition, Semi-Square or Inconjunct Neptune
Vagueness, a lack of clarity and wool-gathering are likely with this aspect, so this person needs to keep as much of a clear head as she can. She should avoid medicinal and other drugs or alcohol that would muddle her thinking even more.

Mercury Square, Opposition, Semi-Square or Inconjunct Pluto
Some people are drawn to excitement and even danger, so this individual might become a journalist or photographer who goes to dangerous places. On the other hand, she may do much to help people discard outmoded ideas.

Mercury Square, Opposition, Semi-Square or Inconjunct Chiron
This person should avoid places where disease abounds, so social work among the homeless or in undeveloped countries is a flawed idea. She needs to stay in a clean, calm environment where she can help others without putting herself in danger.

Venus Aspects

Venus Conjunct Mars
This is a very sexy aspect, so this person may use sex as part of her job, perhaps in the advertising field or by running a nightclub. It makes for an attractive and energetic person who gets on well with everybody.

Venus Conjunct Jupiter
This conjunction characterises an attractive and interesting personality who is successful at marketing her talents. She may be too quick to fall in love without looking too closely at the other person's real nature, but she means well and has a good heart.

Venus Conjunct Saturn
This is a serious person who puts her back into everything she does, so the chances are that she will make a success in her career. Love is not so easy, though, as she may feel sad or restricted in some way by her partners.

Venus Conjunct Uranus
Making money might not be the most important thing for this person, because she wants an interesting job and an exciting life. She may find it easier to make friends than to find stable and reliable lovers, though.

Venus Conjunct Neptune
Romance is the name of the game to this person, and she could turn her wonderful imagination into gold by writing best-selling fiction or wonderful art or music. She would be happiest living near water.

Venus Conjunct Pluto
Intensity marks this conjunction, and so does sexuality, so this person could not endure a relationship with someone who didn't feel as strongly as her or who was a poor lover. There may be some spectacular rows.

Venus Conjunct Chiron

This person needs peace because something has upset her equilibrium. She may have a health problem, or she may have been damaged psychologically in her childhood. She is very loving and will respond well to a gentle and generous partner.

Venus Sextile or Trine Mars

A pleasant personality who can enlist help when it is needed. She may be nice, but she can stand up for herself and fight when the need arises. This person may work as a designer or artist in an unusual field for such work, like aircraft design.

Venus Sextile or Trine Jupiter

A happy personality that makes everyone around her happy. She is attractive to look at and good company as well. Even when times are hard, she keeps smiling; she lands on her feet and finds luck when others cannot.

Venus Sextile or Trine Saturn

This hardworking individual can be somewhat serious, but she gets the job done. She is careful with money and can always find a way of earning it when times are hard. She is earnest about love and romance.

Venus Sextile or Trine Uranus

This subject has a sparkling personality and attractive looks. She can be slightly unconventional at times, but that only adds to her allure. She is forward-looking, and she thinks more deeply than others realise.

Venus Sextile or Trine Neptune

This is the sign of an artist, but her artistry could find expression in any field, even something like garden design. She may be a musician, dress designer or anything else of an artistic nature, but she needs to push herself to succeed.

Venus Sextile or Trine Pluto

This is a magnetic personality who might look rather sexy, especially if she uses this attribute in acting or singing. She can make money easily, but she could sit back and enjoy it a bit too much, thus losing what she has.

Venus Sextile or Trine Chiron
This person may be into health and healing, either by working in the medical field or in the form of complementary therapies. She is a good psychologist who understands how people deal with troubled backgrounds.

Venus Square, Opposition, Semi-Square or Inconjunct Mars
There is a battle of the sexes going on here because this person is spending too much energy on fighting with partners and ex-lovers, and this may impact her financial situation. She needs to relax and let some of the anger go.

Venus Square, Opposition, Semi-Square or Inconjunct Jupiter
The problem here is laziness and self-indulgence, so this person needs to get her act together. There may be trouble in connection with hospitals, schools, religious institutions or foreigners and foreign goods in some way.

Venus Square, Opposition, Semi-Square or Inconjunct Saturn
This puts a dampener on the person's romantic relationships and partnerships, and she may go through some bad experiences before she finds real love. Her relationship with her father may be complicated, assuming he is in her life at all.

Venus Square, Opposition, Semi-Square or Inconjunct Uranus
Love, sex and romance may be challenging to find, and this person may find herself in peculiar situations with oddball people. She really needs to stop and think before getting involved and make sure things are as they should be.

Venus Square, Opposition, Semi-Square or Inconjunct Neptune
At best, this subject would make an excellent hypnotherapist and regression therapist because she has the ability to take people into other worlds. She must take care not to become involved in get-rich-quick schemes.

Venus Square, Opposition, Semi-Square or Inconjunct Pluto
This person should avoid getting into a relationship with someone who she tries to make into the person she wants him to be. She should also avoid being coerced and pushed into things by others. Honesty is the best policy here.

Venus Square, Opposition, Semi-Square or Inconjunct Chiron
This aspect can bring health problems, especially diabetes or kidney problems and even trouble with the throat, neck or Achilles tendon. The person needs to look after her health and not take stupid risks.

Mars Aspects

Mars Conjunct Jupiter
This is an ethical business person who is also very successful. She may work in the legal field or be concerned about such things as ecology, climate change or social issues. She is philanthropic and generous.

Mars Conjunct Saturn
Responsibilities, burdens and a life of hard work characterise this aspect, and the best option is to enlist the help of family and of sensible male partners and friends. This person can be very successful, but her road ahead is a tough one.

Mars Conjunct Uranus
Friends, groups, clubs, societies and like-minded people are part of this person's life, and she may work on something like a town council that benefits the people in her locality. This person has some original and inventive ideas.

Mars Conjunct Neptune
This is an excellent aspect for someone who wants to work in an artistic field or who wants to develop her psychic or spiritual side. However, there is an air of secrecy here, so perhaps she works in a field where confidentiality is needed.

Mars Conjunct Pluto
There may be a touch of self-undoing here because this person may find herself in bad company or with people who take drugs or drink too much. She can make a success of her life as long as she restrains her temper.

Mars Conjunct Chiron
There is an interest in health and healing here, either in the form of surgery or maybe osteopathy or some other form of traditional or

alternative healing. This person may be carrying anger and hurt around from past events.

Mars Sextile or Trine Jupiter
This is a pleasant and lucky aspect, which makes work a pleasure and money fairly easy to find. This person should enjoy sports throughout her life, and she might even take her talents and hard work to the very top of her field.

Mars Sextile or Trine Saturn
Disciplined and well-organised, this person can do well in any form of work. She takes responsibility well and soon works her way up to a position of authority. She gets on well with men of all ages and types.

Mars Sextile or Trine Uranus
This person is independent and intelligent, and she can marshal the aid of friends, colleagues and organisations to help with whatever she sets out to achieve. She would be successful in the field of electronics, computer games and other innovations.

Mars Sextile or Trine Neptune
Mars is an active planet, but Neptune is a laid-back dreamy one, so this person may fluctuate between these two modes of behaviour depending upon her mood. She is imaginative, creative and she has a talent for spiritual healing.

Mars Sextile or Trine Pluto
An intense personality who does well in the world of finance and investment. She might be an accountant or lawyer who helps people deal with the aftermath of a divorce or with business matters that involve partnerships or shareholders.

Mars Sextile or Trine Chiron
This person may teach music or martial arts to young people, and she would bring benefits to the mental and physical health of her students. She is into health and healing, and she may take up spiritual healing as well.

Mars Square, Opposition, Semi-Square or Inconjunct Jupiter
This is a good aspect for someone who is into sports, but she must keep going despite setbacks if she wants to get anywhere. She must avoid becoming big-headed or putting others down who aren't as talented as she is.

Mars Square, Opposition, Semi-Square or Inconjunct Saturn
Battles and fights of one kind or another are inherent in this aspect, and this person must avoid taking out her frustrations on others. She may work in fits and starts rather than working her way through a job.

Mars Square, Opposition, Semi-Square or Inconjunct Uranus
This may be a confrontational personality who gets into fights and arguments at the drop of a hat. She needs to stop, think and consider others before launching herself into yet another battle. She could make an outstanding soldier.

Mars Square, Opposition, Semi-Square or Inconjunct Neptune
This person must take care never to get involved with toxic substances and never to eat or drink anything that isn't absolutely clean and fresh. She must avoid secret activities or weird sexual encounters.

Mars Square, Opposition, Semi-Square or Inconjunct Pluto
There may be phases of irritation and even anger here because things tend to set her off quite easily. However, she also needs to avoid people who would like to control or dominate her. She must take care when using tools and machinery.

Mars Square, Opposition, Semi-Square or Inconjunct Chiron
Health may be an issue for this individual, so she must take immediate action if something is wrong rather than leaving it too long. She should take lessons in self-defence because it is possible that she will come up against dangerous people.

Jupiter Aspects

Jupiter Conjunct Saturn
This is a promising outlook for someone who wants to get on in life because she will work hard in a logical and organised way, and while she will be prepared to take a chance on something, it will only be after doing the necessary research.

Jupiter Conjunct Uranus
These subjects may take too many chances in life, or they may jump to conclusions without stopping to think. On the other hand, they have original ideas that could take off. Foreign affairs and travel will be enjoyable.

Jupiter Conjunct Neptune
It wouldn't be surprising if this person had a spiritual experience that led her to take up some religious practice or to become highly spiritual. It may be an out of body type of event. Alternatively, she can succeed in an artistic field.

Jupiter Conjunct Pluto
Intensity characterises this aspect, so this person will be able to focus on whatever she is doing and block out everything that is going on around her. She can make a success of working in finance or foreign exchange.

Jupiter Conjunct Chiron
Travel for health and healing is part of this aspect, so this person may do just that for herself or set up a travel and tourism business that helps those who need warmth and healing for chronic ailments.

Jupiter Sextile or Trine Saturn

This person is a good student and, in turn, a great teacher. She has a sensible attitude to life and a serious attitude to work. She can make a success of anything, especially if in the legal world or the travel trade.

Jupiter Sextile or Trine Uranus

Unusual ideas may take off and make this person a success. She has an original outlook and a good deal of intuition, but she may do things too quickly at times or trust the wrong person. She needs to take a sensible attitude.

Jupiter Sextile or Trine Neptune

This subject is spiritual and kind-hearted, but she may take on too many lame ducks or try to heal the world as a whole. She needs to be kind to herself as well as to others. Travel is well starred, especially near or on water.

Jupiter Sextile or Trine Pluto

This is a lucky aspect for anyone who has to deal with other people's problems or other people's money, so the best careers would be in finance or the law, especially family law and the law regarding contracts.

Jupiter Sextile or Trine Chiron

There is a desire to heal others and to help the disabled or sick, and this urge is combined with an ability to make money, so this is an ethical worker or business person. This person also loves to make music.

Jupiter Square, Opposition, Semi-Square or Inconjunct Saturn

Jupiter wants to expand, and Saturn wants to limit things, so this makes for a balanced situation where desires that are over the top are trimmed back to make them sensible and workable. Nothing happens quickly here.

Jupiter Square, Opposition, Semi-Square or Inconjunct Uranus

Opportunities abound, but they may be too impractical to get anywhere in reality. This person should link with someone steady who can help her achieve her dreams. She can be surprisingly determined.

Jupiter Square, Opposition, Semi-Square or Inconjunct Neptune

Religion or the religious beliefs of others may be a trial to this person until she finds her own way forward, her own god or goddess and her own philosophy of life. Artistic and musical pursuits will be successful for her.

Jupiter Square, Opposition, Semi-Square or Inconjunct Pluto

This person may take one step forward in life and another back because things don't always work out as she would like, but then opportunities open up, and she needs to take them quickly while there is still time.

Jupiter Square, Opposition, Semi-Square or Inconjunct Chiron

Health may be a problem for this individual, as she may have a chronic illness of her own to cope with, or she may be involved in the health of her loved ones. She understands spirituality and karma and can put up with a lot.

Saturn Aspects

Saturn Conjunct Uranus

This subject has a natural inclination for science and topics such as physics, biology, ecology and research of all kinds. She has a serious frame of mind and can focus on something until she finds the answers she seeks.

Saturn Conjunct Neptune

This combines an interest in art or spirituality with a serious attitude to life, so this subject could take these topics seriously and find a way of making a living at them. This also hints at a somewhat strange family background.

Saturn Conjunct Pluto

A powerful combination that can lead to considerable success, particularly in the world of high finance or politics at a high level. There seems to be a family background of power, wealth or something unusual.

Saturn Conjunct Chiron

Health and healing are issues here, either because the subject has some chronic ailment to cope with or family members who need help. She may choose to work in the field of medicine, or music or teaching.

Saturn Sextile or Trine Uranus

Intellectual and thoughtful, this subject can make a success out of anything scientific or new forms of engineering. The future of the planet may be important to this individual. Otherwise, it makes for an interesting person with a good brain.

Saturn Sextile or Trine Neptune

This person has dreams and ideas that may seem hard to achieve, but her ability to keep her nose to the grindstone means that she does accomplish all that she seeks. She may have interesting parents or a fascinating family background.

Saturn Sextile or Trine Pluto
Scientific research is possible here, and this may lead to a career in forensics or forensic medicine. This is a serious, intellectual person who thinks profoundly and who likes to search for the truth in all things.

Saturn Sextile or Trine Chiron
This person could make a career in medicine, veterinary work, dentistry, optics or complementary therapies of some kind. There is an interest in health and healing, especially osteopathy or orthopaedics.

Saturn Square, Opposition, Semi-Square or Inconjunct Uranus
There may be sudden setbacks in this person's life, so just when she has everything rolling along nicely, something goes wrong. The problem may come from a lover, or it may be a legal obstacle or a health setback.

Saturn Square, Opposition, Semi-Square or Inconjunct Neptune
This person needs sensible and steady people around her because she is likely to be led down the wrong road by those who are glamorous but not really any good. She needs to avoid drink, drugs and pretend psychic people or tricksters.

Saturn Square, Opposition, Semi-Square or Inconjunct Pluto
Dishonest people or difficult political circumstances may have an effect on this person's life, so she needs to keep as far away from such people as possible. She can work in such fields as mining or oil exploration.

Saturn Square, Opposition, Semi-Square or Inconjunct Chiron
Health problems may be a feature of this person's life to the point where she becomes an expert in an unusual medical field. She needs a quiet life without too much hard work because she can't take stress or too much responsibility.

Uranus Aspects

Uranus Conjunct Neptune

This person has an original way of thinking and an artistic or creative temperament. She is interested in New Age ideas, complementary healing and astrology, but also in music, art and travel. She loves to weave dreams and talk in abstract terms.

Uranus Conjunct Pluto

The subject could have an extraordinary life, in which she does something meaningful for the benefit of others or for the planet's benefit. Change will affect her lifestyle, but she will also work towards bringing beneficial changes to everyone she deals with in her lifetime.

Uranus Conjunct Chiron

This individual is a natural healer who wants to help those who are in physical or mental pain. She will go the extra mile for the planet, for humanity and possibly also for animals. She may be musical or interested in conceptual art.

Uranus Sextile or Trine Neptune

This person has a sound mind, but she may spend too much time daydreaming about achieving as much as she could. However, she is a good teacher, and she would make an excellent religious or spiritual leader.

Uranus Sextile or Trine Pluto

This is a powerful aspect to be born under, and it could lead to an interesting life. This subject wants to improve the lot of humanity, and she may be drawn to work in war zones or other places where large numbers of people need help or education.

Uranus Sextile or Trine Chiron

Sometimes people come up with unusual and exciting remedies for ailments or new ways of dealing with stress and worry, and this person may be just the one who makes this kind of breakthrough. She is a wonderful healer.

Uranus Square, Opposition, Semi-Square or Inconjunct Neptune

This is a confusing setup that can make someone want to spend her life doing something for humanity or for the planet, but the reality of daily life and of life's problems keep getting in her way and making it difficult for her to get started on her dreams.

Uranus Square, Opposition, Semi-Square or Inconjunct Pluto

This is an unusual generational aspect that may only occur way ahead in the future, so it is unlikely to affect any of us who live on this earth today. However, it would mean a life of upheaval and revolution, and living through times of significant change.

Uranus Square, Opposition, Semi-Square or Inconjunct Chiron

This is an unusual generational aspect that may only occur way ahead in the future, so it is unlikely to affect any of us who live on this earth today. However, it would mean a life in which health and healing go through some kind of revolution.

Neptune and Pluto Aspects

Neptune Conjunct Pluto
This is an unusual conjunction, but it would belong to someone who is keen to help humanity and the planet in general. She wants to bring positive change to humanity and also to open people's eyes to the worlds of artistry, creativity and spirituality.

Neptune Conjunct Chiron
This would be a wonderful conjunction for someone who wants to work in the fields of healing, music or the arts – say in something like art or music therapy. She would be able to do a great deal of good to those who need it. This person may study something unusual.

Neptune Sextile or Trine Pluto
We will see what these mean when Neptune reaches the later stages of Pisces and enters Aries. It is a generational aspect that will affect people in the future, so its meaning isn't really clear yet.

Neptune Sextile or Trine Chiron
These are unusual generational aspects that will only take effect way ahead in the future.

Neptune Square, Opposition, Semi-Square or Inconjunct Pluto
These generational aspects will occur so far in the future that they aren't worth worrying about for us.

Neptune Square, Opposition, Semi-Square or Inconjunct Chiron
These generational aspects will occur so far in the future that they aren't worth worrying about for us.

Pluto Conjunct Chiron
This won't happen for many generations, so it isn't worth recording.

Pluto Sextile Chiron

The sextile will occur in our lifetime, and it will herald improvements in public health, education, psychology and even fighting drugs and crime. The trine is too far into the future to consider.

Pluto Square, Opposition, Semi-Square or Inconjunct Chiron

These aspects won't occur for many years, probably not in any of our lifetimes.

Conclusion to Volume One

This brings the first volume of the BIG Astrology Guide to a close, but it is only half the story, so you might fancy treating yourself to the second volume at some point in the future.

Some material in this volume is completely new, while some sections are revisions of previous books that have now been heavily updated, renovated and modernised. For instance, the original Rising Sign book didn't say much about the midheaven, but as the years have gone by, I have come to the conclusion that the MC is far more important than astrologers think, so I have gone into it in greater detail – and that is just one item of many that have been expanded and improved.

This book is filled with everything from the most basic data to high levels of information, and it includes many snippets that you might not find anywhere else. So, those who are interested in astrology will find lots of interesting material in these two books to use and enjoy.

Good luck,
Sasha Fenton

Index

CPSIA information can be obtained
at www.ICGtesting.com
Printed in the USA
BVHW091019011121
620447BV00012B/444

9 781903 065938